THE RISK-BASED APPROACH TO

COMBATING MONEY LAUNDERING AND TERRORIST FINANCING

EHI ERIC ESOIMEME

ISBN: 9789486030

ISBN 13: 9789789486038

Published by Eric Press

Manufactured in the United States of America

DEDICATION

I dedicate this book to my mother, Dr Angela Esoimeme. Her support, encouragement, and constant love have sustained me throughout my life.

ACKNOWLEDGEMENTS

I take this opportunity to express my deep sense of gratitude to Mr Ian Ross for the foreword to this book that he has kindly written.

I wish to express my awed gratitude to the editorial team that assisted me in this project. They showed tremendous zeal in the preparatory stages of this work which must be duly recognized. I am grateful to Tomas Barkus, Former Advisor-Interpreter at the National Crime Agency (United Kingdom)/Head of the Financial Crime Unit at EVP International (Lithuania), Emmanuel Sina, NFIU Compliance Analyst and Raghu Vamsy Dasika, AML Specialist/Advocate at the Supreme Court of India.

I would like to express my profound and sincere appreciation to Tom Brown CAMS, for impacting on me, the research skills needed to carry out this project.

TABLE OF CONTENTS

FOREWORD

It is a great honour to write the foreword for a second time for another highly informative and enormously useful book by Ehi Eric Esoimeme.

Ehi Eric Esoimeme is an author who has the rare ability to help us readers gain a grasp of essential theory when we need that delivery. He balances this with his ability to engage us with both evident facts of economic crime and more subtle and even hidden nuances. The emotive impacts as well as the educational needs are also well balanced.

In this book, what is highly impressive is the fearless professional engagement with topics and themes that most others avoid. Terrorist financing is one of the most dangerous schemes of crime there is, and when this is by money laundering the crime is even more dangerous as it moves along money varying laundering channels.

The second achievement of this book is the breakaway from definitions handling, stepping into that wider and more amorphous world of risk. Talking, writing and articulating risk, especially in economic crime and yet more when imbued with terrorist financing, must surely be a skill and awareness asset of every counter-fraud and money laundering professional.   This is the point when tackling money laundering really comes into effect for you, or really ought to.

Thanks again to Ehi Eric Esoimeme for taking us into this professional territory with this superb book. You will gain new knowledge and be guided by such high effort put into it.

Ian Ross

- Director of Investigations: Global Connections Trading Company (GCTC International)

- President: UK & Ireland Chapter: International Institute of Controls ('The IIC')

PREFACE

Governments around the world have made the fight against money laundering and the financing of terrorism a priority. Among its effort is the implementation of the Financial Action Task Force Recommendations, specifically Recommendation 1.

The FATF Recommendations (Recommendation 1) requires that countries mandate financial institutions and designated non-financial businesses and professions (DNFBPs) to identify, assess and take effective action to mitigate their money laundering and terrorist financing risks.

By adopting a risk-based approach, competent authorities, financial institutions and DNFBPs should be able to ensure that measures to prevent or mitigate money laundering and terrorist financing are commensurate with the risks identified, and would enable them to make decisions on how to allocate their own resources in the most effective way.

Purpose of the Book:

The purpose of this book is to:

- Provide a clear understanding of what the risk-based approach involves.

- Differentiate the risk-based approach from the rule based approach. And

- Determine if the risk–based approach interferes with the human rights of high-risk customers.

Target Audience:

The book is aimed at financial institutions and designated non-financial businesses and professions. It is also aimed at both under-graduate and post-graduate researchers.

Content of the Book:

The first chapter analyses the subject of money laundering in relation to its definition, how it occurs, its macroeconomic impact, its relationship with corruption and terrorism financing, and its history.

Chapter two briefly analyses the approach that financial institutions/DNFBPs must adopt to combat money laundering and terrorism financing.

Chapter three gives an explication of how financial institutions and DNFBPs can assess their money laundering and terrorist financing risks in relation to customers.

Chapter four expatiates on how financial institutions and DNFBPs can assess their money laundering and terrorist financing risks in relation to products and services.

Chapter five expatiates on how financial institutions and DNFBPs can assess their money laundering and terrorist financing risks in relation to geographic locations.

Chapter six identifies the individuals responsible for ensuring that firms implement a risk-based approach. It expounds on the need for the risk-based process to be imbedded within the internal controls of financial institutions/DNFBPs.

Chapter seven places emphasis on the need for a firm's training and awareness programme to be proportionate to the risks identified.

Chapter eight differentiates the risk-based approach from the rule-based approach.

Chapter nine determines whether or not the risk-based approach interferes with the human rights of certain individuals.

The Inspiration

Part of my inspiration to put together this outstanding book was drawn from one of my research papers: The Importance of Why Firms Dealing with PEPs must adopt a risk-based approach to their compliance programmes. The paper was written as a research assignment for my LLM degree programme. I had a distinction in that paper.

The paper broadened my interest in the risk assessment topic. It also enabled me to really understand the risk-based process, and its importance in Accountable Institutions. The paper drove me to carry out more extensive research in the area of risk assessment.

The book was also inspired by Tom Brown (CAMS), Tutor & Lecturer in Money Laundering (LLM Masters Degree Level) at Cardiff University and Senior Consultant at Kaizen Compliance Solutions. Tom Brown's lecture classes, focused not only on the dissemination of credible information relating to Money Laundering rules and regulations, but also on research development.

Tom Brown encourages students to think out of the box, and not limit one's thoughts to issues predicated on the subject.

His teachings helped me not only to understand the Anti-Money Laundering principles governing the financial sector but also to develop my research skills and this has helped me to write this book on the Money Laundering subject.

Details of Competing Books, Either Published or in Preparation, and how this book distinguishes itself from these:

Several books have been published on Money Laundering internationally. Notable amongst them are: Alldridge P, Money Laundering Law, Forfeiture, Confiscation, Civil Recovery, Criminal Laundering and Taxation of the proceeds of crime (Hart Publishing 2003), Esoimeme E E, A Comparative Study of the Money Laundering Laws/Regulations in Nigeria, the United States and the United Kingdom (Eric Press 2014), Hopton D, Money Laundering, a Concise Guide for all business (2nd Edition, Ashgate Publishing Ltd 2007) and Lilley P, Dirty Dealing the Untold Truth About Global Money Laundering, International Crime and Terrorism (3rd Edition, Kogan Page Limited, 2006).

Although the above mentioned books may have touched on the risk assessment topic in either one or two chapters, none of them addressed the topic in broad terms as it is done in this book. This book dedicates 9 chapters to the analysis of the risk based approach.

Internationally, this book would be the first comprehensive book on the subject of the Risk-Based Approach. This book would help financial institutions and designated non-financial institutions with any problem regarding the application of the risk-based approach.

Financial institutions/DNFBPs who implement the risk-based approach, in line with the guidance given in this book, will be well-placed to avoid the consequences of inappropriate de-risking behaviour.

I am aware that there are quite a number of reference guides provided by the Financial Action Task Force to assist firms with the implementation of the risk-based approach. Those publications focus mainly on the risk assessment principles. This book is focused on both the principles and the practical aspect of its application.

This book is a must read for every professional specializing in the field of Anti-Money Laundering Compliance. It is also a must read for every individual who intends to know more about the money laundering subject.

Ehi Eric Esoimeme Esq., LLM

Deputy Editor in Chief at DSC Publications Ltd

Member: Association of Certified Anti-Money Laundering Specialists (ACAMS)

Email: ehiesoimeme@yahoo.com

TABLE OF CASES

TABLES OF LEGISLATION

REFERENCES ARE TO PARAGRAPH NUMBERS

AUSTRALIA

PRIMARY LEGISLATION

Anti-Money Laundering and Counter-Terrorism Financing Act 2006 (as amended), 2.0, 8.0, 8.1, 8.2

SECONDARY LEGISLATION

Anti-Money Laundering and Counter-Terrorism Financing Rules Instrument 2007 (as amended), 2.1, 2.2, 2.3, 3.0, 3.1.1, 3.1.2, 3.2, 4.0, 4.1.2.1, 5.0

CANADA

PRIMARY LEGISLATION

Canada Proceeds of Crime (Money Laundering) and Terrorist Financing Act 2000 (as amended), 2.0, 8.0, 8.1, 8.2

TERTIARY LEGISLATION

Officer of the Superintendent of Financial Institutions Canada: Deterring and Detecting Money Laundering and Terrorist Financing, Sound Business and Financial Practices2008, 2.1, 2.2, 2.3, 3.0, 3.1.1, 3.1.2, 3.2, 4.1.2.1, 5.0

CHINA

PRIMARY LEGISLATION

Anti-Money Laundering Law 2007, 3.1

SECONDARY LEGISLATION

Anti-Money Laundering Rules (2007), 8.1, 8.1.2, 8.2

Administrative Rules for Financial Institutions on Customer Identification and Record Keeping of Customer Identity and Transaction Information (2007), 2.0, 2.1, 3.0, 8.0

GERMANY

PRIMARY LEGISLATION

Money Laundering Act 2008 (as amended), 2.0, 8.0, 8.1, 8.2

HONG KONG, CHINA

TERTIARY LEGISLATION

Guideline on Anti-Money Laundering and Counter-Terrorist Financing 2015, 2.0, 2.3, 8.0, 8.1, 8.2

INDIA

SECONDARY LEGISLATION

Prevention of Money-Laundering (Maintenance of Records) Amendment Rules, 2013, 2.0, 8.0, 8.1

NIGERIA

PRIMARY LEGISLATION

Money Laundering Prohibition Act 2011 (as amended), 2.0, 8.0, 8.1, 8.2

SECONDARY LEGISLATION

Central Bank of Nigeria (Anti-Money Laundering and Combating the Financing of Terrorism in Banks and Other Financial Institutions in Nigeria) Regulations, 2013, 2.1, 2.2, 2.3, 3.0, 3.1.1, 3.1.2, 3.2, 4.1.2.1

Special Control Unit against Money Laundering: Anti-Money Laundering/Combating the Financing of Terrorism Regulations for Designated Non-Financial Businesses and Professions in Nigeria 2013, 2.0, 8.0

TERTIARY LEGISLATION

Central Bank of Nigeria's Anti-Money Laundering/Combating the Financing of Terrorism (AML/CFT) Risk Based Supervision (RBS) Framework, 2011, 6.0, 6.1, 6.2

SINGAPORE

TERTIARY LEGISLATION

Notice to Banks, Monetary Authority of Singapore Act, Cap.186, Prevention of Money Laundering and Countering the Financing of Terrorism 2007 (as amended), 2.0, 8.0, 8.1, 8.2

SOUTH AFRICA

PRIMARY LEGISLATION

Financial Intelligence Centre Act, 2001 (as amended), 8.0, 8.1, 8.2

SECONDARY LEGISLATION

Money Laundering and Terrorist Financial Control Regulations, 2002 (as amended), 2.0, 3.1.1, 3.1.2, 4.1.2.1

TERTIARY LEGISLATION

Financial Intelligence Centre Guidance Note 3A, 2005, 2.1, 2.3, 3.2

General Guidance Note Concerning Identification of Clients, 2.0

UNITED STATES

PRIMARY LEGISLATION

Title 22 of the United States Code (the "Act"), 5.3

The Currency and Foreign Transactions Reporting Act of 1970 (which legislative framework is commonly referred to as the 'Bank Secrecy Act' or 'BSA') (as amended), 1.9

SECONDARY LEGISLATION

Codified Bank Secrecy Act Regulations 2010, 8.0, 8.1

TERTIARY LEGISLATION

Federal Financial Institutions Examination Council: Bank Secrecy Act/Anti-Money Laundering Examination Manual 2014, 2.1, 2.2, 2.3, 3.1.1, 3.2, 4.1.2.1, 8.2

UNITED KINGDOM

PRIMARY LEGISLATION

Proceeds of Crime Act 2002 (as amended), 8.0, 8.1

SECONDARY LEGISLATION

Money Laundering Regulations 2007, 8.0, 8.2

TERTIARY LEGISLATION

Joint Money Laundering Steering Group: Prevention of Money Laundering/Combating Terrorist Financing 2014 Revised Version: Guidance for the UK Financial Sector Part I, 2.0, 3.2, 4.1.2.2, 7.1

TABLE OF INTERNATIONAL CONVENTIONS

United Nations Convention against Corruption 2003, 1.9

United Nations Convention against Illicit Traffic in Narcotic Drugs and Psychotropic Substances, 1988, 1.9

United Nations Convention against Transnational Organized Crime and the Protocol There to 2004, 1.9

United Nations International Convention for the Suppression of the Financing of Terrorism 1999, 1.9

LIST OF ABBREVIATIONS

ACH: Automated Clearing House
APG: Asia/Pacific Group on Money Laundering
APT: Asset Protection Trusts
AML: Anti-Money Laundering
BSA: Bank Secrecy Act
CBN: Central Bank of Nigeria
CCO: Chief Compliance Officer
CDD: Customer Due Diligence
CFATF: Caribbean Financial Action Task Force
CFT: Countering the Financing of Terrorism
CIP: Customer Identification Program
CMIR: Currency or Monetary Instruments
CTRs: Currency Transaction Reports
DNFBPs: Designated non-financial business or profession (DNFBPs)
DNFI: Designated non-financial institutions
ECO: Export Control Organization
EDD: Enhanced Due Diligence
ESAAMLG: The Eastern and South Africa 'Anti-Money' Laundering Group
EU: European Union

FATF: Financial Action Task Force
FARC: The Revolutionary Armed Forces of Columbia
FIU: Financial Intelligence Unit
GAFILAT: Financial Action Task Force of Latin America
GDP: Gross Domestic Product
HIFCAs: High Intensity Financial Crime Areas
HIDTAs: High Intensity Drug Trafficking Areas (HIDTAs)
IAT: International ACH Transactions
IBC: International Business Corporations
IMF: International Monetary Fund
IOLTA: Interest on Lawyers' Trust Accounts
IRGC: Iranian Revolutionary Guard Corps
IRGC-QF: Islamic Revolutionary Guard Corps-Qods Force
IRS-SB/SE: Department of the Treasury Internal Revenue Service-Small Business/Self-Employed Division
IVTS: Informal Value Transfer System
KYC: Know Your Customer
MENAFATF: Middle East and North Africa Financial Action Task Force
MIS: Management Information Systems
ML/FT: Money Laundering/Financing of Terrorism
ML/TF: Money Laundering/Terrorist Financing
MNOs: Mobile Network Operators
MSB: Money Service Business
MVTS: Money or Value Transfer Services
NDIP: Non-Deposit Investment Products
NGO: Non-Governmental Organizations
NJDBI: New Jersey Department of Banking and Insurance
NRA: Non-Resident Aliens
ODFI: Originating Depository Financial Institution
OFC: Offshore Financial Centres
OFIs: Other Financial Institutions
OSCE: Organization for Security and Co-operation in Europe

PEPs: Politically Exposed Persons
PICs: Private Investment Companies
PTAs: Payable-Through Accounts
RBA: Risk-Based Approach
RCCs: Remotely Created Cheques
RDC: Remote Deposit Capture
RDFIs: Receiving Depository Financial Institutions
STR: Suspicious Transaction Report
SWIFT: Society for Worldwide Interbank Financial Telecommunication
TIN: Tax Identification Number
TPSP: Third Party Service Provider
UN: United Nations
UNAMID: United Nations-African Union Mission in Darfur Force
UNSCR: United Nations Security Council Resolution
Vienna Convention: The United Nations Convention against Illicit
Traffic in Narcotic Drugs and Psychotropic Substances 1988

CHAPTER 1

MONEY LAUNDERING AND TERRORISM FINANCING

Criminal activities, such as drug trafficking, smuggling, human trafficking, corruption and others, tend to generate large amounts of profits for the individuals or groups carrying out the criminal act. However, by using funds from such illicit sources, criminals risk drawing the authorities' attention to the underlying criminal activity and exposing themselves to criminal prosecution. In order to benefit freely from the proceeds of their crime, they must therefore conceal the illicit origin of these funds.[1]

---

1 International Monetary Fund 'Anti-Money Laundering/Combating the Financing of Terrorism Topics' (http://www.imf.org) http://www.imf.org/external/np/leg/amlcft/eng/aml1.htm. Accessed 10th of March 2015, See also R v. Nabil Zekari, [2010] EWCA Crim 1649, [2011] 1 Cr App R (S) 59 which is to the effect that: hiding proceeds of crime in your car comes within the meaning of concealing criminal property, See Regina v. Fazal [2009] EWCA Crim 1697, [2010] 1 WLR 694 [22] which is to the effect that: where a person allows his account to be deposited and withdrawn with proceeds of fraud, such constitutes converting criminal property. See also R v. Christopher Smale and Ann Smale [2008] EWCA Crim 1235, [2009] 1 Cr App R (S) 25 which is to the effect that: entering into an arrangement could be by agreeing with someone to conceal money. See also Dare v. Crown Prosecution Service [2012] EWHC 2074 (Admin) (2013) 177 JP 37,[2012] Lloyd's Rep FC 718. See Regina v. John Middleton, Veronica, Patricia Rourke [2008] EWCA Crim 233 which is to the effect that: holding a certain amount could amount to possessing criminal property.

1

1.1 WHAT IS MONEY LAUNDERING?

Money laundering is the process that transforms illegal inputs into supposedly legitimate outputs. Proceeds gained by crimes such as fraud, theft, and drug trafficking are made to look as if they were the fruits of honest hard labour—transformed, for instance, into legitimate-looking bank accounts, real estate, or luxury goods. This allows criminals to prosper from their crimes and live their lives without looking like criminals. Moreover, they can use these laundered proceeds to expand their criminal enterprises, thereby increasing their wealth and power, including the power to corrupt and buy protection from the political and law enforcement establishment.

If there were no fraud, no tax crime, no insider trading, no drug trafficking, no corruption, or indeed no proceeds-generating crime at all, there would be no money laundering. The close relationship between the criminal act that gives rise to proceeds and the laundering of these proceeds makes it very difficult to separate the act of money laundering from the underlying crime, although the two are treated legally as separate acts. Money laundering is an essential component of any profit-making crime, because without the laundering, crime really doesn't "pay."

When the underlying—or "predicate"— crime is something like drug trafficking, everyone understands the social costs, which are huge and visible. But the social and economic costs of white-collar crimes like embezzlement, tax evasion, insider trading, and bank fraud, while less obvious, can be massive as well.[2]

1.2 HOW MONEY IS LAUNDERED?

Although money laundering often involves a complex series of transactions, it generally includes three basic steps.

---

2   P Ashin: Dirty Money, Real Pain. Finance and Development, June 2012. 38, 39.

The first step is the physical disposal of cash. This placement might be accomplished by depositing the cash in domestic banks or, increasingly, in other types of formal or informal financial institutions. Or the cash might be shipped across borders for deposit in foreign financial institutions, or used to buy high-value goods, such as artwork, airplanes, and precious metals and stones, that can then be resold for payment by check or bank transfer.

The second step in money laundering is known as layering, carrying out complex layers of financial transactions to separate the illicit proceeds from their source and disguise the audit trail. This phase can involve such transactions as the wire transfer of deposited cash, the conversion of deposited cash into monetary instruments (bonds, stocks, traveler's checks), the resale of high-value goods and monetary instruments, and investment in real estate and legitimate businesses, particularly in the leisure and tourism industries. Shell companies, typically registered in offshore havens, are a common tool in the layering phase. These companies, whose directors often are local attorneys acting as nominees, obscure the beneficial owners through restrictive bank secrecy laws and attorney-client privilege.

The last step is to make the wealth derived from the illicit proceeds appear legitimate. This integration might involve any number of techniques, such as using front companies to "lend" the proceeds back to the owner or using funds on deposit in foreign financial institutions as security for domestic loans. Another common technique is over invoicing or producing false invoices for goods sold—or supposedly sold— across borders.[3]

---

3   D Scott: Money Laundering and International Efforts to fight it. (the World Bank) Note No.48. May 1995.

1.3 MACROECONOMIC IMPACT OF MONEY LAUNDERING

The estimates of the present scale of money laundering transactions are almost beyond imagination—2 to 5 percent of global GDP would probably be a consensus range. This scale poses two sorts of risks: one prudential, the other macroeconomic. Markets and even smaller economies can be corrupted and destabilized. We have seen evidence of this in countries and regions which have harbored large-scale criminal organizations. In the beginning, good and bad monies intermingle, and the country or region appears to prosper, but in the end Gresham's law operates, and there is a tremendous risk that only the corrupt financiers remain. Lasting damage can clearly be done, when the infrastructure that has been built up to guarantee the integrity of the markets is lost. Even in countries that have not reached this point, the available evidence suggests that the impact of money laundering is large enough that it must be taken into account by macroeconomic policy makers. Money subject to laundering behaves in accordance with particular management principles. There is evidence that it is less productive, and therefore that it contributes minimally, to say the least, to optimization of economic growth. Potential macroeconomic consequences of money laundering include, but are not limited to: inexplicable changes in money demand, greater prudential risks to bank soundness, contamination effects on legal financial transactions, and greater volatility of international capital flows and exchange rates due to unanticipated cross-border asset transfers.

1.4 GLOBALIZATION AND MONEY LAUNDERING

Globalization of financial markets is one of the most important contemporary developments. What are its implications for the fight against money laundering? Clearly, globalization implies that the prevention strategies must be universally applied. All countries must participate—and participate enthusiastically—or the money being laundered will flow quickly to the weakest point in the international system. It is in this respect that the Financial Action Task Force (FATF) plays an especially important role. It has developed a comprehensive and authoritative set of international standards for anti-money laundering policies, and procedures for their application and enforcement. Through its so-called "typologies" exercises, the FATF has pooled the intelligence of its members regarding financial instruments and institutions used by the money launderers, and this is reflected in its standards. The FATF has also been energetic in spreading its message beyond its own membership, which is comprised largely of the industrial countries. Like the International Monetary Fund (IMF), it has found the "mission" format, by which groups of FATF experts visit non-member countries, to be valuable in disseminating and promoting its policies. But this process is even more effective when the countries concerned are members of the FATF group—and can enjoy the immediacy, "ownership," and self-evaluation that come with membership. It is therefore a significant achievement that the FATF has established, within the few years since its own formation, two regional offshoots—the Caribbean FATF, and very recently, the Asia/Pacific Group on Money Laundering. These regional bodies will play an important role in promoting the "modern" financial markets—taking into account the special features and state of development of the regional systems.[4]

1.5 CORRUPTION AND MONEY LAUNDERING

Money laundering is the handmaiden of international corruption, and efforts to curb money laundering can help to reduce corruption. The linkage is clear: those who take bribes must find safe international financial channels through which they can bank their ill-gotten gains.

---

4   M Camdessus, 'Money Laundering: the importance of international counter measures' (http://www.imf.org 10th of February 1998) http://www.imf.org/external/np/speeches/1998/021098.htm Accessed 11th of February 2015

Those who provide the bribes may well assist the bribe takers to establish safe financial channels and launder the cash. To a considerable extent, many of the world's largest banks—all of which are headquartered in the leading industrial countries—are used in the global money laundering game. Many of the banks are used unwittingly, in the sense that they have few grounds to suspect that deposits being made have been illegally transferred or are the proceeds of illegal actions or bribery payments.[5]

1.6 TERRORISM FINANCING

In the aftermath of the September 11, 2001 terrorist attacks against American targets, the question of the financing of terrorism took on a new dimension. The sheer magnitude of the attacks and the complex web of preparation they required highlighted the importance of financial resources needed to carry them out. But the international community had not waited until this moment to start working to prevent and punish the financing of such acts. While the September 11 attacks gave renewed urgency to the issue, actions had been started earlier in various United Nations fora. By the end of 2000, two international conventions on relevant topics had been negotiated and opened for signature, and the United Nations Security Council had already put in place a mechanism to identify the assets of terrorists and to require countries to freeze them. Soon after the attacks, the Financial Action Task Force issued a new set of eight Special Recommendations on Terrorist Financing.

The international efforts to curb the financing of terrorism took a comprehensive approach, which combines repressive measures of criminal law with preventive measures. These two approaches have involved the use of different kinds of international instruments. The

---

5   F Vogl, The Supply Side of Global Bribery, (Finance and Development Volume 35, Number 2) June 1998

repressive measures involve agreements among countries to make certain acts criminal offenses in their legislation, and to cooperate among each other by exchanging information and providing mutual legal assistance. The need to ensure uniformity of definitions of the offenses to be criminalized, and the need to organize the greatest degree of cooperation among States in giving each other mutual legal assistance, has led to the use of international treaties to deal with the repressive part of the strategy. Two important international conventions have been negotiated in this respect. They are the International Convention for the Suppression of the Financing of Terrorism (the Financing of Terrorism Convention) and the United Nations Convention against Transnational Organized Crime, also known as the Palermo Convention.

The preventive measures involve the establishment of a regulatory regime for financial institutions that is intended to reduce the scope for using financial systems to collect and transfer funds for terrorism purposes. As these measures must be integrated in the local regulatory framework of each country, they have been contained in more informal arrangements, such as the FATF Recommendations. However, the two approaches are not isolated, and there is constant interaction between them. The FATF requires that countries become parties to the Financing of Terrorism Convention, and that Convention as well as the Palermo Convention contain provisions obligating countries, in very general language, to implement the preventive measures required by the FATF.[6]

1.7 TERRORISM FINANCING AND MONEY LAUNDERING

Money laundering is the process of concealing the illicit origin of proceeds of crimes. Terrorist financing is the collection or the provision

---

6   L Forget, Combating the financing of Terrorism (Seminar on Current Developments in Monetary and Financial Law) 2012, 1-3

of funds for terrorist purposes. In the case of money laundering, the funds are always of illicit origin, whereas in the case of terrorist financing, funds can stem from both legal and illicit sources. The primary goal of individuals or entities involved in the financing of terrorism is therefore not necessarily to conceal the sources of the money but to conceal both the funding activity and the nature of the funded activity.

Similar methods are used for both money laundering and the financing of terrorism. In both cases, the actor makes an illegitimate use of the financial sector. The techniques used to launder money and to finance terrorist activities/terrorism are very similar and in many instances identical. **An effective anti-money laundering/counter financing of terrorism framework must therefore address both risk issues: it must prevent, detect and punish illegal funds entering the financial system and the funding of terrorist individuals, organizations and/or activities.** Also, AML and CFT strategies converge; they aim at attacking the criminal or terrorist organization through its financial activities, and use the financial trail to identify the various components of the criminal or terrorist network. This implies to put in place mechanisms to read all financial transactions, and to detect suspicious financial transfers.[7]

1.8 DETRIMENTAL EFFECTS OF MONEY LAUNDERING AND TERRORIST FINANCING

Money laundering and terrorist financing can have particularly damaging economic and social consequences for developing countries because their economies and financial sectors tend to be less diverse and more susceptible to manipulation than those of more

---

7 International Monetary Fund 'Anti-Money Laundering/Combating the Financing of Terrorism Topics' (http://www.imf.org) http://www.imf.org/external/np/leg/amlcft/eng/aml1.htm Accessed 10th of March 2015

developed countries. Thus, sustainable economic growth and development can be imperiled in countries that are used as money laundering platforms. Experts in the study of money laundering and terrorist financing have found that these activities can have the following impact:

- Potential increase in crime and corruption

- Potential damage to reputation of financial institutions and markets

- Less foreign private investment

- Possible destabilization of financial markets and weaker financial institutions

- Weakened legitimate private sector

- Potential economic distortion

- Loss of tax revenue

- Weakened control over economic policy

- Possible risk to privatization

- Potential reduction of foreign government assistance

- Trigger for international sanctions by the FATF[8]

---

8   The International Bank for Reconstruction and Development/the World Bank: The World Bank in the Global Fight against Money Laundering and Terrorist Financing 2003, 4-5

1.9 INTERNATIONAL AML SITUATION

After the mid-20th century, governments around the world were confronted with the grave situation where the flooding of narcotics became a scourge, and they conducted in-depth examination on the legal policies of preventing narcotics-related crimes. In 1970, the United States passed the Bank Secrecy Act (BSA). BSA reformed on the traditional bank secrecy system, built up the Anti-Money Laundering (AML) foundation in the US and instituted the AML working system led by one government department and participated by various others. Meanwhile, AML was paid much attention by the majority of Western developed economies and emerging economies. During 1980s-1990s, these countries and regions have successively enacted AML laws. Switzerland, famous for its strict bank secrecy arrangements, also accepts the international AML practices under international pressure. Starting from July 1 2004, for those who transfer money above a certain amount through anonymous accounts with banks of Switzerland, the banks should make known their true identity.

Faced with ever-raging money laundering, such international organizations as the Security Council of the United Nations have responded actively as well. In 1988, the UN passed the United Nations Convention against Illicit Traffic in Narcotic Drugs and Psychotropic Substances, which criminalizes money laundering related to narcotics. The Convention is the first international convention against crimes of money laundering in the world. Since 1990s, the international community has paid ever closer attention to money laundering. In 1990, the European Council passed Convention on Laundering, Search, Seizure and Confiscation of Proceeds from Crime. In April 1995, the UN particularly drafted guidelines on preventing money laundering activities, for reference of all countries in the course of AML legislation. In December 1999, the UN General Assembly passed International Convention for the Suppression of the Financing of Terrorism. In November 2000, the UN General Assembly also passed Convention against Transnational Organized Crime, calling for all parties to institute AML program. In October 2003, the UN General Assembly further passed Convention against Corruption, stipulating stricter requirements for AML programs of the parties. Such international organizations as the International Monetary Fund, the World Bank and the Basel Committee on Banking Supervision have also developed an array of principles and guides.

Because of the transnational nature of money laundering, the G-7 Summit in Paris decided in July 1989 to establish the Financial Action Task Force (FATF), in a bid to examine the cooperative results with respect to combating money laundering through banks and the financial system, to improve laws and rules in AML and measures, and to strengthen preventive AML measures through multi-lateral judiciary assistance. In February 1990, the FATF set out a set of Forty Recommendations on Money Laundering ("Forty Recommendations"). First, each country should criminalize money laundering of funds used in severe crimes. Second, governments of all countries should strengthen financial supervision by urging financial institutions to develop and implement feasible internal AML control system and to fulfil the obligation of customer identification, record-keeping of customer information and transactions and detection and reporting of suspicious financial activities. Third, governments should establish Financial Intelligence Unit (FIU) responsible for monitoring unusual and suspicious transactions of funds, so as to achieve coordination and cooperation between appropriate ministries. Fourth, countries should exchange intelligence on money laundering and conduct international cooperation in AML investigation, search and freezing of illegal funds and extradition of suspects. The Forty Recommendations by the FATF has become the most important guiding document in the current international AML sphere, promoting

AML legislation in all countries and regions and development of the international AML system.

After 9/11 terrorist attack, anti-terrorism was combined with AML. Combating terrorist financing has become an important field of AML. AML and combating terrorist financing have become important issues of some international organizations and forums, occupying a significant niche in current international relation. After 9/11 terrorist attack, the United States (US) congress wasted no time in passing the USA PATRIOT Act, strengthening in an all-round way the rules for combating terrorist financing. The legislature of all countries and regions reacted to the movement quickly as well.[9] Besides some international conventions passed by the UN with respect to combating terrorist financing, the FATF drafted specifically 8 more recommendations for combating terrorist financing in October 2001. The FATF Recommendations were revised a second time in 2003 and a third time in 2012. These, together with the Special Recommendations, have been endorsed by over 180 countries, and are universally recognised as the international standard for anti-money laundering and countering the financing of terrorism (AML/CFT).

The FATF Recommendations (2012) require Countries to identify, assess, and understand the money laundering and terrorist financing risks for the country, and should take action, including designating an authority or mechanism to coordinate actions to assess risks, and apply resources, aimed at ensuring the risks are mitigated effectively. Based on that assessment, countries should apply a risk-based approach (RBA) to ensure that measures to prevent or mitigate money laundering and terrorist financing are commensurate with the risks identified.

---

9 Z Xiaochuan: Anti-money laundering in China-the status quo and prospects (BIS Review 50/2004), 2, 3.

CHAPTER 2

THE RISK BASED APPROACH: AN OVERVIEW

The Money Laundering Laws/Regulations of most countries around the world contain language that permits financial institutions/designated non-financial businesses and professions (DNFBPs) to some degree to adopt a risk-based approach to combating money laundering and terrorist financing. That language also authorise financial institutions/DNFBPs to use a risk-based approach to discharging certain of their anti-money laundering (AML) and counter-terrorist financing (CFT) obligations.[1] By adopting a risk-based approach, competent authorities, financial institutions and DNFBPs are able to ensure that measures to prevent or mitigate money laundering and terrorist financing are commensurate to the risks identified. This will allow resources to be allocated in the most efficient ways. The principle is that resources should be directed in accordance with priorities so that the greatest risks receive the highest attention.[2]

Adopting a risk-based approach implies the adoption of a risk management process for dealing with money laundering and terrorist financing. This process encompasses recognising the existence of the

---

1   Australia Anti-Money Laundering and Counter-Terrorism Financing Act 2006 (as amended), s 97, s165, See also Australia Anti-Money Laundering and Counter-Terrorism Financing Rules Instrument 2007 (as amended), paragraph 4.1.3, Canada Proceeds of Crime (Money Laundering) and Terrorist Financing Act 2000 (as amended), s 9.6 (2), See also Officer of the Superintendent of Financial Institutions Canada: Deterring and Detecting Money Laundering and Terrorist Financing 2008, 12, China Administrative Rules for Financial Institutions on Customer Identification and Record Keeping of Customer Identity and Transaction Information (2007), Article 3, Germany Money Laundering Act 2008 (as amended), s 6, Hong Kong, China Guideline on Anti-Money Laundering and Counter-Terrorist Financing 2015, paragraph 3.1, India Prevention of Money-Laundering (Maintenance of Records) Amendment Rules, 2013, rule 13, Nigeria Money Laundering Prohibition Act 2011 (as amended), s 3, s 4, s 5, See Central Bank of Nigeria (Anti-Money Laundering and Combating the Financing of Terrorism in Banks and Other Financial Institutions in Nigeria) Regulations, 2013, Regulation 5, 6, See Nigeria Special Control Unit against Money Laundering: Anti-Money Laundering/Combating the Financing of Terrorism Regulations for Designated Non-Financial Businesses and Professions in Nigeria 2013, Regulation 5.11-5.19, See Singapore Notice to Banks, Monetary Authority of Singapore Act, Cap.186, Prevention of Money Laundering and Countering the Financing of Terrorism 2007 (as amended), paragraph 6,   See also South Africa Money Laundering and Terrorist Financial Control Regulations, 2002 (as amended), Regulation 21, See also South Africa's General Guidance Note Concerning Identification of Clients, 2,3, See United States Federal Financial Institutions Examination Council: Bank Secrecy Act/Anti-Money Laundering Examination Manual 2014, 18, 19, See also United Kingdom Joint Money Laundering Steering Group: Prevention of Money Laundering/Combating Terrorist Financing 2014 Revised Version: Guidance for the UK Financial Sector Part I, paragraph 4.2, 4.8, 4.14-4.18
2   FATF Guidance on the Risk Based Approach to combating money laundering and terrorist financing, (High Level principles and procedures) 2007, paragraph 1.7

risks, undertaking an assessment of the risks and developing strategies to manage and mitigate the identified risks.[3]

Money laundering and terrorist financing risks may be measured using various categories. Application of risk categories provides a strategy for managing potential risks by enabling financial institutions/DNFBPs to subject customers to proportionate controls and oversight. The most commonly used risk criteria are: country or geographic risk; customer risk; and product/services risk. The weight given to these risk categories (individually or in combination) in assessing the overall risk of potential money laundering may vary from one institution to another, depending on their respective circumstances. Consequently, financial institutions/DNFBPs will have to make their own determination as to the risk weights. Parameters set by law or regulation may limit a financial institution's discretion.[4]

While there is no agreed upon set of risk categories, the examples provided herein are the most commonly identified risk categories. There is no one single methodology to apply to these risk categories, and the application of these risk categories is intended to provide a strategy for managing the potential risks.[5]

2.1 CUSTOMER RISK

Although any type of account is potentially vulnerable to money laundering or terrorist financing, by the nature of their business,

---

3 FATF Guidance on the Risk Based Approach to combating money laundering and terrorist financing, (High Level principles and procedures) 2007, paragraph 1.8. See also The Financial Action Task Force (FATF): International Standards On Combating Money Laundering and the financing of terrorism and proliferation,(The FATF Recommendations) 2012, Recommendation 1, See also Basel Committee on Banking Supervision, core principles for effective banking supervision 2012

4 FATF Guidance on the Risk Based Approach to combating money laundering and terrorist financing, (High Level principles and procedures) 2007, paragraph 3.3

5 FATF Guidance on the Risk Based Approach to combating money laundering and terrorist financing, (High Level principles and procedures) 2007, paragraph 3.4

occupation, or anticipated transaction activity, certain customers and entities may pose specific risks.[6]

Financial institutions/DNFBPs must recognise the existence of these risks at the Customer Due Diligence stage, undertake an assessment of the risks at the Enhanced Due Diligence stage and develop strategies to manage and mitigate the identified risks at the Enhanced on-going monitoring stage.[7]

In its internal policies, the firm must define categories of persons whose circumstances warrant enhanced due diligence. This will typically be the case where the circumstances are likely to pose a higher than average risk to a bank.

The circumstances of the following categories of persons are indicators for defining them as requiring Enhanced Due Diligence:

- Cash (and cash equivalent) intensive businesses including:

  o Money services businesses (e.g. remittance houses, currency exchange houses, casas de cambio, bureaux de change, money transfer agents and bank note traders or other businesses offering money transfer facilities).

---

6 Australia Anti-Money Laundering and Counter-Terrorism Financing Rules Instrument 2007 (as amended), Paragraph, paragraph 4.1.3 (1), Officer of the Superintendent of Financial Institutions Canada: Deterring and Detecting Money Laundering and Terrorist Financing 2008, 14, Central Bank of Nigeria's Anti-Money Laundering/Combating the Financing of Terrorism (AML/CFT) Risk Based Supervision (RBS) Framework, 2011, paragraph 5.1

7 Australia Anti-Money Laundering and Counter-Terrorism Financing Act 2006 (as amended), s 165, Officer of the Superintendent of Financial Institutions Canada: Deterring and Detecting Money Laundering and Terrorist Financing 2008, 13, See also the CBN (Anti-Money Laundering and Combating the Financing of Terrorism in Banks and Other Financial Institutions in Nigeria) Regulations, 2013, Regulation 5, 6, 14, 15, 16, See also United States Federal Financial Institutions Examination Council: Bank Secrecy Act/Anti-Money Laundering Examination Manual 2014, 20-21, 57-58

o Casinos, betting and other gambling related activities. And

o Businesses that while not normally cash intensive, generate substantial amounts of cash for certain transactions.

- Charities and other "not for profit" organisations which are not subject to monitoring or supervision (especially those operating on a "cross-border" basis).

- "Gatekeepers" such as accountants, lawyers, or other professionals holding accounts at a financial institution, acting on behalf of their clients, and where the financial institution places unreasonable reliance on the gatekeeper.

- Use of intermediaries within the relationship who are not subject to adequate AML/CFT laws and measures and who are not adequately supervised.

- Persons residing in and/or having funds sourced from countries identified by credible sources as having inadequate AML standards or representing high risk for crime and corruption.

- "Politically Exposed Persons," frequently abbreviated as "PEPs," referring to individuals holding or, as appropriate, having held, senior, prominent, or important public positions with substantial authority over policy, operations or the use or allocation of government-owned resources, such as senior government officials, senior executives of government corporations, senior politicians, important political party officials, etc., as well as their close family and close associates. PEPs from different jurisdictions may be subject to different levels of diligence.[8]

Financial institutions/DNFBPs shall verify customers' basic information regularly according to the level of the customer or the account. Verification on customers or accounts with higher risk level shall be more rigorous. Verification on customers or accounts with the highest risk level shall be carried out at least once per 6 months.[9]

2.2 PRODUCT RISK

The first step of the risk assessment process is to identify the specific products and services unique to the bank. Although attempts to launder money, finance terrorism, or conduct other illegal activities through a bank can emanate from many different sources, certain products and services, may be more vulnerable or have been historically abused by money launderers and criminals. Depending on the specific characteristics of the particular product or service, the risks are not always the same. Various factors, such as the number and volume of transactions, geographic locations, and nature of the customer relationships, should be considered when the bank prepares its risk assessment. The differences in the way a bank interacts with the customer (face-to-face contact versus electronic banking) also should be considered. Because of these factors, risks vary from one bank to another.

---

8 Australia Anti-Money Laundering and Counter-Terrorism Financing Rules Instrument 2007 (as amended), paragraph 4.1.3, See also the Nigerian CBN (Anti-Money Laundering and Combating the Financing of Terrorism in Banks and Other Financial Institutions in Nigeria) Regulations, 2013, Regulation 16, See also South Africa, Financial Intelligence Centre Guidance Note 3A: Guidance for Accountable Institutions on Client Identification and Verification and Related Matters, paragraph 4

9 China Administrative Rules for Financial Institutions on Customer Identification and Record Keeping of Customer Identity and Transaction Information (2007), Article 18

The second step of the risk assessment process entails a more detailed analysis of the data obtained during the identification stage in order to more accurately assess Anti-Money Laundering (AML) risk. This step involves evaluating data pertaining to the bank's activities (e.g., number of: domestic and international funds transfers; private banking customers; foreign correspondent accounts; payable through accounts; and domestic and international geographic locations of the bank's business area and customer transactions) in relation to Customer Identification Program (CIP) and customer due diligence (CDD) information.

Management should structure the bank's AML compliance program to adequately address its risk profile, as identified by the risk assessment. Management should understand the bank's AML risk exposure and develop the appropriate policies, procedures, and processes to monitor and control AML risks. For example, the bank's monitoring systems to identify, research, and report suspicious activity should be risk-based, with particular emphasis on higher-risk products and services as identified by the bank's AML risk assessment.[10]

2.3 COUNTRY OR GEOGRAPHIC RISK

There is no universally agreed definition by either competent authorities or financial institutions/DNFBPs that prescribes whether a particular country or geographic area (including the country within

---

10 Australia Anti-Money Laundering and Counter-Terrorism Financing Rules Instrument 2007 (as amended), Paragraph 4.1.3 (5), Officer of the Superintendent of Financial Institutions Canada: Deterring and Detecting Money Laundering and Terrorist Financing 2008, 15, See Central Bank of Nigeria's Anti-Money Laundering/Combating the Financing of Terrorism (AML/CFT) Risk Based Supervision (RBS) Framework, 2011, paragraph 5.1, See also the Central Bank of Nigeria's (Anti-Money Laundering and Combating the Financing of Terrorism in Banks and Other Financial Institutions in Nigeria) Regulations, 2013, Regulation 5,6,19,20, See also United States Federal Financial Institutions Examination Council: Bank Secrecy Act/Anti-Money Laundering Examination Manual 2014, 19-20

which the financial institution operates) represents a higher risk. Country risk, in conjunction with other risk factors, provides useful information as to potential money laundering and terrorist financing risks. Factors that may result in a determination that a country poses a higher risk include:

- Countries subject to sanctions, embargoes or similar measures issued by, for example, the United Nations ("UN"). In addition, in some circumstances, countries subject to sanctions or measures similar to those issued by bodies such as the UN, but which may not be universally recognized, may be given credence by a financial institution because of the standing of the issuer and the nature of the measures.

- Countries identified by credible sources as lacking appropriate AML/CFT laws, regulations and other measures.

- Countries identified by credible sources as providing funding or support for terrorist activities that have designated terrorist organisations operating within them.

- Countries identified by credible sources as having significant levels of corruption, or other criminal activity.[11]

This would be discussed in more detail in chapter 5.

---

11 FATF Guidance on the Risk Based Approach to combating money laundering and terrorist financing, (High Level principles and procedures) 2007, paragraph 3.5. Australia Anti-Money Laundering and Counter-Terrorism Financing Rules Instrument 2007 (as amended), Paragraph 4.1.3 (7), Officer of the Superintendent of Financial Institutions Canada: Deterring and Detecting Money Laundering and Terrorist Financing 2008, 16, See Central Bank of Nigeria (Anti-Money Laundering and Combating the Financing of Terrorism in Banks and Other Financial Institutions in Nigeria) Regulations, 2013, Regulation 5, 6, 17, See also United States Federal Financial Institutions Examination Council: Bank Secrecy Act/Anti-Money Laundering Examination Manual 2014, 21-22

Case 2.1: Financial Crimes Enforcement Network v. HSBC Bank USA N.A. Number 2012-02

The Financial Crimes Enforcement Network determined that HBUS wilfully violated the Bank Secrecy Act since at least mid-2006 by: (1) lacking an effective anti-money laundering program reasonably designed to manage risks of money laundering and other illicit activity, in violation of Title 31, United States Code, Section 5318(h) and 31 C.F.R. § 1020.210; (2) failing to conduct due diligence on certain foreign correspondent accounts, in violation of Title 31, United States Code, Section 5318(i) and 31 C.F.R. § 1010.610.

HBUS provided a full range of consumer and commercial products and services to individuals, corporations, financial institutions, non-profit organizations, and governments in the United States and abroad, including in jurisdictions with weak anti-money laundering and counter-terrorist financing ("AML/CTF") controls. HBUS did not effectively conduct enterprise-wide, risk-based assessments of potential money laundering risks, given its clients, products, and geographic reach, and HBUS failed to adequately identify potential money laundering vulnerabilities. The Bank's failure to adequately assess risk negatively impacted the effectiveness of its transaction monitoring, which already suffered from additional systemic weaknesses.

Customer Risk. The Bank's written policies, procedures, and controls did not effectively risk rate customers. The Bank's risk rating methodologies were not designed to evaluate customers based on specific customer information and balanced consideration of all relevant factors, including country/jurisdictional risk, products and services provided, expected transaction volume, and nature of customer profiles. Failure to consistently gather reasonably accurate and complete customer documentation undermined the Bank's ability to conduct customer risk assessments. These deficiencies prevented the Bank from performing adequate analysis of the risks associated with particular customers and from determining whether transactions lacked an apparent business or lawful purpose or fell within the particular customer's normal and expected range of conduct.

For example, Group affiliate HSBC Mexico S.A. Banco ("HBMX") was an HBUS respondent bank. The account that HBMX maintained with HBUS accepted bulk deposits of U.S. currency and processed wire transfers. HBMX operated in Mexico, a country that was the subject of publicly available cautionary information about drug trafficking and money laundering vulnerabilities. HBMX's branch in the Cayman Islands operated under a Cayman Islands Monetary Authority license limiting authority to do business to non-residents of the Cayman Islands. Potentially high-risk Mexican casas de cambio and other money transmitter and dollar-exchange businesses were HBMX customers. Despite these risks, until 2009, HBUS treated HBMX as a "standard" money laundering risk and did not effectively detect and report suspicious activity.

Product Risk. Some of the Bank's products and services involved significant anti-money laundering risks, including but not limited to: correspondent accounts, embassy banking, wire transfers, automated clearing house ("ACH") transfers, banknotes, lockboxes, clearing of bulk traveler's checks, bearer share accounts, pre-paid cards, foreign exchange, cash letters, international pouch activity, and remote deposit capture. HBUS failed to take appropriate steps to adequately assess the AML/CFT risks posed with respect to many of its products and services.

For instance, the Bank failed to manage money laundering risks associated with its pouch services and did not provide for appropriate controls and monitoring to address the underlying risks posed by this transaction activity. In one example, until November 2008, the Bank cleared traveler's checks received from a foreign respondent

bank without monitoring systems in place that were reasonably designed to detect, investigate, and report evidence of money laundering. Several individuals purchased sequentially numbered traveler's
checks at a Russian bank in transactions totaling more than $290
million over several years. These traveler's checks were signed in a
uniform illegible scrawl and made payable to approximately 30 different customers of a Japanese bank. The Japanese bank was a HBUS
correspondent customer and for several years regularly delivered
multi-hundred-thousand-dollar batches of these sequentially numbered traveler's checks to HBUS via pouch. During the relevant
period of time, HBUS knew or should have known that uniformly
signed, sequentially numbered traveler's checks in such high volume
are a money laundering "red flag."

Country Risk. The Bank lacked adequate country risk rating processes reasonably designed to capture readily available information about
countries' AML/CFT risks and failed to ensure uniform compliance
with risk rating standards through complete internal reviews. The
Bank lacked a precise structure to ensure systematic country risk assessments, including updates, as prudent and necessary, which resulted in HBUS making inappropriate country risk assessments in some
instances. The Bank used four labels ("standard," "medium," "cautionary," or "high" risk) to identify a country's anti-money laundering
risk. From 2002 until 2009, HBUS rated Mexico as having "standard" anti-money laundering risk, the lowest of the Bank's four possible country risk ratings, despite publicly-available information to the
contrary. In 2006, the Financial Crimes Enforcement Network issued
an advisory, FIN-2006-A003, notifying financial institutions of the
potential threat of narcotics-based money laundering between Mexico
and the United States. In addition, the United States Department of
State International Narcotics Control Strategy Reports dating back
to 2002 have consistently rated Mexico as a country of primary concern for money laundering and financial crimes. The inappropriate

country risk rating, together with other AML/CFT deficiencies, including the monitoring failures described above, resulted in HBUS failing to identify and thereby facilitating the flow of illicit proceeds between Mexico and the United States.

The Financial Crimes Enforcement Network determined that a civil money penalty in the amount of five hundred million dollars is warranted for HBUS's violations of the Bank Secrecy Act and its implementing regulations, as described in the ASSESSMENT.

> **BOX 2.1: DELIVERY CHANNEL RISK/BUSINESS RELATIONSHIP RISK**
>
> Application of risk categories provides a strategy for managing potential risks by enabling financial institutions/DNFBPs to subject customers to proportionate controls and oversight. The most commonly used risk criteria are: country or geographic risk; customer risk; and product/services risk.[12]
>
> Although countries like Australia, Canada, Hong Kong, India, Nigeria and South Africa have identified other risk categories in addition to the ones stated above.[13] It is not mandatory for a financial institution/DNFBP to provide

---

12 See United States Federal Financial Institutions Examination Council: Bank Secrecy Act/Anti-Money Laundering Examination Manual 2014, 19-22, See also United Kingdom Joint Money Laundering Steering Group: Prevention of Money Laundering/Combating Terrorist Financing 2014 Revised Version: Guidance for the UK Financial Sector Part I, paragraph 4.29

13 Australia Anti-Money Laundering and Counter-Terrorism Financing Rules Instrument 2007 (as amended), paragraph 4.1.3, See Officer of the Superintendent of Financial Institutions Canada: Deterring and Detecting Money Laundering and Terrorist Financing 2008, 15, Hong Kong, China Guideline on Anti-Money Laundering and Counter-Terrorist Financing 2015, paragraph 3.5, India Prevention of Money-Laundering (Maintenance of Records) Amendment Rules, 2013, rule 13, See Central Bank of Nigeria (Anti-Money Laundering and Combating the Financing of Terrorism in Banks and Other Financial Institutions in Nigeria) Regulations, 2013, Regulation 5, See also South Africa, Financial Intelligence Centre Guidance Note 3A, 2005, paragraph 3

for such additional criteria as same can be used to assess other risk categories.

For example the Delivery Channel Risk Criteria as identified by Australia, Hong Kong, India and Nigeria can be used to assess product and services risk while the Business Relationship Risk Criteria identified by Canada and South Africa can be used to assess customer risk.

Money Laundering risk in relation to products increases where that product can be used to quickly move funds around the world, to make purchases and to access cash (both directly and indirectly) through the Automated Teller Machine (ATM) network.

Money Laundering risk in relation to customers increases where a client frequently exchanges currencies.

BOX 2.2: DE-RISKING

A global trend has emerged whereby banks are closing accounts deemed high risk, which are often those of nongovernmental organizations, foreign embassies, correspondent banks, and money transfer businesses. This practice, referred to as de-risking, is perhaps an inevitable response from the financial services industry given the ascendance of AML/CFT in recent years, coupled with the 2008 financial crisis, which prompted the sector to rethink the way it defines and manages risk.[14]

---

14 Global Center on Cooperative Security: Understanding Bank De-risking and its Effects on Financial Inclusion, January 2015

De-risking refers to the phenomenon of financial institutions terminating or restricting business relationships with clients or categories of clients to avoid, rather than manage, risk in line with the FATF's risk-based approach.

"De-risking" should never be an excuse for a bank to avoid implementing a risk-based approach, in line with the Financial Action Task Force (FATF) standards. The FATF Recommendations only require financial institutions to terminate customer relationships, on a case-by-case basis, where the money laundering and terrorist financing risks cannot be mitigated. This is fully in line with AML/CFT objectives. What is not in line with the FATF standards is the wholesale cutting loose of entire classes of customer, without taking into account, seriously and comprehensively, their level of risk or risk mitigation measures for individual customers within a particular sector.

The risk-based approach should be the cornerstone of an effective AML/CFT system, and is essential to properly managing risks. The FATF expects financial institutions to identify, assess and understand their money laundering and terrorist financing risks and take commensurate measures in order to mitigate them. This does not imply a "zero failure" approach.[15]

---

15 Financial Action Task Force 'FATF clarifies risk-based approach: case-by-case, not wholesale de-risking' (http://www.fatf-gafi.org 23rd October 2014)http://www.fatf-gafi.org/documents/documents/rba-and-de-risking.html Accessed 3rd of March 2015

CHAPTER 3

CUSTOMER RISK

Any type of account is potentially vulnerable to money laundering or terrorist financing. By the nature of their business, occupation or anticipated transaction activity, certain customers and entities may pose specific risks. At this stage of the risk assessment process, it is essential that the financial institution/DNFBP exercises judgment and neither define nor treat all members of a specific category of customer as posing the same level of risk.

In assessing customer risk, financial institutions/DNFBPs are required to consider other variables such as services sought and geographic locations.[1]

Financial institutions/DNFBPs will determine the due diligence requirements appropriate to each customer. This may include:

---

1 Australia Anti-Money Laundering and Counter-Terrorism Financing Rules Instrument 2007 (as amended), Paragraph 4.1.3, Officer of the Superintendent of Financial Institutions Canada Guideline: Deterring and Detecting Money Laundering and Terrorist Financing 2008, 14, Central Bank of Nigeria's Anti-Money Laundering/Combating the Financing of Terrorism (AML/CFT) Risk Based Supervision (RBS) Framework, 2011, paragraph 5.1

- A standard level of due diligence, to be applied to all customers.[2]

- An increased level of due diligence in respect of those customers that are determined to be of higher risk. This may be the result of the customer's business activity, ownership structure, anticipated or actual volume or types of transactions, including those transactions involving higher risk countries or defined by applicable law or regulation as posing higher risk, such as:

O Correspondent banking relationships; and O PEPs.[3]

- The standard level being reduced in recognized lower risk scenarios, such as:

    o Publicly listed companies subject to regulatory disclosure requirements.

    o Other financial institutions (domestic or foreign) subject to an AML/CFT regime consistent with the FATF Recommendations.

    o Individuals whose main source of funds is derived from salary, pension, social benefits from an identified and

---

2 Australia Anti-Money Laundering and Counter-Terrorism Financing Rules Instrument 2007 (as amended), paragraphs 4.2.3-4.2.9, Officer of the Superintendent of Financial Institutions Canada Guideline: Deterring and Detecting Money Laundering and Terrorist Financing 2008, 18, CBN (Anti-Money Laundering and Combating the Financing of Terrorism in Banks and Other Financial Institutions in Nigeria) Regulations, 2013, Regulation 14

3 Australia Anti-Money Laundering and Counter-Terrorism Financing Rules Instrument 2007 (as amended), paragraph 4.13.3, Officer of the Superintendent of Financial Institutions Canada Guideline: Deterring and Detecting Money Laundering and Terrorist Financing 2008, 18, 23, CBN (Anti-Money Laundering and Combating the Financing of Terrorism in Banks and Other Financial Institutions in Nigeria) Regulations, 2013, Regulation 16

appropriate source and where transactions are commensurate with the funds.

o Transactions involving de minimis amounts for particular types of transactions (e.g. small insurance premiums).[4]

3.1 STANDARD DUE DILIGENCE

Financial institutions/DNFBPs shall apply a standard level of due diligence to all customers.

3.1.1 NATURAL PERSONS

An anti-money laundering and counter-terrorist financing ("AML/CTF") program must include appropriate risk-based systems and controls that are designed to enable financial institutions/designated non-financial institutions to be reasonably satisfied, where a customer is an individual, that the customer is the individual that he or she claims to be.

The type of information that would normally be needed to perform this function would be:

- Legal name and any other names used (such as maiden name);

- Permanent address (full address shall be obtained and the use of a post office box number only, is not sufficient);

- Telephone number, fax number, and email address;

---

4 Australia Anti-Money Laundering and Counter-Terrorism Financing Rules Instrument 2007 (as amended), paragraph 48.2, 50.3, Central Bank of Nigeria (Anti-Money Laundering and Combating the Financing of Terrorism in Banks and Other Financial Institutions in Nigeria) Regulations, 2013, Regulation 24, Officer of the Superintendent of Financial Institutions Canada Guideline: Deterring and Detecting Money Laundering and Terrorist Financing 2008, 22

- Date and place of birth;

- Nationality

- Occupation, public position held and name of employer;

- An official personal identification number or other unique identifier contained in an unexpired official document such as passport, identification card, residence permit, social security records or drivers' licence that bears a photograph of the customer;

- Type of account and nature of the banking relationship; and

- Signature.[5]

An AML/CTF program must include a procedure for the reporting entity to verify, at a minimum, the following Customer Due Diligence (CDD) information about a customer:

- the customer's full name; and

- either:

  o the customer's date of birth; or

  o the customer's residential address.

---

5 Australia Anti-Money Laundering and Counter-Terrorism Financing Rules Instrument 2007 (as amended), paragraph 4.2.3-4.2.5, Officer of the Superintendent of Financial Institutions Canada Guideline: Deterring and Detecting Money Laundering and Terrorist Financing 2008, 20, CBN (Anti-Money Laundering and Combating the Financing of Terrorism in Banks and Other Financial Institutions in Nigeria) Regulations, 2013, Schedule II Paragraph 1 (1). See also South Africa Money Laundering and Terrorist Financial Control Regulations, 2002 (as amended), Regulation 3, See United States Federal Financial Institutions Examination Council: Bank Secrecy Act/Anti-Money Laundering Examination Manual 2014, 48-49

A financial Institution/DNFBP shall verify the information referred to above, by at least one of the following methods –

- Confirming the full name and date of birth from an official document (such as birth certificate, passport, identity card, social security records);

- Confirming the permanent address (such as utility bill, tax assessment, bank statement, a letter from a public authority);

- Contacting the customer by telephone, by letter or by e-mail to confirm the information supplied after an account has been opened (such as a disconnected phone, returned mail, or incorrect e-mail address shall warrant further investigation);

- Confirming the validity of the official documentation provided through certification by an authorized person such as embassy official, notary public.[6]

The examples quoted above are not the only possibilities. There may be other documents of an equivalent nature which may be produced as satisfactory evidence of customers' identity.

---

6 Australia Anti-Money Laundering and Counter-Terrorism Financing Rules Instrument 2007 (as amended), paragraphs 4.2.6 - 4.2.13, Officer of the Superintendent of Financial Institutions Canada Guideline: Deterring and Detecting Money Laundering and Terrorist Financing 2008, 21, CBN (Anti-Money Laundering and Combating the Financing of Terrorism in Banks and Other Financial Institutions in Nigeria) Regulations, 2013, Schedule II Paragraph 1 (2), See also South Africa Money Laundering and Terrorist Financial Control Regulations, 2002 (as amended), Regulation 4, See United States Federal Financial Institutions Examination Council: Bank Secrecy Act/Anti-Money Laundering Examination Manual 2014, 49-50

BOX 3.1: WHEN TO UNDERTAKE CUSTOMER DUE DILIGENCE?

Client identification and verification must be done at the outset of the business relationship or single transaction. It is good business practice to date documents relating to the verification of a client. This is an indicator that the account opening and verification of the client was done simultaneously.

BOX 3.2: WHERE CDD MEASURES ARE NOT COMPLETED

Where a financial institution/designated non-financial institution are unable to complete CDD measures, it shall terminate the business relationship and consider if the circumstances are suspicious so as to warrant the filing of a Suspicious Transaction Report (STR).[7]

3.1.2 BENEFICIAL OWNERS

Beneficial ownership, for AML purposes, must be established for all accounts. Beneficial owners will ordinarily include the individuals (i) who generally have ultimate control through ownership or other means over the funds in the account and/or (ii) who are the ultimate source of funds for the account and whose source of wealth should be subject to due diligence. Mere signature authority does not necessarily constitute control for these purposes. The meaning of beneficial ownership for purposes of determining who should be subject to due

---

7 See China Anti-Money Laundering Law 2007, Article 16, See also Singapore Notice to Banks, Monetary Authority of Singapore Act, Cap.186, Prevention of Money Laundering and Countering the Financing of Terrorism 2007, paragraph 4.34,

diligence is dependent on the circumstances and due diligence must be done on all beneficial owners identified.[8]

3.1.2.1 LEGAL ENTITIES

Where the client is a private investment company, a financial Institution/DNFBP will understand the structure of the company sufficiently to determine the provider of funds, the beneficial owner(s) of the assets held by the company and those with the power to give direction to the directors of the company. This principle applies regardless of whether the share capital is in registered or bearer form.[9]

The type of information that would normally be needed to perform this function would be:

- Name of the institution

- Principal place of the institution's business operations;

- Mailing address of the institution;

- Contact telephone and fax numbers;

- Some form of official identification number, if available such as tax identification number;

- The original or certified copy of the certificate of incorporation and memorandum and articles of association;

---

8 Australia Anti-Money Laundering and Counter-Terrorism Financing Rules Instrument 2007 (as amended), paragraphs 4.3.1-4.8.8, See also the CBN (Anti-Money Laundering and Combating the Financing of Terrorism in Banks and Other Financial Institutions in Nigeria) Regulations, 2013, Regulation 15

9 The Wolfsberg Group: Wolfsberg Anti-Money Laundering Principles for Private Banking (2012), paragraph 1.2.3

- The resolution of the board of directors to open an account and identification of those who have authority to operate the account; and

- Nature and purpose of business and its legitimacy.[10]

A financial Institution/DNFBP shall verify the information above, by at least one of the following methods:

- For established corporate entities, reviewing a copy of the latest report and audited accounts, if available;

- Conducting an enquiry by a business information service or an undertaking from a reputable and known firm of lawyers or accountants confirming the documents submitted;

- Undertaking a company search and/or other commercial enquiries to see that the institution has not been, or is not in the process of being dissolved, struck off, wound up or terminated;

- Utilising an independent information verification process, such as accessing public and private databases;

- Obtaining prior bank references;

- Visiting the corporate entity; and

---

10 Australia Anti-Money Laundering and Counter-Terrorism Financing Rules Instrument 2007 (as amended), paragraph 4.3.1-4.3.4, Officer of the Superintendent of Financial Institutions Canada Guideline: Deterring and Detecting Money Laundering and Terrorist Financing 2008, 21, CBN (Anti-Money Laundering and Combating the Financing of Terrorism in Banks and Other Financial Institutions in Nigeria) Regulations, 2013, Schedule II Paragraph 3 (1). See also South Africa Money Laundering and Terrorist Financial Control Regulations, 2002 (as amended), Regulation 7

- Contacting the corporate entity by telephone, mail or e-mail.[11]

Financial institutions/DNFBPs shall also take reasonable steps to verify the identity and reputation of any agent that opens an account on behalf of a corporate customer, if that agent is not an officer of the corporate customer.[12]

3.1.2.2 PARTNERSHIPS

Where the client is a partnership, a financial Institution/DNFBP will understand the structure of the partnership sufficiently to determine the provider of funds and the general partners.[13]

The information needed to carry out these function includes:

- the full name of the partnership;

- the full business name (if any) of the partnership as registered under any State or Territory business names legislation;

- the country in which the partnership was established;

- in respect of one of the partners - the information required to be collected from an individual under the applicable customer

---

11 Australia Anti-Money Laundering and Counter-Terrorism Financing Rules Instrument 2007 (as amended), paragraph 4.3.5-4.3.13, Officer of the Superintendent of Financial Institutions Canada Guideline: Deterring and Detecting Money Laundering and Terrorist Financing 2008, 21-22, CBN (Anti-Money Laundering and Combating the Financing of Terrorism in Banks and Other Financial Institutions in Nigeria) Regulations, 2013, Schedule II Paragraph 3 (2), See also South Africa Money Laundering and Terrorist Financial Control Regulations, 2002 (as amended), Regulation 8

12 Australia Anti-Money Laundering and Counter-Terrorism Financing Rules Instrument 2007 (as amended), paragraph 4.3.5, CBN (Anti-Money Laundering and Combating the Financing of Terrorism in Banks and Other Financial Institutions in Nigeria) Regulations, 2013, Schedule II Paragraph 3 (3)

13 CBN (Anti-Money Laundering and Combating the Financing of Terrorism in Banks and Other Financial Institutions in Nigeria) Regulations, 2013, Schedule II Paragraph 4 (1)

identification procedure with respect to individuals set out in an AML/CTF program; and

- the full name and residential address of each partner in the partnership except where the regulated status of the partnership is confirmed through reference to the current membership directory of the relevant professional association.[14]

An AML/CTF program must include a procedure for the reporting entity to verify at a minimum:

- the full name of the partnership from the partnership agreement, certified copy or certified extract of the partnership agreement, reliable and independent documents relating to the partnership or reliable and independent electronic data; and

- information about one of the partners in accordance with the applicable customer identification procedure with respect to individuals set out in an AML/CTF program.[15]

An AML/CTF program must include appropriate risk-based systems and controls for the reporting entity to determine whether, and to what extent, in addition to the CDD information referred to above, any other CDD information collected in respect of the partnership should be verified.[16]

---

14 Australia Anti-Money Laundering and Counter-Terrorism Financing Rules Instrument 2007 (as amended), paragraph 4.5.3, See also South Africa Money Laundering and Terrorist Financial Control Regulations, 2002 (as amended), Regulation 13

15 Australia Anti-Money Laundering and Counter-Terrorism Financing Rules Instrument 2007 (as amended), paragraph 4.5.5

16 Australia Anti-Money Laundering and Counter-Terrorism Financing Rules Instrument 2007 (as amended), paragraph 4.5.6

An AML/CTF program must require that the verification of information about a partnership be based on:

- a partnership agreement, certified copy or certified extract of a partnership agreement;

- a certified copy or certified extract of minutes of a partnership meeting;

- reliable and independent documents relating to the partnership;

- reliable and independent electronic data; or

- a combination of the above.[17]

For the purposes of this section, reliable and independent documents relating to the partnership 'includes a disclosure certificate that verifies information about a partnership where:

- the information to be verified is not otherwise reasonably available from the sources described above.[18]

3.1.2.3 TRUSTS

Where the client is a trust, a financial institution/DNFBP will understand the structure of the trust sufficiently to determine (i) the provider of funds (e.g. settlor), (ii) those who have control over the funds (e.g. trustees), (iii) any persons or entities who have the power

---

17 Australia Anti-Money Laundering and Counter-Terrorism Financing Rules Instrument 2007 (as amended), paragraph 4.5.7, See also South Africa Money Laundering and Terrorist Financial Control Regulations, 2002 (as amended), Regulation 14

18 Australia Anti-Money Laundering and Counter-Terrorism Financing Rules Instrument 2007 (as amended), paragraph 4.5.8

to remove the trustees and (iv) the persons for whose benefit the trust is established.[19]

An AML/CTF program must include a procedure for the reporting entity to collect, at a minimum, the following CDD information from a customer:

- the full name of the trust;

- the full business name (if any) of the trustee in respect of the trust;

- the type of the trust;

- the country in which the trust was established;

- the full name of the settlor of the trust, unless:

  - o the material asset contribution to the trust by the settlor at the time the trust is established is less than ten thousand dollars; or

  - o the settlor is deceased; or

  - o the trust is verified using the simplified trustee verification procedure described below.

- if any of the trustees is an individual, then in respect of one of those individuals – the information required to be collected from an individual under the applicable customer

---

19 The Wolfsberg Group: Wolfsberg Anti-Money Laundering Principles for Private Banking (2012), paragraph 1.2.2

identification procedure with respect to individuals set out in an AML/CTF program;

- if any of the trustees is a company, then in respect of one of those companies – the information required to be collected from a company under the applicable customer identification procedure with respect to companies set out in an AML/CTF program; and

- if the trustees comprise individuals and companies then in respect of either an individual or a company – the information required to be collected from the individual or company (as the case may be) under the applicable customer identification with respect to the individual or company set out in an AML/CTF program.[20]

An AML/CTF program must include a procedure for the reporting entity to verify, at a minimum:

- the full name of the trust from a trust deed, certified copy or certified extract of the trust deed, reliable and independent documents relating to the trust or reliable and independent electronic data;

- if any of the trustees is an individual, then in respect of one of those individuals – information about the individual in accordance with the applicable customer identification procedure with respect to individuals set out in an AML/CTF program;

20 Australia Anti-Money Laundering and Counter-Terrorism Financing Rules Instrument 2007 (as amended), paragraph 4.4.3, CBN (Anti-Money Laundering and Combating the Financing of Terrorism in Banks and Other Financial Institutions in Nigeria) Regulations, 2013, Schedule II Paragraph 5 (1), See also South Africa Money Laundering and Terrorist Financial Control Regulations, 2002 (as amended), Regulation 15

- if any of the trustees is a company, then in respect of one of those companies – information about the company in accordance with the applicable customer identification procedure with respect to companies set out in an AML/CTF program;

- if the trustees comprise individuals and companies then in respect of either an individual or a company – the information about the individual or company (as the case may be) in accordance with the applicable procedures with respect to the individual or company set out in an AML/CTF program; and

- the full name of the settlor of the trust, unless:

- the material asset contribution to the trust by the settlor at the time the trust is established is less than ten thousand dollars; or

- the settlor is deceased; or

- the trust is verified using the simplified trustee verification procedure described below.[21]

Simplified Trustee Verification Procedure requires the reporting entity to verify that the trust is:

o   a managed investment scheme registered by the relevant authority in that country;

o   a managed investment scheme that is not registered by the relevant authority in that country and that:

---

21 Australia Anti-Money Laundering and Counter-Terrorism Financing Rules Instrument 2007 (as amended), paragraph 4.4.5 – 4.4.16,CBN (Anti-Money Laundering and Combating the Financing of Terrorism in Banks and Other Financial Institutions in Nigeria) Regulations, 2013, Schedule II Paragraph 5 (2), See also South Africa Money Laundering and Terrorist Financial Control Regulations, 2002 (as amended), Regulation 16

o   only has wholesale clients; and

o   registered and subject to the regulatory oversight of a Commonwealth statutory regulator in relation to its activities as a trust; or

o   a government superannuation fund established by legislation.

3.1.2.4 UNINCORPORATED ASSOCIATIONS

The type of information that would normally be needed to perform standard due diligence on the above institutions include:

- Name of account;

- Mailing address;

- Contact telephone and fax numbers;

- Some form of official identification number, such as tax identification number;

- Description of the purpose or activities of the account holder as stated in a formal constitution; and

- Copy of documentation confirming the legal existence of the account holder such as register of charities.[22]

Financial institutions/DNFBPs shall verify the information referred to above, by at least one of the following –

---

22 Australia Anti-Money Laundering and Counter-Terrorism Financing Rules Instrument 2007 (as amended), paragraph 4.6.3, CBN (Anti-Money Laundering and Combating the Financing of Terrorism in Banks and Other Financial Institutions in Nigeria) Regulations, 2013, Schedule II Paragraph 5 (1)

- Obtaining an independent undertaking from a reputable and known firm of lawyers or accountants confirming the documents submitted;

- Obtaining prior bank references; and

- Accessing public and private databases or official sources.[23]

In each of the above cases, a financial institution/DNFBP will make a reasonable judgment as to the need for further due diligence. This would be explained in more detail in the next section.

BOX 3.3: AIMS AND OBJECTIVES OF STANDARD DUE DILIGENCE

Information obtained from the customer due diligence process would enable financial institutions/DNFBPs differentiate between high risk, medium risk and low risk clients.

For example if a client tells the financial institution/ DNFBP that he is a Senior Government Official, the financial institution/DNFBP would have to classify him as a high risk customer. But if the customer says his source of income is dependent on a pension scheme, and that information has been verified by the firm, then the financial institution/DNFBP would classify the customer as low risk. Customers who are neither classified as high risk or low risk automatically become medium risk customers.

23 Australia Anti-Money Laundering and Counter-Terrorism Financing Rules Instrument 2007 (as amended), paragraph 4.6.5 - 4.6.8, CBN (Anti-Money Laundering and Combating the Financing of Terrorism in Banks and Other Financial Institutions in Nigeria) Regulations, 2013, Schedule II Paragraph 5 (2)

Financial institutions/DNFBPs must ensure that they monitor medium risk customers so as not to be caught unawares when a medium risk customer becomes a high risk customer.

For example, a customer who works in a publishing firm may venture into politics later in the future. A financial institution/DNFBP that monitors medium risk customers would be able to know when such transition happens.

Financial institutions/DNFBPs can monitor medium risk customers by conducting extensive research occasionally on such customers. Watching local news would enable a financial institution/DNFBP to determine if a client who was working in a publishing firm is now working as a top government official.

BOX 3.4: POINTS TO CONSIDER IN MAKING A PEP DETERMINATION

Financial institutions/DNFBPs must take "reasonable measures" to determine if a customer is a Politically Exposed Person (PEP). Reasonable measures could include:

- Asking the individual for information that could indicate PEP status, such as existing or previous connections to the prescribed relationships;

- Screening the individual's name and other personal information against a commercially or publicly available database to gather more information about the individual; or

- a combination of both.

About asking the Client

If a financial institution/DNFBP chooses to ask the individual for information, the financial institution/DNFBP should keep in mind that clients should not be expected to know the criteria that determine whether they are PEPs. Financial institutions/DNFBPs should also note that there is no obligation imposed on them to disclose to a client that a determination must be made, or needs to be made.

A reasonable approach would be to ask the client if the client has or has ever had a prescribed connection to a foreign state, government, military or judiciary. The questions could be expanded to cover family members with any similar connections. If the responses are not clear or inconclusive, additional assessment or due diligence may be necessary before finalizing the determination. The additional measures could range from asking the applicant for more information, to internet searches, to running the individual(s') name(s) against a public database.

About consulting a commercial database

Financial institutions/DNFBPs that choose to screen names and other personal information against a commercial or publicly available database should ensure they:

- Determine whether the provider identifies in the database individuals who fit the definition of PEPs. Most of these databases are built using open source (i.e. public) information. If the family members of a PEP are not well known, there is no guarantee that a database will know about them.

- Establish the frequency and methodology used to update the information in the database, including whether the provider removes names from the database when office-holders leave office or die. If names are removed, the database may not capture persons who "have ever been" PEPs.

- Establish a process to discard false positive hits, and identify other steps to be taken if the information in the database is inconclusive.

- Are able to screen the names of clients in all business lines against this list, especially if the financial institution/DNFBP has manual procedures, legacy systems, or uses the database to screen for the names of designated persons under anti-terrorist regulations.

Regulatory authorities do not expect financial institutions to depend on a client database in making a PEP determination where the information obtained from the client shows that the client is a PEP. Clients, who initially provide information that clearly establishes them to be PEPs, must be determined to be PEPs and need not be scrubbed through databases unless it is done merely to obtain background or additional information.

Financial institutions/DNFBPs should also ensure that, where a client is determined to be a PEP, and the financial institution/DNFBP is aware that the client has family members who are also PEPs by reason of the definition in the relevant Money Laundering Laws/Regulations applicable in that country, the names of such family members are scrubbed against the financial institution's client databases to determine if accounts are held in such names by the financial institution/DNFBP.

Financial institutions/DNFBPs that use agents or mandataries (deposit brokers, mortgage brokers or others) to identify their clients and remit client identification information to them retain responsibility for PEP determination. Financial institutions/ DNFBPs may assign responsibility for collecting the information necessary for the financial institution to determine if the client is a PEP, but the financial institution, not the agent, is responsible for making the determination and for applying the prescribed measures accordingly. Financial institutions/DNFBPs should ensure that where agents or mandataries are responsible for gathering the information, the agents understand what is required to be done and the financial institution/DNFBP satisfies itself that its agents are doing what is required. If a client's name is contained in a public database, but the financial institution/ DNFBP does not determine the client is a PEP, the financial institution/DNFBP may wish to make a note of the "hit" for future reference or to guide it in any future risk assessment.[24]

3.2 ENHANCED DUE DILIGENCE

The Enhanced Due Diligence (EDD) should give financial institutions/DNFBPs a greater understanding of the customer and their associated risk than standard due diligence. It should provide more certainty that the customer and/or beneficial owner is who they say they are and that the purposes of the business relationship are legitimate; as well as increasing opportunities to identify and deal with concerns that they are not.[25]

---

24 Officer of the Superintendent of Financial Institutions Canada: Deterring and Detecting Money Laundering and Terrorist Financing, Sound Business and Financial Practices 2008, 29, 30

25 Australia Anti-Money Laundering and Counter-Terrorism Financing Rules Instrument 2007 (as amended), paragraph 4.13.1, Officer of the Superintendent of Financial Institutions Canada: Deterring and Detecting Money Laundering and Terrorist Financing 2008, 23, See also the CBN (Anti-Money Laundering and Combating the Financing of Terrorism in Banks and Other Financial Institutions in Nigeria) Regulations, 2013, Regulation 16, See also South Africa, Financial Intelligence Centre Guidance Note 3A: Guidance for Accountable Institutions on Client Identification and Verification and Related Matters, paragraph 4

Financial institutions/DNFBPs must apply EDD measures on a risk-sensitive basis in any situation which by its nature can present a higher risk of money laundering or terrorist financing. As part of this, a financial institution/DNFBP may conclude, under its risk-based approach, that the information it has collected as part of the customer due diligence process is insufficient in relation to the money laundering or terrorist financing risk, and that it must obtain additional information about a particular customer, the customer's beneficial owner, where applicable, and the purpose and intended nature of the business relationship.

In its internal policies, financial institutions/DNFBPs must define categories of persons whose circumstances warrant enhanced due diligence. This will typically be the case where the circumstances are likely to pose a higher than average risk to a bank.

Indicators

The circumstances of the following categories of persons are indicators for defining them as requiring Enhanced Due Diligence:

- Cash (and cash equivalent) intensive businesses including:

    o Money services businesses (MSB) (e.g. remittance houses, currency exchange houses, casas de cambio, bureaux de change, money transfer agents and bank note traders or other businesses offering money transfer facilities).

    o Casinos, betting and other gambling related activities. And

    o Businesses that while not normally cash intensive, generate substantial amounts of cash for certain transactions.

- Charities and other "not for profit" organisations which are not subject to monitoring or supervision (especially those operating on a "cross-border" basis).

- "Gatekeepers" such as accountants, lawyers, or other professionals holding accounts at a financial institution, acting on behalf of their clients, and where the financial institution places unreasonable reliance on the gatekeeper.

- Use of intermediaries within the relationship who are not subject to adequate AML/CFT laws and measures and who are not adequately supervised.

- Persons residing in and/or having funds sourced from countries identified by credible sources as having inadequate AML standards or representing high risk for crime and corruption.

- "Politically Exposed Persons," frequently abbreviated as "PEPs," referring to individuals holding or, as appropriate, having held, senior, prominent, or important public positions with substantial authority over policy, operations or the use or allocation of government-owned resources, such as senior government officials, senior executives of government corpo rations, senior politicians, important political party officials, etc., as well as their close family and close associates. PEPs from different jurisdictions may be subject to different levels of diligence.[26]

---

26 Australia Anti-Money Laundering and Counter-Terrorism Financing Rules Instrument 2007 (as amended), paragraph 4.1.3, See also the Nigerian CBN (Anti-Money Laundering and Combating the Financing of Terrorism in Banks and Other Financial Institutions in Nigeria) Regulations, 2013, Regulation 16, See also South Africa, Financial Intelligence Centre Guidance Note 3A: Guidance for Accountable Institutions on Client Identification and Verification and Related Matters, paragraph 4

It is for each Accountable Institution to decide the steps it takes to determine whether a customer is seeking to establish a business relationship for legitimate reasons. Financial institutions/DNFBPs should in any case take adequate meaningful measures to establish the source of funds and source of wealth.[27] Financial institutions/DNFBPs may wish to refer to information sources such as asset and income declarations, which some jurisdictions expect certain senior public officials to file and which often include information about an official's source of wealth and current business interests. Financial institutions/DNFBPs should note that not all declarations are publicly available and that a high risk customer may have a legitimate reason for not providing a copy.[28]

Financial institutions/DNFBPs may also perform on-site visits for out-of-state, high-risk MSB customers, several of which could be located in High Intensity Drug Trafficking Areas ('HIDTAs') and High Intensity Financial Crime Areas ('HIFCAs).

Once the source of wealth and source of funds are established financial institutions/DNFBPs will need to analyse the information for "red flag" for corrupt activity.[29] In all cases if a financial institution/DNFBP suspects that the funds are proceeds of criminal activity, the financial institution/DNFBP is required to file a Suspicious Transaction

---

27 Australia Anti-Money Laundering and Counter-Terrorism Financing Rules Instrument 2007 (as amended), paragraph 4.13.3 (3), Officer of the Superintendent of Financial Institutions Canada Guideline: Deterring and Detecting Money Laundering and Terrorist Financing 2008, 23, See also the CBN (Anti-Money Laundering and Combating the Financing of Terrorism in Banks and Other Financial Institutions in Nigeria) Regulations, 2013, Regulation 18 (6), See also South Africa Money Laundering and Terrorist Financial Control Regulations, 2002 (as amended), Regulation 21 (3). See United States Federal Financial Institutions Examination Council: Bank Secrecy Act/Anti-Money Laundering Examination Manual 2014, 57-58

28 Joint Money Laundering Steering Group Guidance for the UK Financial Sector Part 1, Paragraph 5.5.29. Other sources of income or wealth (e.g., inheritance, divorce settlement, property sale)

29 T S Greenberg: Stolen Asset Recovery, Politically Exposed Persons, A policy paper on strengthening preventive measures

Report with the Financial Intelligence Unit.[30] A risk-based approach for the reporting of suspicious activity under these circumstances is not applicable.[31] A risk-based approach is however appropriate for the purpose of identifying suspicious activity, for example by directing additional resources at those areas a financial institution/DNFBP has identified as higher risk and in this case to customers who have been found to be high risk.[32]

3.2.1 SENIOR MANAGEMENT APPROVAL

The FATF standard requires a financial institution/DNFBP to obtain senior management approval for establishing a business relationship with PEPs and continuing a business relationship with a customer who is subsequently found to be a PEP or becomes a PEP.[33] The group AML/CTF officer should be involved in the PEP approval process since he is in the best position to say that a person should not be accepted regardless of the size of the account.[34]

---

30 See also the CBN (Anti-Money Laundering and Combating the Financing of Terrorism in Banks and Other Financial Institutions in Nigeria) Regulations, 2013, Regulation 18 (7). See also T S Greenberg: Stolen Asset Recovery, Politically Exposed Persons, A policy paper on strengthening preventive measures

31 FATF Guidance on the Risk Based Approach to combating money laundering and terrorist financing, (High Level principles and procedures) 2007, paragraph 3.16.

32 FATF Guidance on the Risk Based Approach to combating money laundering and terrorist financing, (High Level principles and procedures) 2007, paragraph 3.17, Australian Anti-Money Laundering and Counter-Terrorism Financing Rules Instrument 2007 (as amended), paragraph 4.13.3 (2)

33 The Financial Action Task Force (FATF): International Standards On Combating Money Laundering and the financing of terrorism and proliferation,(The FATF Recommendations) 2012, Recommendation 12, See also the CBN (Anti-Money Laundering and Combating the Financing of Terrorism in Banks and Other Financial Institutions in Nigeria) Regulations, 2013, Regulation 18 (4)

34 See T S Greenberg: Stolen Asset Recovery, Politically Exposed Persons, A policy paper on strengthening preventive measures

Financial institutions/DNFBPs are also required to obtain senior management approval for establishing a business relationship with other high-risk customers like money service businesses.

3.2.2 ENHANCED ON-GOING MONITORING

Once a business relationship has been established with a high-risk customer, financial institutions/DNFBPs must conduct enhanced on-going monitoring of the business relationship. [35]

The principle aim of monitoring in a risk-based system is to respond to enterprise wide issues based on each financial institution's analysis of major risks and in this case the major risks are the high-risk customers.[36]

Monitoring should identify information, transactions or attempted transactions that are unusual or potentially suspicious and that require further analysis. Monitoring criteria should cover all relevant indicators. Relevant indicators could include:

- frequent and unexplained movement of accounts to different financial institutions;

- frequent and unexplained movement of funds between different financial institutions in various geographic locations;

---

35 The Financial Action Task Force (FATF): International Standards On Combating Money Laundering and the financing of terrorism and proliferation,(The FATF Recommendations) 2012, Recommendation 12, Australia Anti-Money Laundering and Counter-Terrorism Financing Rules Instrument 2007 (as amended), paragraph 4.13.3,See also See also the CBN (Anti-Money Laundering and Combating the Financing of Terrorism in Banks and Other Financial Institutions in Nigeria) Regulations, 2013, Regulation 18 (7)

36 FATF Guidance on the Risk Based Approach to combating money laundering and terrorist financing, (High Level principles and procedures) 2007, paragraph 3.13.

- a client wishes to have credit and debit cards sent to destinations other than his or her address;

- a client has numerous accounts and makes or receives cash deposits in each of them amounting to a large aggregated amount;

- a client frequently exchanges currencies;

- a client wishes to have unusual access to safe deposit facilities;

- a client's accounts show virtually no normal business related activities, but are used to receive or disburse large sums;

- a client has accounts that have a large volume of deposits in bank cheques, postal orders or electronic funds transfers;

- a client is reluctant to provide complete information regarding the client's activities;

- a client's financial statements differ noticeably from those of similar businesses;

- a business client's representatives avoid contact with the branch;

- a client's deposits to, or withdrawals from, a corporate account are primarily in cash, rather than in the form of debit and credit normally associated with commercial operations;

- a client maintains a number of trustee accounts or client subaccounts;

- a client makes a large volume of seemingly unrelated deposits to several accounts and frequently transfers a major portion of the balances to a single account at the same bank or elsewhere.

- a client makes a large volume of cash deposits from a business that is not normally cash intensive;

- a small business in one location makes deposits on the same day at different branches;

- there is a remarkable transaction volume and a significant change in a client's account balance;

- a client's accounts show substantial increase in deposits of cash or negotiable instruments by a company offering professional advisory services;

- a client's accounts show a sudden and inconsistent change in transactions or patterns.

The examples referred to above may be legitimate features of certain categories of businesses, or may make business sense if viewed in the context of the client's business activities. However, it is equally possible that these features would be unexpected in relation to certain categories of businesses, or would have no apparent business purpose, given a particular client's business activities. **The purpose of obtaining additional information concerning certain clients in these circumstances is to assist the financial institution/designated non-financial institution to more accurately identify truly suspicious behaviour or relationships and transactions that pose a risk of money laundering, on the basis of a broader profile of the client than the mere client identification particulars.**

The information that a financial institution/designated non-financial institution must obtain in such circumstances must be adequate to reasonably enable a financial institution/DNFBP to determine whether transactions involving a client are consistent with a financial institution's knowledge of that client and that client's business activities and must include particulars concerning:

- the source of that client's income; and

- the source of the funds that the particular client expects to use in concluding the single transaction or transactions in the course of the business relationship.[37]

Case 3.1: Financial Services Authority v. Coutts & Company (Coutts) FSA/PN/032/2012

In October 2010, the United Kingdom Financial Services Authority (FSA) visited Coutts as part of its thematic review into banks' management of high money-laundering risk situations. Following that visit, the FSA's investigation identified that Coutts did not apply robust controls when starting relationships with high risk customers and did not consistently apply appropriate monitoring of those high risk relationships. In addition, the FSA determined that the AML team at Coutts failed to provide an appropriate level of scrutiny and challenge.

The FSA identified deficiencies in nearly three quarters of the PEP and high risk customer files reviewed. Specifically, in one or more of each inadequate file Coutts failed to:

---

37 South Africa Financial Intelligence Centre Guidance Note 3A Guidance for accountable institutions on client identification and verification and related matters 2013, paragraph 4.

i. gather sufficient information to establish the source of wealth and source of funds of its prospective PEP and other high risk customers;

ii. identify and/or assess adverse intelligence about prospective and existing high risk customers properly and take appropriate steps in relation to such intelligence;

iii. keep the information held on its existing PEP and other high risk customers up-to-date; and

iv. scrutinise transactions made through PEP and other high risk customer accounts appropriately.

Tracey McDermott, acting director of enforcement and financial crime, said:

"Coutts' failings were significant, widespread and unacceptable. Its conduct fell well below the standards we expect and the size of the financial penalty demonstrates how seriously we view its failures.

"Coutts was expanding its customer base which increased the number of high risk customer relationships. The regulatory environment in relation to financial crime had also changed. It is therefore particularly disappointing that Coutts failed to take appropriate steps to manage its AML risks. This penalty should serve as a warning to other firms that, not only should they ensure they constantly review and adapt their controls to changing financial crime risks within their businesses, but that they must also make changes to reflect changing regulatory or other legal standards."

As a result of the FSA's review, a number of improvements and recommendations have already been, or are being, implemented. These include significant remedial amendments to PEP and other high risk customer files to ensure that appropriate due diligence information about Coutts' customers has been assessed and recorded.

Coutts agreed to settle at an early stage and therefore qualifies for a 30% discount. Were it not for this discount, the FSA would have imposed a financial penalty of twelve million, five hundred thousand pounds.

Case 3.2: Financial Crimes Enforcement Network v. First Bank of Delaware Number 2012-01

The Financial Crimes Enforcement Network determined that First Bank failed to implement and maintain transaction monitoring systems necessary to effectively monitor customer transactions.

In light of its deficient customer documentation and across-the-board risk ratings, the Bank ran the risk of failing to effectively monitor its customers' transactions to determine if the actual activity was commensurate with expected activity and/or lacked any apparent business or legal purpose. First Bank's transaction monitoring practices put the Bank at risk of failing to comply with BSA suspicious activity reporting requirements. The Bank's software system merely identified customer deviations from a peer group average and did not compare a customer's actual ongoing activity to the customer's transaction history for inexplicable deviations or spikes. The detection system did not allow for report analysis by name, address, or phone number fields. The Bank's automated system allowed for stratification and evaluation of customer risk ratings, but these functions were not adequately utilized.

3.3 SIMPLIFIED DUE DILIGENCE

Simplified due diligence means not having to apply Customer Due Diligence (CDD) measures. In practice, this means not having to verify the customer's identity, or, where relevant, that of a beneficial owner, nor having to obtain information on the purpose or intended nature of the business relationship. It is, however, still necessary to conduct ongoing monitoring of the business relationship. Financial institutions/DNFBPs must have reasonable grounds for believing that the customer, transaction or product relating to such transaction falls within one of the categories set out in the Regulations, and may have to demonstrate this to their supervisory authority. Clearly, for operating purposes, a financial institution/DNFBP will nevertheless need to maintain a base of information about the customer.

Simplified due diligence may be applied to:

(i) Financial institutions - provided they are subject to the requirements for the combat of money laundering and terrorist financing which are consistent with the provisions of the relevant Money Laundering Regulations in that country and are supervised for compliance with them;

(ii) Public companies (listed on a stock exchange or similar situations) that are subject to regulatory disclosure requirements;

(iii) Insurance policies for pension schemes which there is no surrender-value clause and the policy cannot be used as collateral; and

(iv) Individuals whose main source of funds is derived from salary, pension, social benefits from an identified and appropriate source and where transactions are commensurate with the funds.

There is no exemption from the obligation to verify identity where a financial institution/DNFBP knows or suspects that a proposed relationship or occasional transaction involves money laundering or terrorist financing, or where there are doubts about the veracity or accuracy of documents, data or information previously obtained for the purposes of customer verification.

An exemption from the basic verification obligation does not extend to the obligation to conduct ongoing monitoring of the business relationship, or to the duty to report knowledge or suspicion of money laundering or terrorist financing.[38]

BOX 3.5: NEED FOR FINANCIAL INSTITUTIONS/ DNFBPS TO BE ALERT WHEN A LOW RISK CUSTOMER BECOMES A HIGH RISK CUSTOMER

An effective monitoring system enables financial institutions/DNFBPs to detect when a low risk customer becomes a high-risk customer. For example, a customer whose source of income is dependent on a pension scheme may later occupy a political position. This makes the customer a politically exposed person requiring enhanced AML measures to be applied to those customers. In a situation where the bank failed to monitor the account of the low risk customer, it may not be able to detect if the income received into the account has increased or is still the same.

Financial institutions/DNFBPs are also required to pay close attention to the news during the election periods. This would enable them know candidates who were

---

38 Australia Anti-Money Laundering and Counter-Terrorism Financing Rules Instrument 2007 (as amended), paragraph 48.2, 50.3, Officer of the Superintendent of Financial Institutions Canada Guideline: Deterring and Detecting Money Laundering and Terrorist Financing 2008, 22, See also the CBN (Anti-Money Laundering and Combating the Financing of Terrorism in Banks and Other Financial Institutions in Nigeria) Regulations, 2013, Regulation 24

successful at the elections. Banks need to verify if those candidates are among those designated as low risk customers. In an event where they are among, banks would need to apply enhanced AML measures to such customers so as to mitigate the money laundering and terrorist financing risks associated with such customers.

CHAPTER 4

PRODUCT/SERVICE RISK

An overall risk assessment should also include determining the potential risks presented by products and services offered by a financial institution. Financial institutions should be mindful of the risk associated with new or innovative products or services not specifically being offered by financial institutions, but that make use of the institution's services to deliver the product. Determining the risks of products and services should include a consideration of such factors as:

- Services identified by competent authorities or other credible sources as being potentially higher risk, including, for example:

    o Private banking services.

    o Services that inherently have provided more anonymity or can readily cross international borders, such as online banking, stored value cards, international wire transfers, private investment companies and trusts. And o Correspondent banking services involving transactions such as commercial payments for non-customers (for example, acting as an intermediary bank) and pouch activities.[1]

4.1 PRIVATE BANKING

Private banking can be broadly defined as providing personalized financial services to wealthy clients. In particular, a financial institution must establish appropriate, specific and (where necessary) Enhanced Due Diligence (EDD) policies, procedures and controls that are reasonably designed to enable the financial institution to detect and report instances of money laundering through such accounts.[2]

Enhanced scrutiny is required to detect and, if appropriate, report transactions that may involve proceeds of foreign corruption for private banking accounts that are requested or maintained by or on behalf of a senior foreign/local political figure or the individual's immediate family and close associates.

A private banking account is an account (or any combination of accounts) maintained at a financial institution that satisfies all the three criteria:

(*i*) Requires a minimum aggregate deposit of funds or other assets of not less than fifty thousand US dollars or its equivalent;

(*ii*) Is established on behalf of or for the benefit of one or more individuals who are direct or beneficial owners of the account; and

---

1 FATF Guidance on the Risk Based Approach to combating money laundering and terrorist financing, (High Level principles and procedures) 2007, paragraph 3.7, Australia Anti-Money Laundering and Counter-Terrorism Financing Rules Instrument 2007 (as amended), paragraph 4.1.3 (5) (6)

2 Central Bank of Nigeria's Anti-Money Laundering/Combating the Financing of Terrorism (AML/CFT) Risk Based Supervision (RBS) Framework, 2011, paragraph 5.33

(*iii*) Is assigned to, or is administered by, in whole or in part, an officer, employee, or agent of a financial institution acting as a liaison between a financial institution covered by the regulation and the direct or beneficial owner of the account.

If an account satisfies the last two criteria in the definition of a private banking account as described above, but the institution does not require a minimum balance of fifty thousand US dollars or its equivalent, then the account does not qualify as a private banking account under this rule. However, the account is subject to the internal controls and risk-based due diligence included in the institution's general AML Compliance program.[3]

4.1.1 RISK FACTORS

Five factors in private banking increase its vulnerability to money laundering: the role of private bankers as client advocates, a powerful clientele which discourages tough questions, a corporate culture of secrecy, a corporate culture of lax controls, and the competitive nature of the industry.

Private Bankers As Client Advocates. Private bankers are the linchpin of the private bank system. They are trained to service their clients' needs and to set up accounts and move money around the world using sophisticated financial systems and secrecy tools. Private banks encourage their bankers to develop personal relationships with their clients, visiting the clients' homes, attending weddings and graduations, and arranging their financial affairs. The result is that private bankers may feel loyalty to their clients for both professional and personal reasons, leading them to miss or minimize warning signs. In addition, private bankers may use their expertise in bank

---

3 Central Bank of Nigeria's Anti-Money Laundering/Combating the Financing of Terrorism (AML/CFT) Risk Based Supervision (RBS) Framework, 2011, paragraph 3.12

systems to evade what they may perceive as unnecessary "red tape" hampering the services their clients want, thereby evading controls designed to detect or prevent money laundering.

Powerful Clients. Private bank clients are, by definition, wealthy. Many also exert political or economic influence which may make banks anxious to satisfy their requests and reluctant to ask hard questions. If a client is a government official with influence over the bank's in-country operations, the bank has added reason to avoid offense.

Culture of Secrecy. A culture of secrecy pervades the private banking industry. Numbered accounts at Swiss banks are but one example. There are other layers of secrecy that private banks and clients routinely use to mask accounts and transactions. For example, private banks routinely create shell companies and trusts to shield the identity of the beneficial owner of a bank account. Private banks also open accounts under code names and will, when asked, refer to clients by code names or encode account transactions.

Secrecy Jurisdictions. In addition to shell corporations and codes, a number of private banks also conduct business in secrecy jurisdictions such as Switzerland and the Cayman Islands, which impose criminal sanctions on the disclosure of bank information related to clients and restrict U.S. bank oversight. The secrecy laws are so tight, they even restrict internal bank oversight. For example, if a bank's own employee uncovers a problem in an office located in a secrecy jurisdiction, that employee is barred from conveying any client-specific information to colleagues in the United States, even though they are part of the same banking operation. The bank's auditors and compliance officers operate under the same restrictions; any audit or compliance report sent out of the country must first be cleansed of client-specific information.

Culture of Lax Anti-Money Laundering Controls. In addition to a culture of secrecy, private banking operates in a corporate culture that is at times indifferent or resistant to anti-money laundering controls, such as due diligence requirements and account monitoring.

The problem begins with the private banker who, in most private banks, is responsible for the initial enforcement of anti-money laundering controls. It is the private banker who is charged with researching the background of prospective clients, and it is the private banker who is asked in the first instance to monitor existing accounts for suspicious activity. But it is also the job of the private banker to open accounts and expand client deposits.

The fundamental problem is that private bankers are being asked to fill contradictory roles -- to develop a personal relationship with a client and increase their deposits with the bank, while also monitoring their accounts for suspicious activity and questioning specific transactions.

Human nature makes these contradictory roles difficult to perform, and anti-money laundering duties often suffer.

Competition and Profitability. A final factor creating money laundering concerns is the ongoing competition among private banks for clients, due to the profitability of the business. As the target market for private banking is growing, so is the level of competition among institutions that provide private banking services." The dual pressures of competition and expansion are disincentives for private banks to impose tough anti-money laundering controls that may discourage new business or cause existing clients to move to other institutions.

Private Banking Products and Services

In addition to the general factors cited above, the actual products and services offered by the private bank also create opportunities for money laundering.

Multiple Accounts. A striking feature of the private bank accounts examined is their complexity. Private bank clients often have many accounts in many locations. Some are personal checking, money market or credit card accounts. Others are in the name of one or more shell companies. Multiple investment accounts are common, including mutual funds, stocks, bonds and time deposits.

The reality right now is that private banks allow clients to have multiple accounts in multiple locations under multiple names and do not aggregate the information. This approach creates vulnerabilities to money laundering by making it difficult for banks to have a comprehensive understanding of their own client's accounts. In addition, it complicates regulatory oversight and law enforcement, by making it nearly impossible for an outside reviewer to be sure that all private bank accounts belonging to an individual have been identified.

Secrecy Products. Most private banks offer a number of products and services that shield a client's ownership of funds. They include offshore trusts and shell corporations, special name accounts, and codes used to refer to clients or fund transfers.

Private banks usually make routine use of shell corporations for their clients. These shell corporations are often referred to as "private investment corporations" or PICs. They are usually incorporated in jurisdictions such as the Cayman Islands or Channel Islands which restrict disclosure of a PIC's beneficial owner. Private banks then open bank accounts in the name of the PIC, allowing the PIC's owner to avoid identification as the accountholder.

It is not unusual for private bank clients to have multiple PICs and use these PICs to hold accounts and conduct transactions. Some private banks will open accounts only for PICs they incorporate and manage, while others will do so for PICs incorporated and managed by someone else, such as the client. These so-called "client-managed PICs" create additional money laundering risks, because the private banks do not control and may not even know the activities, assets and complete ownership of the PIC holding the account at the private bank. Some private banks go a step further and open accounts for client-managed PICs whose ownership is determined by whomever has physical possession of the PIC's shares. These so-called "bearer-share PICs" pose still greater money-laundering risks because, unless a bank maintains physical possession of the shares, it is impossible to know with certainty who, at any given moment, is the PIC's true owner.

Movement of Funds. Client account transactions at private banks routinely' involve large sums of money. The size of client transactions increases the bank's vulnerability to money laundering by providing an attractive venue for money launderers who want to move large sums without attracting notice. In addition, most private banks provide products and services that facilitate the quick, confidential and hard-to-trace movement of money across jurisdictional lines.

For example, private banks routinely facilitate large wire transfers into, out of and among client accounts, in multiple countries. Many of these transfers take place with minimal or no notice from the client and sometimes involve parties and accounts with which the private banker is unfamiliar. It is a situation that invites money laundering.

Some private banks move funds for clients through concentration or suspense accounts, which are accounts, established by private banks for administrative purposes to hold funds from various destinations prior to depositing them into the proper accounts. Client funds which come into a private bank may pass through a concentration account on the way to the client's own account. The problem arises when a private bank allows clients to move funds through the bank's concentration account and onto another destination, without ever passing through an account belonging to the client. When that happens, the funds are never associated in bank records with a particular client. The Federal Reserve has warned against this practice, stating:

"[I]t is inadvisable from a risk management and control perspective for institutions to allow their clients to direct transactions through the organization's suspense accounts(s). Such practices effectively prevent association of the clients' names and account numbers with specific account activity, could easily mask unusual transactions and flows, the monitoring of which is essential to sound risk management in private banking, and could easily be abused."

Credit. Another common private bank service involves the extension of credit to clients. Private banks usually urge their private bankers to convince clients to leave their deposits in the bank and use them as collateral for large loans.

This practice enables the bank to earn a fee not only on the deposits under their management, but also on the loan. This practice also, however, creates vulnerabilities for money laundering, by allowing a client to deposit questionable funds and replace them with "clean" money from a loan.

In addition, because the client loans are fully collateralized by assets on deposit with the bank, the bank may not scrutinize the loan purpose and repayment prospects as carefully as for a conventional loan, and may unwittingly further a money launderer's efforts to hide illicit proceeds behind seemingly legitimate transactions.[4]

4.1.2 RISK MITIGATION

The bank will endeavour to accept only those clients whose source of wealth and funds can be reasonably established to be legitimate. The primary responsibility for this lies with the private banker who sponsors the client for acceptance. Mere fulfilment of internal review procedures does not relieve the private banker of this basic responsibility.

Bank policy must require a private banker to perform CDD on clients before establishing a business relationship with them,[5]

4.1.2.1 CUSTOMER DUE DILIGENCE

CDD is an effective measure to mitigate the Money Laundering/ Terrorist Financing ML/TF risk associated with private banking accounts.

A private banker must ensure that his duty to expand client deposits does not conflict with his duty to carry out the appropriate CDD measures on his clients.

A private banker would need to obtain the following information in relation to natural persons opening private bank accounts:

---

4 Permanent Sub-committee on Investigations of the Committee on Governmental Affairs United States Senate: Private Banking and Money Laundering 'A Case Study of Opportunities and Vulnerabilities 1999, 5-12.

5 The Wolfsberg Group: Wolfsberg Anti-Money Laundering Principles for Private Banking (2012), paragraph 1.1

- Legal name and any other names used (such as maiden name);

- Permanent address (full address shall be obtained and the use of a post office box number only, is not sufficient);

- Telephone number, fax number, and email address;

- Date and place of birth;

- Nationality

- Occupation, public position held and name of employer;

- An official personal identification number or other unique identifier contained in an unexpired official document such as passport, identification card, residence permit, social security records or drivers' licence that bears a photograph of the customer;

- Type of account and nature of the banking relationship; and

- Signature.[6]

An anti-money laundering and counter-terrorist financing ("AML/CTF") program must include a procedure for the reporting entity to verify, at a minimum, the following CDD information about a customer:

---

6 Australia Anti-Money Laundering and Counter-Terrorism Financing Rules Instrument 2007 (as amended), paragraph 4.2.3-4.2.5, Officer of the Superintendent of Financial Institutions Canada Guideline: Deterring and Detecting Money Laundering and Terrorist Financing 2008, 20, CBN (Anti-Money Laundering and Combating the Financing of Terrorism in Banks and Other Financial Institutions in Nigeria) Regulations, 2013, Schedule II Paragraph 1 (1). See also South Africa Money Laundering and Terrorist Financial Control Regulations, 2002 (as amended), Regulation 3, See United States Federal Financial Institutions Examination Council: Bank Secrecy Act/Anti-Money Laundering Examination Manual 2014, 48-49

- the customer's full name; and

- either:

  o the customer's date of birth; or

  o the customer's residential address.

The financial institution shall verify the information referred to above, by at least one of the following methods –

- Confirming the full name and date of birth from an official document (such as birth certificate, passport, identity card, social security records);

- Confirming the permanent address (such as utility bill, tax assessment, bank statement, a letter from a public authority);

- Contacting the customer by telephone, by letter or by e-mail to confirm the information supplied after an account has been opened (such as a disconnected phone, returned mail, or incorrect e-mail address shall warrant further investigation);

- Confirming the validity of the official documentation provided through certification by an authorized person such as embassy official, notary public.[7]

---

7 Australia Anti-Money Laundering and Counter-Terrorism Financing Rules Instrument 2007 (as amended), paragraphs 4.2.6 - 4.2.13, Officer of the Superintendent of Financial Institutions Canada Guideline: Deterring and Detecting Money Laundering and Terrorist Financing 2008, 21, CBN (Anti-Money Laundering and Combating the Financing of Terrorism in Banks and Other Financial Institutions in Nigeria) Regulations, 2013, Schedule II Paragraph 1 (2), See also South Africa Money Laundering and Terrorist Financial Control Regulations, 2002 (as amended), Regulation 4, See United States Federal Financial Institutions Examination Council: Bank Secrecy Act/Anti-Money Laundering Examination Manual 2014, 49-50

A private banker must also perform CDD functions on customers who are beneficial owners.

> ## BOX 4.1: CONFLICT OF INTEREST
>
> Since it is the private banker who is charged with opening accounts and expanding client deposits, and it is the private banker who is charged with researching the background of prospective clients. Bank policies must emphasize the need for private bankers to place top priority on the later role.
>
> Banks must avoid making policies that may encourage private bankers to flout their AML responsibilities.
>
> A bank policy which mandates private bankers to expand client deposits or risk being dismissed from service would encourage private bankers to disregard their AML responsibilities. Banks should therefore avoid such policies.

4.1.2.2 ENHANCED DUE DILIGENCE

The Enhanced Due Diligence (EDD) should give financial institutions a greater understanding of the customer and their associated risk than standard due diligence. It should provide more certainty that the customer and/or beneficial owner is who they say they are and that the purposes of the business relationship are legitimate; as well as increasing opportunities to identify and deal with concerns that they are not.[8]

Financial institutions must apply EDD measures on a risk-sensitive basis in any situation which by its nature can present a higher risk of money laundering or terrorist financing. As part of this, a financial institution may conclude, under its risk-based approach, that the information it has collected as part of the customer due diligence process is insufficient in relation to the money laundering or terrorist financing risk, and that it must obtain additional information about a particular customer, the customer's beneficial owner, where applicable, and the purpose and intended nature of the business relationship.

In its internal policies, financial institutions must define categories of persons whose circumstances warrant enhanced due diligence. This will typically be the case where the circumstances are likely to pose a higher than average risk to a bank.

Indicators

The circumstances of the following categories of persons are indicators for defining them as requiring Enhanced Due Diligence:

- Cash (and cash equivalent) intensive businesses including:

    o   Money services businesses (e.g. remittance houses, currency exchange houses, casas de cambio, bureaux de

---

8 Australia Anti-Money Laundering and Counter-Terrorism Financing Rules Instrument 2007 (as amended), paragraph 4.13.1, Officer of the Superintendent of Financial Institutions Canada: Deterring and Detecting Money Laundering and Terrorist Financing 2008, 23, See also the CBN (Anti-Money Laundering and Combating the Financing of Terrorism in Banks and Other Financial Institutions in Nigeria) Regulations, 2013, Regulation 16, See also South Africa, Financial Intelligence Centre Guidance Note 3A: Guidance for Accountable Institutions on Client Identification and Verification and Related Matters, paragraph 4

change, money transfer agents and bank note traders or other businesses offering money transfer facilities).

o Casinos, betting and other gambling related activities. And

o Businesses that while not normally cash intensive, generate substantial amounts of cash for certain transactions.

- Charities and other "not for profit" organisations which are not subject to monitoring or supervision (especially those operating on a "cross-border" basis).

- "Gatekeepers" such as accountants, lawyers, or other professionals holding accounts at a financial institution, acting on behalf of their clients, and where the financial institution places unreasonable reliance on the gatekeeper.

- Use of intermediaries within the relationship who are not subject to adequate AML/CFT laws and measures and who are not adequately supervised.

- Persons residing in and/or having funds sourced from countries identified by credible sources as having inadequate AML standards or representing high risk for crime and corruption.

- "Politically Exposed Persons," frequently abbreviated as "PEPs," referring to individuals holding or, as appropriate, having held, senior, prominent, or important public positions with substantial authority over policy, operations or the use or allocation of government-owned resources, such as senior government officials, senior executives of government corporations, senior politicians, important political party officials, etc., as well as their close family and close associates. PEPs from different jurisdictions may be subject to different levels of diligence.[9]

It is for each financial institution to decide the steps it takes to determine whether a customer is seeking to establish a business relationship for legitimate reasons. Financial institutions should in any case take adequate meaningful measures to establish the source of funds and source of wealth.[10] Financial institutions may wish to refer to information sources such as asset and income declarations, which some jurisdictions expect certain senior public officials to file and which often include information about an official's source of wealth and current business interests. Financial institutions should note that not all declarations are publicly available and that a high risk customer may have a legitimate reason for not providing a copy.[11]

Once the source of wealth and source of funds are established banks will need to analyse the information for "red flag" for corrupt activity.[12] In all cases if a financial institution suspects that the funds are

---

9 Australia Anti-Money Laundering and Counter-Terrorism Financing Rules Instrument 2007 (as amended), paragraph 4.1.3, See also the Nigerian CBN (Anti-Money Laundering and Combating the Financing of Terrorism in Banks and Other Financial Institutions in Nigeria) Regulations, 2013, Regulation 16, See also South Africa, Financial Intelligence Centre Guidance Note 3A: Guidance for Accountable Institutions on Client Identification and Verification and Related Matters, paragraph 4

10 Australia Anti-Money Laundering and Counter-Terrorism Financing Rules Instrument 2007 (as amended), paragraph 4.13.3 (3), Officer of the Superintendent of Financial Institutions Canada Guideline: Deterring and Detecting Money Laundering and Terrorist Financing 2008, 23, See also the CBN (Anti-Money Laundering and Combating the Financing of Terrorism in Banks and Other Financial Institutions in Nigeria) Regulations, 2013, Regulation 18 (6), See also South Africa Money Laundering and Terrorist Financial Control Regulations, 2002 (as amended), Regulation 21 (3). See United States Federal Financial Institutions Examination Council: Bank Secrecy Act/Anti-Money Laundering Examination Manual 2014, 57-58

11 Joint Money Laundering Steering Group Guidance for the UK Financial Sector Part 1, Paragraph 5.5.29.

12 T S Greenberg: Stolen Asset Recovery, Politically Exposed Persons, A policy paper on strengthening preventive measures

proceeds of criminal activity, the financial institution is required to file a Suspicious Transaction Report with the Financial Intelligence Unit.[13] A risk-based approach for the reporting of suspicious activity under these circumstances is not applicable.[14] A risk-based approach is however appropriate for the purpose of identifying suspicious activity, for example by directing additional resources at those areas a financial institution has identified as higher risk and in this case to customers who have been found to be high risk.[15]

4.1.2.2.1 SENIOR MANAGEMENT APPROVAL

The FATF standard requires financial institutions to obtain senior management approval for establishing a business relationship with PEPs and continuing a business relationship with a customer who is subsequently found to be a PEP or becomes a PEP.[16] The group AML/CTF officer should be involved in the PEP approval process since he is in the best position to say that a person should not be accepted regardless of the size of the account.[17]

---

13 See also the CBN (Anti-Money Laundering and Combating the Financing of Terrorism in Banks and Other Financial Institutions in Nigeria) Regulations, 2013, Regulation 18 (7). See also T S Greenberg: Stolen Asset Recovery, Politically Exposed Persons, A policy paper on strengthening preventive measures

14 FATF Guidance on the Risk Based Approach to combating money laundering and terrorist financing, (High Level principles and procedures) 2007, paragraph 3.16.

15 FATF Guidance on the Risk Based Approach to combating money laundering and terrorist financing, (High Level principles and procedures) 2007, paragraph 3.17, Australia Anti-Money Laundering and Counter-Terrorism Financing Rules Instrument 2007 (as amended), paragraph 4.13.3 (2)

16 The Financial Action Task Force (FATF): International Standards On Combating Money Laundering and the financing of terrorism and proliferation,(The FATF Recommendations) 2012, Recommendation 12, See also the CBN (Anti-Money Laundering and Combating the Financing of Terrorism in Banks and Other Financial Institutions in Nigeria) Regulations, 2013, Regulation 18 (4)

17 See T S Greenberg: Stolen Asset Recovery, Politically Exposed Persons, A policy paper on strengthening preventive measures

Financial institutions/DNFBPs are also required to obtain senior management approval for establishing a business relationship with other high-risk customers like money service businesses.

4.1.2.2.2 ENHANCED ON-GOING MONITORING

Once a business relationship has been established with a high-risk customer, banks must conduct enhanced on-going monitoring of the business relationship. [18]

The principle aim of monitoring in a risk-based system is to respond to enterprise wide issues based on each financial institution's analysis of major risks and in this case the major risks are the high-risk customers.[19]

Monitoring should identify information, transactions or attempted transactions that are unusual or potentially suspicious and that require further analysis. Monitoring criteria should cover all relevant indicators. Relevant indicators could include:

- frequent and unexplained movement of accounts to different financial institutions;

- frequent and unexplained movement of funds between different financial institutions in various geographic locations;

---

18   The Financial Action Task Force (FATF): International Standards On Combating Money Laundering and the financing of terrorism and proliferation,(The FATF Recommendations) 2012, Recommendation 12, Australia Anti-Money Laundering and Counter-Terrorism Financing Rules Instrument 2007 (as amended), paragraph 4.13.3,See also See also the CBN (Anti-Money Laundering and Combating the Financing of Terrorism in Banks and Other Financial Institutions in Nigeria) Regulations, 2013, Regulation 18 (7)

19   FATF Guidance on the Risk Based Approach to combating money laundering and terrorist financing, (High Level principles and procedures) 2007, paragraph 3.13.

- a client wishes to have credit and debit cards sent to destinations other than his or her address;

- a client has numerous accounts and makes or receives cash deposits in each of them amounting to a large aggregated amount;

- a client frequently exchanges currencies;

- a client wishes to have unusual access to safe deposit facilities;

- a client's accounts show virtually no normal business related activities, but are used to receive or disburse large sums;

- a client has accounts that have a large volume of deposits in bank cheques, postal orders or electronic funds transfers;

- a client is reluctant to provide complete information regarding the client's activities;

- a client's financial statements differ noticeably from those of similar businesses;

- a business client's representatives avoid contact with the branch;

- a client's deposits to, or withdrawals from, a corporate account are primarily in cash, rather than in the form of debit and credit normally associated with commercial operations;

- a client maintains a number of trustee accounts or client subaccounts;

- a client makes a large volume of seemingly unrelated deposits to several accounts and frequently transfers a major portion of the balances to a single account at the same bank or elsewhere.

- a client makes a large volume of cash deposits from a business that is not normally cash intensive;

- a small business in one location makes deposits on the same day at different branches;

- there is a remarkable transaction volume and a significant change in a client's account balance;

- a client's accounts show substantial increase in deposits of cash or negotiable instruments by a company offering professional advisory services;

- a client's accounts show a sudden and inconsistent change in transactions or patterns.

The examples referred to above may be legitimate features of certain categories of businesses, or may make business sense if viewed in the context of the client's business activities. However, it is equally possible that these features would be unexpected in relation to certain categories of businesses, or would have no apparent business purpose, given a particular client's business activities. **The purpose of obtaining additional information concerning certain clients in these circumstances is to assist the financial institution to more accurately identify truly suspicious behaviour or relationships and transactions that pose a risk of money laundering, on the basis of a broader profile of the client than the mere client identification particulars.**

The information that a financial institution must obtain in such circumstances must be adequate to reasonably enable a financial institution to determine whether transactions involving a client are consistent with the financial institution's knowledge of that client and that client's business activities and must include particulars concerning:

- the source of that client's income; and

- the source of the funds that the particular client expects to use in concluding the single transaction or transactions in the course of the business relationship.[20]

4.2 PREPAID CARDS

The term prepaid card generally refers to an access device linked to funds held in a pooled account, which is the type of product most frequently offered by banking organizations. Prepaid cards can cover a variety of products, functionalities and technologies. Prepaid cards operate within either an open or closed system.

Open-system prepaid cards can be used for purchases at any merchant or to access cash at any automated teller machine (ATM) that connects to the affiliated global payment network. Examples of open system cards are payroll cards and gift cards that can be used anywhere a credit card can be used. Some prepaid cards may be reloaded, allowing the cardholder to add value.

Closed-system cards generally can only be used to buy goods or services from the merchant issuing the card or a select group of merchants or service providers that participate in a specific network.

---

20 South Africa Financial Intelligence Centre Guidance Note 3A Guidance for accountable institutions on client identification and verification and related matters 2013, paragraph 4.

Examples of closed system cards include merchant-specific retail gift cards, mall cards and mass transit system cards.

Some prepaid card Programmes may combine multiple features, such as a flexible spending account card that can be used to purchase specific health services as well as products at a variety of merchants. These Programmes are often referred to as hybrid cards.

Prepaid cards provide a compact and transportable way to maintain and access funds. They also offer individuals without bank accounts an alternative to cash and money orders. As an alternate method of cross-border funds transmittal, prepaid card Programmes may issue multiple cards per account, so that persons in another country or jurisdiction can access the funds loaded by the original cardholder via ATM withdrawals of cash or merchant purchases.

Many financial institutions that offer prepaid card Programmes do so as issuer or issuing bank. Most payment networks require that their branded prepaid cards be issued by a bank that is a member of that payment network. In addition to issuing prepaid cards, banks may participate in other aspects of a card Programme such as marketing and distributing cards issued by another financial institution. Banks often rely on multiple third parties to accomplish the design, implementation and maintenance of their prepaid card Programmes. These third parties may include Programme managers, distributors, marketers, merchants and processors. Under payment network requirements, the issuing bank or other financial institution may have due diligence and other responsibilities relative to these third parties.[21]

---

21 Central Bank of Nigeria's Anti-Money Laundering/Combating the Financing of Terrorism (AML/CFT) Risk Based Supervision (RBS) Framework, 2011, paragraph 5.27

4.2.1 RISK FACTORS

This section identifies a range of risk factors that help to identify the money laundering/terrorist financing (ML/TF) risks associated with prepaid cards.

Non-face-to-face relationships and anonymity

As with many banking methods, prepaid cards can allow for non-face-to-face business relationships. Depending on their characteristics, prepaid cards can be used to quickly move funds around the world, to make purchases and access to cash (both directly and indirectly) through the ATM network. The absence of face-to-face contact may indicate a higher money laundering/terrorist financing (ML/TF) risk situation. If customer identification and verification measures do not adequately address the risks associated with non-face-to-face contact, such as impersonation fraud, the ML/TF risk increases, as does the difficulty in being able to trace the funds.

While monitoring and reporting mechanisms can be put in place to identify suspicious activity, an absence of CDD increases the difficulty for the service provider to do so. For example, this impacts on the ability of the service provider to identify instances of customers holding multiple accounts simultaneously.

The risk posed by anonymity (not identifying the customer) can occur when the card is purchased, registered, loaded, reloaded, or used by the customer. The level of risk posed by anonymity is relative to the functionality of the card and existence of AML/CFT risk mitigation measures such as funding or purchasing limits, reload limits, cash access, and whether the card can be used outside the country of issue. Prepaid cards can be funded in various ways with different degrees of CDD including through banks, the Internet, at small retail shops, or at ATMs.

Prepaid cards can easily be passed on to third parties that are unknown to the issuer, including, but not restricted to, 'twin cards' which are specifically designed to allow third parties remittances, and may advertise anonymity as a feature of the product. This is concerning when the providers of these products are based in countries where prepaid card providers are insufficiently regulated and supervised for AML/CFT purposes, but sell their products internationally.

Geographical reach

The extent to which prepaid cards can be used globally for making payments or transferring funds is an important factor to take into account when determining the level of risk.

Open-loop prepaid cards often enable customers to effect payments at domestic and foreign points of sales through global payment networks. These cards are accepted as a means of payment everywhere a similarly-branded card (debit or credit) is accepted. Providers of prepaid cards may be based in one country and sell their product internationally through agents or the Internet. These cards can then be used to purchase goods and services, or access cash, internationally. Additionally, some prepaid card programmes allow cardholders to transfer funds from person-to-person. This global reach of some prepaid cards to make payments, access cash and transfer funds are all features that make those products attractive for ML/TF purposes. The compact physical size of prepaid cards also makes them potentially vulnerable to misuse by criminals who use them, instead of cash, to make physical cross-border transportations of value. Prepaid cards which can be used to access funds internationally are particularly vulnerable due to the logistical benefits of transporting a discreet number of prepaid cards that have accounts loaded with high fund values which cannot be determined from the card itself, rather than transporting large, bulky amounts of cash using cash couriers. Countries should also consider whether Recommendation 32 applies to certain prepaid access products, such as prepaid cards, that would qualify as bearer negotiable instruments.

Methods of Funding

The ML/TF risk posed by prepaid cards is increased by allowing cash funding and, in some rare cases, reloadability without any limit on the value placed on the card account or CDD requirements. This makes prepaid cards vulnerable to abuse by criminals who can use them, for example, as a means to launder the proceeds of crime by placing those proceeds into the financial system or using the prepaid cards as an alternative to the physical cross-border transportation of cash.

Access to cash

Access to cash through the international ATM network increases the level of ML/TF risk. Such access to cash may be direct, as in the case of prepaid cards which can allow funding in one country and cash withdrawals in another.

Segmentation of services

Prepaid cards may involve several parties for the execution of payments including the programme manager, issuer, acquirer, payment network, distributor and agents, while mobile payments service providers must often coordinate with a number of interrelated service providers, and partner with international counterparts to provide cross-border transactions.

A large number of parties involved in the provision of prepaid services, especially when spread across several countries, can increase the

ML/TF risk of the product due to the potential of segmentation and the potential loss of customer and transaction information. This is a particular concern when it is not clearly established which of the entities involved are subject to AML/CFT obligations, who is responsible for complying with such obligations, and what country among those involved in the transaction process is responsible for regulating and supervising for compliance with AML/CFT measures.

Using agents and relying on unaffiliated third parties for establishing customer relationships and reloading raises potential ML/TF risks, particularly if the collected information is not shared with the entity responsible for AML/CFT requirements. A service provider that can take responsibility for all aspects of the customer relationship (i.e. registration, cash-in/cash-out and transactions) can pose a lower risk. Of relevance is the organizational structure and processes set up for the training, management and control of the network of agents.

Additionally, entities providing prepaid cards often come from sectors, such as Mobile Network Operators (MNOs), which are unfamiliar with AML/CFT controls. Consequently, CDD know-how could be limited in comparison to, for example, the traditional banking sector, and CDD generally may remain restricted to analysing atypical transactions and feedback from distributors. In addition, the chain of information could create difficulties in tracing the funds. For example, the chain of information for a single financial transaction could involve more entities; some of which may be located in different countries. This could slow down the investigation process, which is further complicated by the speed of money flows, and the challenges of trying to seize and freeze criminal proceeds which can be quickly transferred or transported to another country using the services of prepaid cards.

Prepaid card providers maintain bank accounts and use the banking system for periodic transactions to settle accounts with agents and Money or Value Transfer Services (MVTS) partners. However, while a bank settling wholesale transactions between prepaid card providers has CDD obligations in relation to the prepaid card provider, it has no, or limited visibility into the prepaid card providers' customers and is unable to oversee transactions between the prepaid card provider and their customers.

4.2.2 RISK MITIGATION

The overall degree of risk of prepaid cards is, in a given context, the cumulative effect of combining each of the risk factors described above. In addition, procedures to mitigate risk should be proportionate to the level of risk posed by the product or service. Adopting proportionality criteria allows the risks posed by prepaid cards to be addressed, while maintaining the functionality which is aimed at customer convenience and ease of use. Against these considerations, within national or applicable regulatory frameworks, private sector institutions should take into account the ML/TF risks of a product or service while it is still in its project phase, with a view to designing it in such a way that these vulnerabilities are kept to a minimum. This section provides guidance on possible risk mitigation measures that private sector institutions should take into account during the product design phase.

Financial institutions should identify, assess and understand the risks posed by the prepaid card services they provide before establishing their CDD processes and procedures. In particular, financial institutions should undertake this risk assessment, with a particular focus on ML/TF risks posed by new products and business practices, including delivery mechanisms, and the use of new technologies, prior to their launch. This is an essential step in this process which enables financial institutions to establish appropriate risk-based AML/CFT measures in proportion to the level of risk identified.

4.2.2.1 CUSTOMER DUE DILIGENCE

CDD is an effective measure to mitigate ML/TF risk associated with prepaid cards. Under the risk-based approach, the extent to which the prepaid card providers should take measures to identify and verify their customer's identity will vary depending on the level of risk posed by the product, in line with the FATF Recommendations and the Money Laundering Laws/Regulations of the country concerned.

It is important to note that the FATF Recommendations allow financial institutions in non-face- to-face scenarios to verify the identity of the customer following the establishment of the business relationship (rather than before or during the course of establishing a business relationship) when essential to not interrupt the normal conduct of business and provided that the ML/TF risks are effectively managed.

The greater the functionality of the pre-paid card, the greater the need may be for more enhanced CDD. Non-face-to-face verification of customer identity often requires corroborating information received from the customer with information in third party databases or other reliable sources, and potentially tracing the customer's Internet Protocol (IP) address, and even searching the Web for corroborating information, provided that the data collection is in line with national privacy legislation. It may be appropriate to use multiple techniques to effectively verify the identity of customers. In situations where higher ML/TF risk is identified, enhanced CDD should be carried out in proportion to that risk.

In all cases, transaction monitoring and suspicious activity reporting is essential. Its importance is even greater, however, where obtaining reliably information on the customer may be difficult. This may be the case in countries that have no reliable identity card scheme, or alternative reliable forms of identification.

Prepaid card services are commonly distributed using a wide network of agents or distributors which the service provider may then use to undertake the CDD during the face-to-face transaction. In such cases, distributors or agents are carrying out the CDD obligations on behalf of the provider, and the programme manager or issuer should include the distributors or agents in its AML/CFT programme and monitor their compliance with applicable CDD measures.

Using an agent gives institutions a chance to conduct CDD while the customer is physically present. When using the Internet, the mobile service provider will have to rely on non-face-to-face identification and verification.

BOX 4.2: VERIFYING THE IDENTITY OF THE CUSTOMER FOLLOWING THE ESTABLISHMENT OF THE BUSINESS RELATIONSHIP

One of the very popular prepaid cards in the United Kingdom is the Cashplus prepaid card.

Cashplus is issued by APS Financial Ltd (AFL) pursuant to license by MasterCard International Incorporated. AFL is authorised by the Financial Conduct Authority under the Electronic Money Regulations 2011 for the issuing of electronic money. Cards are serviced by Advanced Payment Solutions Ltd (APS) which operates the card on behalf of AFL.

Although almost anyone that lives in the UK and is aged 18 or over will be approved to receive a Cashplus prepaid

---

card, some features and services are only available to customers who have been fully identified and verified.[22]

For example, the maximum loading limit for customers who have not been fully identified and verified is two thousand pounds while the maximum loading limit for customers who have been fully identified and verified is five thousand pounds.[23]

The above measures adopted by APS could mitigate the money laundering and terrorist financing risks associated with the non-verification of accounts before the establishment of a business relationship.

4.2.2.2 LOADING, VALUE AND GEOGRAPHICAL LIMITS

Placing limits on prepaid cards can be an effective mechanism to mitigate ML/TF risk, as long as it is combined with other AML/CFT measures such as account and transaction monitoring, and the filing of suspicious transaction reports. Setting geographical or reloading limitations also mitigates the risk that prepaid cards may be misused for ML/TF purposes. Limiting the functionality of prepaid cards to certain geographical areas or for the purchase of certain goods and services decreases the attractiveness of the product to money launderers or terrorist financiers. Although, it is important to recognise that such limitations can also limit the attractiveness of the product generally, and financial institutions and countries should consider the adverse effect of any limitations on legitimate customer activity. These measures should be considered and implemented, as appropriate, during the design phase of prepaid cards.

---

22 Cashplus 'Cashplus prepaid Gold MasterCard®, the only prepaid card you'll ever need' (http://www.mycashplus.co.uk/) http://www.mycashplus.co.uk/ Accessed 21st of May 2015

23 Cashplus 'Upgrade your Cashplus Account's access level' (http://www.mycashplus.co.uk) http://www.mycashplus.co.uk/help/upgrade-your-account.aspx Accessed 21st of May 2015

Given that the ML/TF risk increases as the functionality of the pre-paid card increases, financial institutions could consider establishing individual tiers of service provided to customers. This should be developed on a case-by-case basis during the design phase of the prepaid card. In this way, financial institutions may consider applying different restrictions, for example thresholds, for prepaid cards to ensure that a product remains lower risk, therefore allowing them to apply simplified CDD. In such a scenario, the extent of CDD and other AML/CFT measures should increase as the functionality, and therefore risk, increases.

Many prepaid card programmes already envisage loading and duration limits to ensure that the outstanding prepaid value does not present undue ML/TF risk. Other common measures include limitations on the amount that is prepaid and accessible via the card as well as a restriction on the ability to reload funds onto the prepaid card. Both loading and duration limits, as well as limits placed on the ability to make cash withdrawals, can make prepaid cards less attractive for criminals.

Thresholds are an effective measure for setting the maximum that can be loaded onto a prepaid card, and held on one card at one time or over a defined period. The level of such thresholds should be determined on a risk-sensitive basis and will vary depending on the existence of other AML/CFT measures. Due regard, however, should be given to consumer protection to ensure that customers have access to their funds as they need it, and appropriate recourse should be considered where customers are denied access to funds held on prepaid cards.

In addition, the possibility that some prepaid card programmes allow funds to be transferred from person-to-person may represent a high risk of misuse for ML/TF purposes. Especially where it is envisaged that person-to-person funds transfers can be made through a prepaid card, limits imposed on the possible transfers can be an effective measure to mitigate the ML/TF risk, especially if they are treated as cash. This can be enhanced through combining transfer limits with loading or withdrawal limits. In adopting the risk-based approach, the maximum value that can be transferred person-to-person using prepaid cards may also vary depending on the existence of other AML/CFT measures, such as geographical limitations.

BOX 4.3: LOADING LIMITS

On the 14th of June 2010, Barclaycard Commercial launched its prepaid card, providing organisations with a simple way to improve efficiency and gain more control over their spending and the way funds are distributed.[24]

The Maximum loading limit on the Barclays Travel Money Card is two thousand five hundred pounds.[25]

The above measures adopted by Barclays could reduce the money laundering and terrorist financing risks associated with prepaid cards.

4.2.2.3 SOURCE OF FUNDING

Prepaid providers should consider the source of funding when assessing the ML/TF risk of prepaid cards and could consider restricting the permissible sources of funding for that product. Anonymous sources of funding such as cash that are anonymous increase ML/TF

---

24 Barclay Card 'Barclaycard launch new Prepaid card' (http://www.barclaycard.com 14th June 2010) http://www.barclaycard.com/news/new-barclaycard-prepaid-card.html Accessed 21st May 2015

25 R Marday 'Barclays Travel Money Card – Visa' (http://www.what-prepaid-card.co.uk 23rd August 2013) http://www.what-prepaid-card.co.uk/travel-news/barclays-prepaid.html Accessed 21st May 2015

risk. Prepaid card providers should take a holistic view to the mitigation of ML/TF risk through these measures and such restrictions could be combined with other limitations outlined above.

When cash is used by an individual to add value to prepaid cards, for which there are limited safeguards, the prepaid card services provider could consider requiring the person to be identified if the cash exceeds a predetermined cash load limit either for an individual account, either for one or a series of transactions in a day.

Record Keeping, transaction monitoring and reporting Transaction and CDD records are key to AML/CFT efforts and support law enforcement investigations. At a minimum the transaction record of a payment or funds transfer should include information identifying the parties to the transaction, any account(s) involved, the nature and date of the transaction, and the amount transferred. The relative size of a transaction does not necessarily equal the value of the transaction record to law enforcement, so recordkeeping should be kept for all transactions irrespective of the value. The records that are retained should be sufficient to allow the tracing of funds through the reconstruction of transactions.

The electronic nature of prepaid cards provides in principle a good foundation for effective record keeping and the monitoring of transactions. Prepaid card providers should keep all records relating to transactions and CDD information for a minimum period of 5 years, as is required by Recommendation 11, or the length required by the laws in the applicable country.

Prepaid card providers should consider putting in place transaction monitoring systems which can detect suspicious activity based on money laundering and terrorism financing typologies and indicators. Such monitoring systems should take into consideration customer risks, country or geography risks, and product, service transaction or delivery channel risks. The transaction monitoring system could also be used to identify multiple accounts or products held by an individual or group, such as holding multiple prepaid cards.

Prepaid card providers should consider analysing the information and records retained to determine unusual patterns or activity. Where the prepaid card provider identifies a transaction which it suspects, or has reasonable grounds to suspect, that the funds involved are the proceeds of criminal activity or are related to terrorist financing, it should report its suspicions to the relevant financial intelligence unit in accordance with the FATF Recommendations and the laws in the applicable country.

Prepaid card providers should be vigilant to transactions or activity for which there is no apparent legitimate or economic rationale. In particular, providers should consider situations where prepaid card services appear to be used as a substitute for bank accounts for no apparent legitimate purpose. For example, a prepaid card which appears to be used in an uncharacteristic manner (such as frequent high value transactions), may be considered unusual in some circumstances given that prepaid cards may not offer similar levels of protection (i.e. deposit insurance protections) or same benefits (such as interest) that might be provided to bank accounts in many jurisdictions. Providers should consider the rationale for using prepaid cards and the circumstances in the jurisdiction in which they operate.[26]

BOX 4.4: PAYPOINT

Cash can be directly loaded into a prepaid card in any one of the 28,000 PayPoints up and down the United Kingdom.[27]

26 FATF 'Guidance for a Risk Based Approach Prepaid Cards, Mobile Payments and Internet-Based Payment Services' 2013

27 Pockit 'How to load cash by PayPoint' (http://www.pockit.com 2015) http://www.pockit.com/affiliates/money?utm_source=money&utm_medium=affiliate&utm_campaign=standard#FAQCollapse-1 Accessed 21st of May 2015

> PayPoint have taking steps to mitigate the money laundering risks associated with cash payments.
>
> PayPoint.net only process transactions in accordance with Scheme Rules and its Anti-Money Laundering Requirements.[28]

4.3 CORRESPONDENT BANKING

Correspondent banking relationships are established between banks to facilitate, among other things, transactions between banks made on their own behalf; transactions on behalf of their clients; and making services available directly to clients of other banks. Examples of these services include: inter-bank deposit activities; international electronic funds transfers; cash management; cheque clearing and payment services; collections; payment for foreign exchange services; processing client payments (in either domestic or foreign currency); and payable-through accounts.

According to the Core Principles, banks should only establish correspondent relationships with foreign banks that are effectively supervised by the relevant authorities. For their part, respondent banks should have effective customer acceptance and Know Your Customer (KYC) policies.[29]

In particular, the Core Principles provide that banks should refuse to enter into or continue a correspondent banking relationship with a bank incorporated in a jurisdiction in which it has no physical presence and which is unaffiliated with a regulated financial group (i.e. shell banks).

---

28 PayPoint.net 'PayPoint.net Merchant Operating Guide' 2011, paragraph 2

29 Wolfsberg Anti-Money Laundering Principles for Correspondent Banking

Banks should pay particular attention when continuing relationships with respondent banks located in jurisdictions that have poor KYC standards or have been identified by FATF as being "non co-operative" in the fight against anti-money laundering.

4.3.1 RISK FACTORS

The Wolfsberg principles set out the following risk indicators that a Bank shall consider, to ascertain what reasonable due diligence or enhanced due diligence it will undertake:

- the correspondent banking client's domicile - the jurisdiction where the correspondent banking client is based and/or where its ultimate parent is headquartered may present greater risk. Certain jurisdictions are internationally recognised as having inadequate anti-money laundering standards, insufficient regulatory supervision, or presenting greater risk for crime, corruption or terrorist financing. Institutions will review pronouncements from regulatory agencies and international bodies, such as the FATF, to evaluate the degree of risk presented by the jurisdiction in which the correspondent banking client is based and/or in which its ultimate parent is headquartered.

- the correspondent banking client's ownership and management structures - the location of owners, their corporate legal form and the transparency of ownership structure may present greater risks. The involvement of a PEP in the management or ownership of certain correspondent banking clients may also increase the risk.

- the correspondent banking client's business and customer base - the type of businesses the correspondent banking client engages in, as well as the type of the markets the correspondent banking client serves, may present greater risks. Consequently, a correspondent banking client that derives a substantial part of its business income from higher risk clients may present greater risk.

Higher risk clients are those clients of a correspondent banking client that may be involved in activities or are connected to jurisdictions that are identified by credible sources as activities or countries being especially susceptible to money laundering. Each institution may give the appropriate weight to each risk factor, as it deems necessary.

4.3.2 RISK MITIGATION

FATF Recommendation 13 states that financial institutions such as banks should, in addition to performing normal due diligence measures, do the following in relation to cross-border correspondent banking and other similar relationships:

- gather sufficient information about a respondent bank to understand fully the nature of the respondent's business and to determine from publicly available information the reputation of the bank and the quality of supervision, including whether the institution has been subject to a money-laundering or terrorist-financing investigation or regulatory action;

- assess the respondent bank's anti-money laundering and terrorist-financing controls;

- obtain approval from senior management before establishing new correspondent relationships;

- document the respective responsibilities of each bank;

- with respect to "payable-through accounts" (correspondent accounts that are used directly by third parties to transact business on their own behalf), be satisfied that the respondent bank has verified the identity of and performed on-going due diligence on the customers having direct access to accounts of the correspondent bank and that the respondent bank is able to provide relevant customer identification data upon request to the correspondent bank.

Case 4.1: Financial Crimes Enforcement Network v. Oppenheimer and Co., Inc. Number 2015-01

Foreign correspondent accounts are gateways to the United States (U.S) financial system. As part of their Anti-Money Laundering (AML) obligations, U.S. broker-dealers maintaining correspondent accounts in the United States for Foreign Financial Institutions (FFIs) must apply due diligence to those correspondent accounts. 31 U.S.C. § 5318(i)(1). Broker-dealers must develop risk-based policies, procedures, and controls that are reasonably designed to gather all relevant due diligence information concerning such foreign correspondent accounts, employ this due diligence information to determine whether an account is subject to enhanced due diligence, conduct assessments of money laundering risks for each account, and comply with suspicious activity reporting requirements. 31 C.F.R. §§ 1010.610(a) (1), (2), and (3).

Oppenheimer's written AML policy required special due diligence on FFIs and restricted activity in accounts held by FFIs to proprietary business for the entity that opened the account, unless it was granted one of the exceptions detailed in the Firm's AML procedures. As noted above, Oppenheimer designated Gibraltar, a Bahamas-based broker-dealer, as a high-risk account in July 2007 because it was a foreign broker-dealer. Gibraltar began trading in its Oppenheimer account in

May 2008. Gibraltar is one of the Oppenheimer customers that engaged in the illegal penny stock trading. Despite expressly acknowledging the high risk that Gibraltar's account presented, however, Oppenheimer took no steps to assess Gibraltar's risk as an FFI and further failed to conduct adequate due diligence when it opened the account. Oppenheimer did not inquire into the AML or supervisory regime of Gibraltar's country of jurisdiction or consider Gibraltar's AML policies and procedures. 31 C.F.R. § 1010.610(a) (1) - (3).

Oppenheimer's policies also required its AML unit to conduct periodic reviews of all FFI accounts. Notwithstanding these written policies, Oppenheimer did not put adequate procedures in place to actually implement them. This resulted in the failure to monitor and detect suspicious and prohibited activity. Oppenheimer failed to adequately monitor Gibraltar's transactions and consequently failed to detect or investigate the numerous suspicious transactions conducted through the account, including prohibited third-party activity. Gibraltar used its account at Oppenheimer to act as an agent for undisclosed principals, repeatedly depositing and liquidating securities for the benefit of third parties. By failing to conduct appropriate due diligence for the Gibraltar account and failing to adequately monitor transactions conducted by the account, Oppenheimer violated the Bank Secrecy Act.

In view of the above facts, FinCEN determined that Oppenheimer willfully violated requirements under the Bank Secrecy Act to implement an adequate anti-money laundering program and an adequate due diligence program for a foreign correspondent account, and willfully violated the notification requirements in rules imposing Special Measures under Section 311 of the USA PATRIOT Act, as described in the CONSENT, and that grounds exist to assess a civil money penalty for these violations. 31 U.S.C. § 5321 and 31 C.F.R. § 1010.820. FinCEN determined that the penalty in this matter will be twenty million dollars.

CHAPTER 5

COUNTRY OR GEOGRAPHIC RISK

Identifying geographic locations that may pose a higher risk is essential to a financial institution's AML/CFT Compliance Program. Financial institutions/DNFBPs are required to understand and evaluate the specific risks associated with doing business in, opening accounts for customers from or facilitating transactions involving certain geographic locations. However, geographic risk alone does not necessarily determine a customer's or transaction's risk level, either positively or negatively.[1]

There is no universally agreed definition by either competent authorities or Accountable Institutions that prescribes whether a particular country or geographic area (including the country within which the financial institution operates) represents a higher risk. Country risk, in conjunction with other risk factors, provides useful information as to potential money laundering and terrorist financing risks. Factors

---

1 Australia Anti-Money Laundering and Counter-Terrorism Financing Rules Instrument 2007 (as amended), paragraph 4.1.3 (7), Officer of the Superintendent of Financial Institutions Canada: Deterring and Detecting Money Laundering and Terrorist Financing 2008, 16,Central Bank of Nigeria's Anti-Money Laundering/Combating the Financing of Terrorism (AML/CFT) Risk Based Supervision (RBS) Framework, 2011, paragraph 5.1

that may result in a determination that a country poses a higher risk include:

1. Countries subject to sanctions, embargoes or similar measures issued by, for example, the United Nations ("UN"). In addition, in some circumstances, countries subject to sanctions or measures similar to those issued by bodies such as the UN, but which may not be universally recognized, may be given credence by a financial institution because of the standing of the issuer and the nature of the measures.

2. Countries identified by credible sources as lacking appropriate AML/CFT laws, regulations and other measures.

3. Countries identified by credible sources as providing funding or support for terrorist activities that have designated terrorist organisations operating within them.

4. Countries identified by credible sources as having significant levels of corruption, or other criminal activity.[2]

This chapter analyses each of the above risk factors.

BOX 5.1: DIRECT DISCRIMINATION

The geographic risk factor alone cannot solely determine the level of risk of a client. An Accountable Institution would have to assess a client's risk with other risk factors like services sought and the type of business the client is involved in. For example, if a client informs the accountable institution that his country of origin is

---

2 FATF Guidance on the Risk Based Approach to combating money laundering and terrorist financing, (High Level principles and procedures) 2007, paragraph 3.5

Afghanistan.[3] An Accountable Institution should not use that information alone to classify the customer as high-risk. Accountable institutions should assess this information with other information obtained from the customer like the customer's occupation. A client who works as a Nurse poses little or no threat to the bank. But a client who works as a minister in a government office does pose a threat to the Accountable Institution as such individual could abuse his position in the country. Assessing customer risk with geographic risk alone may violate the human rights of certain clients, specifically the right to equality. A customer should not be judged with respect to his country of origin. He should be judged based on the business he carries out or the services he intends to utilize in the firm.

5.1 COUNTRIES SUBJECT TO SANCTIONS, EMBARGOES OR SIMILAR MEASURES

Sanctions are restrictions on exports implemented for political reasons by countries and international organisations to maintain international peace and security.

Sanctions measures include arms embargoes and other trade control restrictions.

It is a criminal offence to export licensable goods without a licence.

An arms embargo is a prohibition or sanction against the export of weaponry and dual-use items - goods which have both a civil and military use. An arms embargo might be imposed via various routes such

---

3 Afghanistan has been identified by the Financial Action Task Force as lacking appropriate AML/CFT Laws/Regulations. See paragraph 5.2 for more details on this topic

as by the United Nations, European Union or the Organization for Security and Co-operation in Europe (OSCE) and where the United Kingdom (UK) has imposed regulations as a result.

This section details specific countries where sanctions have been imposed and where there are stricter trade controls in place.

Financial institutions/DNFBPs are however advised to visit the UN, EU and OSCE websites regularly. This would keep them up-to-date with any changes on the sanctions list.

Sudan

Sudan is the largest country in Africa and the UK's 87th largest export market. In 2008, bilateral trade was worth £142 million.

For decades, a civil war has been fought between the country's northern and southern areas, costing 1.5 million lives. Since 2003, the resumption of the war in the Darfur region has caused 200,000 deaths and the displacement of 2 million people, according to UN estimates.

A UN arms embargo has been imposed on Sudan, which is incorporated into EU and UK law. The embargo bans the export of strategic goods to the Sudan, although certain dual-use military goods can be exported under licence for humanitarian and other purposes.

This section explains what items are banned for export to Sudan under the embargo, and how dual-use items are licensed by the Export Control Organisation (ECO).

Extent of the arms embargo on Sudan

An arms embargo is a ban on the export of 'arms and related material' (i.e. military ammunition, weapons and goods). This can be put in place by either the UN, the EU, the Organisation on Security and Co-operation in Europe, or at a UK national level.

The UK interprets an arms embargo as covering all goods and items on the UK Military List (which forms part of the UK Strategic Export Control Lists), unless stated otherwise.

Some items not on the UK Military List may still need an export licence. This is known as the Military End-Use Control. You will need a licence to export items to Sudan under the following circumstances:

- dual-use items that are or may be for use with military equipment

- dual-use items that may be for use as parts of military goods illegally obtained from the UK

If you know or suspect that your exports to Sudan fall under either of these categories, you must tell the ECO, which will tell you if you need a licence.

Prohibitions

The Sudan arms embargo also prohibits:

- technical assistance, brokering services and other military-related services

- financing or financial assistance related to military activities for use in Sudan

The embargo does not prohibit:

- non-lethal military equipment for humanitarian or protective use, eg by the United Nations-African Union Mission in Darfur force (UNAMID) and the EU

- material for crisis management operations

- mine clearance equipment and material

- protective clothing, such as flak jackets and military helmets, for use by personnel from the UN, EU, EU member states, media organisations, and members of humanitarian and development organisations

Trade Control restrictions

Sudan is also subject to Trade Controls under Schedule 4 Part 2 of the Export Control Order 2008. This means that the destination is both embargoed and subject to transit control for military goods.

Sudan arms embargo key legislation

UN Security Council resolutions

After fighting broke out in the Sudanese region of Darfur in 2003, in a renewal of the country's civil war, an arms embargo was imposed by the UN Security Council.

The embargo came into force in 2004, with the passing of UN Security Council Resolution (UNSCR) 1556. It was extended in 2005 with Resolution 1591.

UK legislation

Under UK legislation, the latest implementing regulation is the Export Control (Sudan, South Sudan and Central African Republic Sanctions) (SI2014/3258).

As well as the arms embargo, Sudan is subject to other international restrictions, including:

- a ban on providing services relating to the supply of technical, financial and other assistance related to military activities in Sudan

- freezing of funds

- travel restrictions on people infringing the arms embargo and human rights

You can view a current list of asset freeze targets designated by the United Nations (UN), European Union and United Kingdom, under legislation relating to Sudan.[4]

Lebanon

An arms embargo is in force on Lebanon.[5]

Other Countries subject to Arms Embargo include:

Armenia

Azerbaijan

---

4   Gov.UK Guidance: Embargoes and sanctions on Sudanhttps://www.gov.uk/arms-embargo-on-sudan

5   Gov.UK Guidance: Embargoes and sanctions on Lebanon https://www.gov.uk/arms-embargo-on-lebanon

Burma (Myanmar)

Democratic Republic of the Congo

Ivory Coast (Côte d'Ivoire)

Uzbekistan

Zimbabwe.[6]

> **BOX 5.2: ENHANCED DUE DILIGENCE (1)**
>
> Although Risk factor 1 has no direct link with customers who are not involved in the business of exporting arms, Risk factor 1 does have a direct link with customers involved in the business of exporting weaponry and dual-use items - goods which have both a civil and military use.
>
> Financial institutions/DNFBPs must therefore obtain additional information from such customers, to determine if such customers have the required licence to carry out their respective businesses.

5.2 COUNTRIES IDENTIFIED BY CREDIBLE SOURCES AS LACKING APPROPRIATE AML/CFT LAWS, REGULATIONS AND OTHER MEASURES

The Financial Action Task Force (FATF) is the global standard setting body for anti-money laundering and combating the financing of terrorism (AML/CFT). In order to protect the international financial system from money laundering and financing of terrorism (ML/FT) risks and to encourage greater compliance with the AML/CFT standards,

---

6   UK Export Control Order 2008, Schedule 4

the FATF identified jurisdictions that have strategic deficiencies and works with them to address those deficiencies that pose a risk to the international financial system.

As part of its on-going review of compliance with the AML/CFT standards, the FATF has to date identified the following jurisdictions which have strategic AML/CFT deficiencies for which they have developed an action plan with the FATF. While the situations differ among each jurisdiction, each jurisdiction has provided a written high-level political commitment to address the identified deficiencies. The FATF welcomes these commitments.

A large number of jurisdictions have not yet been reviewed by the FATF. The FATF continues to identify additional jurisdictions, on an on-going basis, that pose a risk to the international financial system.

This section gives a breakdown of those jurisdictions identified by the FATF as having strategic AML/CFT deficiencies.

Financial institutions/DNFBPs are however advised to visit the FATF website regularly. This will keep them up-to-date with regards to countries identified by the FATF as having strategic AML deficiencies.

Afghanistan

In June 2012, Afghanistan made a high-level political commitment to work with the Financial Action Task Force (FATF) and Asia/Pacific Group on Money Laundering (APG) to address its strategic AML/CFT deficiencies. However, the FATF has determined that certain strategic AML/CFT deficiencies remain. Afghanistan should continue to work on implementing its action plan to address its strategic AML/CFT deficiencies, including by: (1) adequately criminalising money laundering; (2) establishing and implementing an adequate legal framework for identifying, tracing and freezing terrorist assets; (3) implementing an adequate AML/CFT supervisory and oversight programme for all financial sectors; (4) establishing and implementing adequate procedures for the confiscation of assets related to money laundering; and (5) establishing and implementing effective controls for cross-border cash transactions. The FATF encourages Afghanistan to address its remaining deficiencies and continue the process of implementing its action plan.

Angola

In June 2010 and again in February 2013 in view of its revised action plan, Angola made a high-level political commitment to work with the FATF and the Eastern and South Africa 'Anti-Money' Laundering Group (ESAAMLG) to address its strategic AML/CFT deficiencies. However the FATF has determined that a strategic AML/CFT deficiency remains. Angola should continue to work on implementing its action plan to address this deficiency by ensuring that appropriate laws and procedures are in place to provide mutual legal assistance. The FATF encourages Angola to address its remaining deficiency and continue the process of implementing its action plan.

Guyana

In October 2014, Guyana made a high-level political commitment to work with the FATF and the Caribbean Financial Action Task Force (CFATF) to address its strategic AML/CFT deficiencies. However, the FATF has determined that certain strategic deficiencies remain. Guyana should continue to work on implementing its action plan to address these deficiencies, including by: (1) adequately criminalising money laundering and terrorist financing; (2) establishing and implementing adequate procedures for the confiscation of assets related to money laundering; (3) establishing and implementing an adequate legal framework for identifying, tracing and freezing terrorist assets; (4) establishing a fully operational and effectively functioning financial intelligence unit; (5) establishing effective measures for customer due diligence and enhancing financial transparency; (6) strengthening suspicious transaction reporting requirements; and (7) implementing an adequate supervisory framework. The FATF encourages Guyana to address its remaining deficiencies and continue the process of implementing its action plan.

Indonesia

Since February 2010, when Indonesia made a high-level political commitment to work with the FATF and APG to address its strategic AML/CFT deficiencies, Indonesia has made significant progress to improve its AML/CFT regime. Indonesia has substantially addressed its action plan at a technical level, including by: (1) adequately criminalising money laundering and terrorist financing; (2) establishing adequate procedures to identify and freeze terrorist assets; and (3) enacting laws or other instruments to fully implement the 1999 International Convention for the Suppression of Financing of Terrorism. The FATF will conduct an on-site visit to confirm that the process of implementing the required reforms and actions is underway to address deficiencies previously identified by the FATF.

Iraq

In October 2013, Iraq made a high-level political commitment to work with the FATF and the Middle East and North Africa Financial Action Task Force (MENAFATF) to address its strategic AML/CFT deficiencies. However, the FATF has determined that certain strategic AML/CFT deficiencies remain. Iraq should continue to work on implementing its action plan to address these deficiencies, including by: (1) adequately criminalising money laundering and terrorist financing; (2) establishing and implementing an adequate legal framework for identifying, tracing and freezing terrorist assets; (3) establishing effective customer due diligence measures; (4) establishing a fully operational and effectively functioning financial intelligence unit; (5) establishing suspicious transaction reporting requirements; and (6) establishing and implementing an adequate AML/CFT supervisory and oversight programme for all financial sectors. The FATF encourages Iraq to address its remaining deficiencies and continue the process of implementing its action plan.

Lao PDR

In June 2013, the Lao PDR made a high-level political commitment to work with the FATF and APG to address its strategic AML/CFT deficiencies. Since October 2014, the Lao PDR has taken steps towards improving its AML/CFT regime, including by enacting AML/CFT legislation. However, the FATF has determined that certain strategic AML/CFT deficiencies remain. The Lao PDR should continue to work on implementing its action plan to address these deficiencies, including by: (1) adequately criminalising money laundering and terrorist financing; (2) establishing and implementing adequate procedures for the confiscation of assets related to money laundering; (3) establishing and implementing an adequate legal framework for identifying, tracing and freezing terrorist assets; (4) establishing a fully operational and effectively functioning financial intelligence unit; (5) establishing suspicious transaction reporting requirements; (6) implementing an adequate AML/CFT supervisory and oversight programme for all financial sectors; and (7) establishing and implementing effective controls for cross-border currency transactions. The FATF encourages the Lao PDR to address its AML/CFT deficiencies and continue the process of implementing its action plan.

Panama

In June 2014, Panama made a high-level political commitment to work with the FATF and the Financial Action Task Force of Latin America(GAFILAT) to address its strategic AML/CFT deficiencies. Since October 2014, Panama has taken steps towards improving its AML/CFT regime, including by issuing guidance to reporting entities on filing Suspicious Transaction Reports (STRs), improving the capacity of the Financial Intelligence Unit (FIU) and issuing regulations on bearer shares. However, the FATF has determined that strategic AML/CFT deficiencies remain. Panama should continue to work on implementing its action plan to address these deficiencies, including by: (1) adequately criminalising money laundering and terrorist financing; (2) establishing and implementing an adequate legal framework for freezing terrorist assets; (3) establishing effective measures for customer due diligence in order to enhance transparency; (4) establishing a fully operational and effectively functioning financial intelligence unit; (5) establishing suspicious transaction reporting requirements for all financial institutions and DNFBPs; and (6) ensuring effective legal mechanisms for international co-operation. The FATF encourages Panama to address its remaining deficiencies and continue the process of implementing its action plan.

Papua New Guinea

In February 2014, Papua New Guinea made a high-level political commitment to work with the FATF and APG to address its strategic AML/CFT deficiencies. However, the FATF has determined that certain strategic AML/CFT deficiencies remain. Papua New Guinea should continue to work on implementing its action plan to address these deficiencies, including by: (1) adequately criminalising money laundering and terrorist financing; (2) establishing and implementing adequate procedures for the confiscation of assets related to money laundering;

(3) establishing and implementing an adequate legal framework for identifying, tracing and freezing terrorist assets; (4) establishing a fully operational and effectively functioning financial intelligence unit; (5) establishing suspicious transaction reporting requirements; (6) implementing an adequate AML/CFT supervisory and oversight programme for all financial sectors; and (7) establishing and implementing effective controls for cross-border currency transactions. The FATF encourages Papua New Guinea to address its remaining deficiencies and continue the process of implementing its action plan.

Sudan

In February 2010 and again in June 2013 in view of its revised action plan, Sudan made a high-level political commitment to work with the FATF and MENAFATF to address its strategic AML/CFT deficiencies. Since October 2014, Sudan has taken steps towards improving its AML/CFT regime, including by issuing customer due diligence circulars and guidelines for mutual legal assistance. However, the FATF has determined that strategic AML/CFT deficiencies remain. Sudan should continue to work on implementing its action plan to address these deficiencies, including by: (1) ensuring implementation of recent procedures established to freeze terrorist assets and (2) ensuring a fully operational and effectively functioning financial intelligence unit. The FATF encourages Sudan to address its remaining deficiencies and continue the process of implementing its action plan.

Syria

Since February 2010, when Syria made a high-level political commitment to work with the FATF and MENAFATF to address its strategic AML/CFT deficiencies, Syria has made progress to improve its AML/CFT regime. In June 2014, the FATF determined that Syria had substantially addressed its action plan at a technical level, including by criminalising terrorist financing and establishing procedures for freezing terrorist assets. While the FATF determined that Syria has completed its action plan agreed upon with the FATF, due to the security situation, the FATF has been unable to conduct an on-site visit to assess whether the process of implementing the required reforms and actions is underway. The FATF will continue to monitor the situation.

Yemen

Since February 2010, when Yemen made a high-level political commitment to work with the FATF and MENAFATF to address its strategic AML/CFT deficiencies, Yemen has made progress to improve its AML/CFT regime. In June 2014, the FATF determined that Yemen had substantially addressed its action plan at a technical level, including by adequately criminalising money laundering and terrorist financing; establishing procedures to identify and freeze terrorist assets; improving its customer due diligence and suspicious transaction reporting requirements; issuing guidance; developing the monitoring and supervisory capacity of the financial sector supervisory authorities and the financial intelligence unit (FIU); and establishing a fully operational and effectively functioning FIU. While the FATF determined that Yemen has completed its action plan agreed upon with the FATF, due to the security situation, the FATF has been unable to conduct an on-site visit to assess whether the process of implementing the required reforms and actions is underway. The FATF will continue to monitor the situation.

Jurisdictions not making sufficient progress

The FATF is not yet satisfied that the following jurisdiction has made sufficient progress on its action plan agreed upon with the FATF. The most significant action plan items and/or the majority of the action plan items have not been addressed. If this jurisdiction does not take sufficient action to implement significant components of its action plan by June 2015, then the FATF will identify this jurisdiction as being out of compliance with its agreed action plan and will take the additional step of calling upon its members to consider the risks arising from the deficiencies associated with the jurisdiction.

Uganda

Despite Uganda's high-level political commitment to work with the FATF and ESAAMLG to address its strategic AML/CFT deficiencies, the FATF is not yet satisfied that Uganda has made sufficient progress in improving its AML/CFT regime, and certain strategic AML/CFT deficiencies remain. Uganda should continue to work on implementing its action plan to address these deficiencies, including by: (1) adequately criminalising terrorist financing; (2) establishing and implementing an adequate legal framework for identifying, tracing and freezing terrorist assets; (3) ensuring effective record-keeping requirements; (4) establishing a fully operational and effectively functioning financial intelligence unit; (5) ensuring adequate suspicious transaction reporting requirements; (6) ensuring an adequate and effective AML/CFT supervisory and oversight programme for all financial sectors; and (7) ensuring that appropriate laws and procedures are in place with regard to international co-operation for the financial intelligence unit and supervisory authorities. The FATF encourages Uganda to address its remaining AML/CFT deficiencies and continue the process of implementing its action plan.

Jurisdictions no Longer Subject to the FATF's On-Going Global AML/CFT Compliance Process

Albania

The FATF welcomes Albania's significant progress in improving its AML/CFT regime and notes that Albania has established the legal and regulatory framework to meet its commitments in its action plan regarding the strategic deficiencies that the FATF had identified in June 2012. Albania is therefore no longer subject to the FATF's monitoring process under its on-going global AML/CFT compliance process. Albania will work with MONEYVAL as it continues to address the full range of AML/CFT issues identified in its mutual evaluation report.

Cambodia

The FATF welcomes Cambodia's significant progress in improving its AML/CFT regime and notes that Cambodia has established the legal and regulatory framework to meet its commitments in its action plan regarding the strategic deficiencies that the FATF had identified in June 2011. Cambodia is therefore no longer subject to the FATF's monitoring process under its on-going global AML/CFT compliance process. Cambodia will work with APG as it continues to address the full range of AML/CFT issues identified in its mutual evaluation report.

Kuwait

The FATF welcomes Kuwait's significant progress in improving its AML/CFT regime and notes that Kuwait has established the legal and regulatory framework to meet its commitments in its action plan regarding the strategic deficiencies that the FATF had identified in June 2012. Kuwait is therefore no longer subject to the FATF's monitoring process under its on-going global AML/CFT compliance process. Kuwait will work with MENAFATF as it continues to address the full range of AML/CFT issues identified in its mutual evaluation report, in particular, fully implementing United Nations Security Council (UNSC) Resolution 1373.

Namibia

The FATF welcomes Namibia's significant progress in improving its AML/CFT regime and notes that Namibia has established the legal and regulatory framework to meet its commitments in its action plan regarding the strategic deficiencies that the FATF had identified in June 2011. Namibia is therefore no longer subject to the FATF's monitoring process under its on-going global AML/CFT compliance process. Namibia will work with ESAAMLG as it continues to address the full range of AML/CFT issues identified in its mutual evaluation report.

Nicaragua

The FATF welcomes Nicaragua's significant progress in improving its AML/CFT regime and notes that Nicaragua has established the legal and regulatory framework to meet its commitments in its action plan regarding the strategic deficiencies that the FATF had identified in June 2011. Nicaragua is therefore no longer subject to the FATF's monitoring process under its on-going global AML/CFT compliance process. Nicaragua will work with GAFILAT as it continues to address the full range of AML/CFT issues identified in its mutual evaluation report.

Pakistan

The FATF welcomes Pakistan's significant progress in improving its AML/CFT regime and notes that Pakistan has established the legal and regulatory framework to meet its commitments in its action plan regarding the strategic deficiencies that the FATF had identified in June 2010. Pakistan is therefore no longer subject to the FATF's monitoring process under its on-going global AML/CFT compliance process. Pakistan will work with APG as it continues to address the full range of AML/CFT issues identified in its mutual evaluation report, in particular, fully implementing UNSC Resolution 1267.

Zimbabwe

The FATF welcomes Zimbabwe's significant progress in improving its AML/CFT regime and notes that Zimbabwe has established the legal and regulatory framework to meet its commitments in its action plan regarding the strategic deficiencies that the FATF had identified in June 2011. Zimbabwe is therefore no longer subject to the FATF's monitoring process under its on-going global AML/CFT compliance process. Zimbabwe will work with ESAAMLG as it continues to address the full range of AML/CFT issues identified in its mutual evaluation report.[7]

Case 5.1: Financial Services Authority v. Habib Bank AG Zurich (Habib) and its former Money Laundering Reporting Officer (MLRO) Syed Itrat Hussain FSA/PN/055/2012

The FSA's investigation identified that during the period 15 December 2007 to 15 November 2010, Habib failed to establish and maintain adequate controls for assessing the level of money laundering risk posed by its customers. In particular, Habib maintained a high risk country list which excluded certain high risk countries on the basis that it had group offices in them. However, Habib's local knowledge of these countries did not negate the higher risk of money laundering they presented.

As MLRO, Hussain was responsible for oversight of Habib's AML systems and controls, but failed to ensure that these systems and controls

---

7   FATF: High-risk and non-cooperative jurisdictions: Improving Global AML/CFT Compliance: on-going process 2015, http://www.fatf-gafi.org/topics/high-riskandnon-cooperativejurisdictions/documents/fatf-compliance-february-2015.html

were adequate. The FSA imposed a financial penalty on Hussain for these failings. He has now retired from the financial services industry.

Tracey McDermott, acting director of enforcement and financial crime, said:

"Habib's failings were unacceptable. Habib's belief that local knowledge of a country through a group office mitigated the higher money laundering risk posed by that country was entirely misconceived.

"Firms must take a dynamic approach to assessing money laundering risk so they can adapt to the ever-evolving risks of financial crime. It is a basic requirement that firms know their customers and understand the risks they pose. The requirement for enhanced due diligence recognises that some customers present a greater risk of money laundering than others and that firms therefore need to do more to identify, manage and control that risk. Habib fell short in this regard.

"It is critical that Money Laundering Reporting Officers properly evaluate, on an ongoing basis, the adequacy and effectiveness of the AML systems and controls which they are responsible for. MLROs have a key role to play in ensuring that firms take appropriate action to minimise the financial crime risks they face. Where individuals fail to meet their regulatory responsibilities we will not hesitate to take action."

Habib and Hussain agreed to settle at an early stage and therefore qualified for a 30% discount. Were it not for this discount, the FSA would have imposed a financial penalty of seven hundred and fifty thousand pounds on Habib and twenty five thousand pounds on Hussain.

BOX 5.3: ENHANCED DUE DILIGENCE (2)

A financial institution/DNFBP that does business with foreign institutions which do not apply the provisions of FATF Recommendations shall take measures, including the following-

- Stringent requirements for identifying clients and enhancement of advisories, including jurisdiction-specific financial advisories to financial institutions for identification of the beneficial owners before business relationships are established with individuals or companies from that jurisdiction;

- Enhance relevant reporting mechanisms or systematic reporting of financial transactions on the basis that financial transactions with such countries are more likely to be suspicious;

- In considering requests for approving the establishment of subsidiaries or branches or representative offices of financial institutions, in countries applying the counter measure shall take into account the fact that the relevant financial institution is from a country that does not have adequate AML/CFT systems; and

- Warn that non-financial sector businesses that transact with natural or legal persons within that country might run the risk of money laundering; limiting business relationships or financial transactions with the identified country or persons in that country.[8]

---

8 CBN (Anti-Money Laundering and Combating the Financing of Terrorism in Banks and Other Financial Institutions in Nigeria) Regulations, 2013, Regulation 17 (3)

5.3 COUNTRIES IDENTIFIED BY CREDIBLE SOURCES AS PROVIDING FUNDING OR SUPPORT FOR TERRORIST ACTIVITIES THAT HAVE DESIGNATED TERRORIST OR-GANISATIONS OPERATING WITHIN THEM.

U.S. law requires the Secretary of State to provide Congress, by April 30 of each year, a full and complete report on terrorism with regard to those countries and groups meeting criteria set forth in the legislation.[9] This annual report is entitled Country Reports on Terrorism. Beginning with the report for 2004, it replaced the previously published Patterns of Global Terrorism.[10]

The 'Country Reports on Terrorism' gives an overview of countries that have been designated by the US Secretary of State as state sponsors of terrorism.

To designate a country as a State Sponsor of Terrorism, the US Secretary of State must determine that the government of such country has repeatedly provided support for acts of international terrorism. Once a country is designated, it remains a State Sponsor of Terrorism until the designation is rescinded in accordance with statutory criteria. A wide range of sanctions are imposed as a result of a State Sponsor of Terrorism designation, including:

- A ban on arms-related exports and sales;

- Controls over exports of dual-use items, requiring 30-day Congressional notification for goods or services that could

---

9 Title 22 of the United States Code, Section 2656f (the "Act"), which requires the Department of State to provide to Congress a full and complete annual report on terrorism for those countries and groups meeting the criteria of the Act.

10 US Department of State: Country Reports on Terrorism http://www.state.gov/j/ct/rls/crt/ Accessed 6th April 2015

significantly enhance the designated country's military capability or ability to support terrorism;

- Prohibitions on economic assistance; and

- Imposition of miscellaneous financial and other restrictions.

Cuba

Cuba was designated as a State Sponsor of Terrorism in 1982. Reports in 2012 suggested that the Cuban government was trying to distance itself from Basque Fatherland and Liberty (ETA) members living on the island by employing tactics such as not providing services including travel documents to some of them. The Government of Cuba continued to provide safe haven to approximately two dozen ETA members.

In past years, some members of the Revolutionary Armed Forces of Colombia (FARC) were allowed safe haven in Cuba and safe passage through Cuba. In November, the Government of Cuba began hosting peace talks between the FARC and Government of Colombia.

There was no indication that the Cuban government provided weapons or paramilitary training to terrorist groups.

The Cuban government continued to harbor fugitives wanted in the United States. The Cuban government also provided support such as housing, food ration books, and medical care for these individuals.

The Financial Action Task Force (FATF) has identified Cuba as having strategic anti-money laundering/combating the financing of terrorism deficiencies. In 2012, Cuba became a member of the Financial

Action Task Force of South America against Money Laundering, a FATF-style regional body. With this action, Cuba has committed to adopting and implementing the FATF Recommendations.

Iran

Designated as a State Sponsor of Terrorism in 1984, Iran increased its terrorist-related activity, including attacks or attempted attacks in India, Thailand, Georgia, and Kenya. Iran provided financial, material, and logistical support for terrorist and militant groups in the Middle East and Central Asia. Iran used the Islamic Revolutionary Guard Corps-Qods Force (IRGC-QF) and militant groups to implement foreign policy goals, provide cover for intelligence operations, and stir up instability in the Middle East. The IRGC-QF is the regime's primary mechanism for cultivating and supporting terrorists abroad.

In 2012, Iran was implicated in planned attacks in India, Thailand, Georgia, and Kenya. On February 13, in New Delhi, India, a magnetic bomb placed under the vehicle of an Israeli diplomat's wife exploded, seriously injuring her and three Indian nationals. On February 14, a similar device was discovered under a vehicle belonging to the Israeli embassy in Tbilisi, Georgia, and safely defused. Also on February 14, Thai police arrested three Iranian nationals in connection with explosions in a Bangkok private residence that revealed bomb-making materials and makeshift grenades intended for use in attacks against Israeli targets. On June 19, Kenyan authorities arrested two Iranian nationals in connection with explosives stockpiled for a suspected terrorist attack. According to press reports, the individuals were members of the IRGC-QF.

On October 17, Iranian-born U.S. dual-national Mansour Arbabsiar was arrested by U.S. authorities and pled guilty in a New York court to participating in a 2011 plot to murder the Saudi ambassador to the United States. Arbabsiar held several meetings with an associate whom Iranian officials believed was a narcotics cartel member. This associate, in fact, was a confidential source for U.S. law enforcement. Arbabsiar admitted to working on behalf of the IRGC-QF to carry out the plot. An IRGC-QF officer who remains at large was also indicted. The thwarted plot demonstrated Iran's interest in using international terrorism – including in the United States – to further its foreign policy goals.

In 2012, the IRGC-QF trained Taliban elements on small unit tactics, small arms, explosives, and indirect fire weapons, such as mortars, artillery, and rockets. Since 2006, Iran has arranged arms shipments to select Taliban members, including small arms and associated ammunition, rocket propelled grenades, mortar rounds, 107mm rockets, and plastic explosives. Iran has shipped a large number of weapons to Kandahar, Afghanistan, aiming to increase its influence in this key province.

Despite its pledge to support Iraq's stabilization, Iran trained, funded, and provided guidance to Iraqi Shia militant groups. The IRGC-QF, in concert with Lebanese Hizballah, provided training outside of Iraq as well as advisors inside Iraq for Shia militants in the construction and use of sophisticated improvised explosive device technology and other advanced weaponry.

Regarding Syria, Iran provided extensive support, including weapons, funds, and training to assist the Asad regime in its brutal crackdown that has resulted in the death of more than 70,000 civilians. Iran provided weapons, training, and funding to Hamas and other Palestinian terrorist groups, including the Palestine Islamic Jihad and the Popular Front for the Liberation of Palestine-General Command. Since the end of the 2006 Israeli-Hizballah conflict, Iran has assisted in rearming Hizballah, in direct violation of UNSCR 1701. Iran has provided hundreds of millions of dollars in support of Hizballah in Lebanon and has trained thousands of Hizballah fighters at camps in Iran.

Iran actively supported members of the Houthi tribe in northern Yemen, including activities intended to build military capabilities, which could pose a greater threat to security and stability in Yemen and the surrounding region. In July 2012, the Yemeni Interior Ministry arrested members of an alleged Iranian spy ring, headed by a former member of the IRGC.

Iran remained unwilling to bring to justice senior al-Qa'ida (AQ) members it continued to detain, and refused to publicly identify those senior members in its custody. Iran allowed AQ facilitators Muhsin al-Fadhli and Adel RadiSaqr al-Wahabi al-Harbi to operate a core facilitation pipeline through Iran, enabling AQ to move funds and fighters to South Asia and to Syria. Al-Fadhli is a veteran AQ operative who has been active for years. Al-Fadhli began working with the Iran-based AQ facilitation network in 2009 and was later arrested by Iranian authorities. He was released in 2011 and assumed leadership of the Iran-based AQ facilitation network.

Since 2009, the Financial Action Task Force (FATF) has called for its members and the international community to institute counter-measures to protect their respective financial sectors and the global financial system from the risks – in particular the terrorist financing threat – posed by Iran. In October 2012, the FATF strengthened its language and again called for countermeasures against Iran. Iran has had some limited engagement regarding anti-money laundering/ combating the financing of terrorism and has responded to overtures by multilateral entities such as the UN's Global Programme against Money Laundering, but it has failed to criminalize terrorist financing and require that financial institutions and other obliged entities file suspicious transaction reports. Iran has not engaged with FATF and was not a member of a FATF-style regional body.

Iran remains a state of proliferation concern. Despite multiple UNSCRs requiring Iran to suspend its sensitive nuclear proliferation activities, Iran continues to violate its international obligations regarding its nuclear program. For further information, see the Report to Congress on Iran-related Multilateral Sanctions Regime Efforts (February 2013), and the Report on the Status of Bilateral and Multilateral Efforts Aimed at Curtailing the Pursuit of Iran of Nuclear Weapons Technology (September 2012).

Sudan

Sudan was designated as a State Sponsor of Terrorism in 1993. Sudanese officials regularly discussed counterterrorism issues with U.S. counterparts in 2012 and were generally responsive to international community concerns about counterterrorism efforts. Sudan remained a cooperative counterterrorism partner on certain issues, including al-Qa'ida (AQ)-linked terrorism, and the outlook for continued cooperation on those issues remained somewhat positive. The Government of Sudan continued to pursue counterterrorism operations directly involving threats to U.S. interests and personnel in Sudan. Sudanese officials have indicated that they view continued cooperation with the United States as important and recognize the potential benefits of U.S. training and information-sharing. While the counterterrorism relationship remained solid in many aspects, hard-line Sudanese officials continued to express resentment and distrust over actions by the United States and questioned the benefits of continued cooperation. Their assessment reflected disappointment that Sudan's cooperation on counterterrorism, as well as the Sudanese government's decision to allow for the successful referendum on Southern independence leading to an independent Republic of South Sudan in July 2011, have not resulted in Sudan's removal from the list of state sponsors of terrorism. Nonetheless, there was little indication that the government would curtail its AQ-related counterterrorism cooperation despite tensions in the overall bilateral relationship.

Elements of designated terrorist groups, including AQ-inspired terrorist groups, remained in Sudan. The Government of Sudan took steps to limit the activities of these organizations, and has worked to disrupt foreign fighters' use of Sudan as a logistics base and transit point to Mali and Afghanistan. Gaps remained in the government's knowledge of, and ability to identify and capture these individuals, however. There was some evidence to suggest that individuals who were active participants in the Iraqi insurgency have returned to Sudan and are in a position to use their expertise to conduct attacks within Sudan or to pass on their knowledge. There was also evidence that Sudanese extremists participated in terrorist activities in Somalia and Mali, activities that the Sudanese government has also attempted to disrupt.

In May, the U.S. government alerted U.S. citizens residing in Sudan that it had received credible reports that extremists were planning to carry out kidnapping operations targeting westerners in greater Khartoum. No such kidnapping had occurred by year's end. The Government of Sudan was responsive to U.S. concerns about the threat. In September, violent extremists attacked the German and U.S. Embassies in Khartoum to protest an American-made film they deemed offensive to the Prophet Mohammed, as well as a Berlin Administrative Court's decision not to ban the use of images of the Prophet by a right-wing group when its members protested outside of a Berlin-area mosque. Demonstrators caused extensive damage to both embassies, and the press reported that local police killed three demonstrators outside of the U.S. Embassy. The British Embassy also suffered minor damage during the events, due to its proximity to the German Embassy. In December, the Sudanese government announced that its security services had disrupted a terrorist training camp in Sudan's Dinder National Park, approximately 186 miles southeast of the capital. Authorities said they killed 13 violent extremists and arrested another 25. Security officials said the terrorists were planning to assassinate Sudanese government officials and were planning to target Western diplomatic missions in the country.

With the exception of Hamas, the government does not appear to support the presence of violent extremist elements. In November, Hamas political chief Khaled Meshal visited Khartoum during a meeting of Sudan's Islamic Movement, and Meshal met with several senior members of the Sudanese government during his visit.

The United States continued to monitor Sudan's relationship with Iran, itself designated as a State Sponsor of Terrorism. In October 2012, two Iranian warships docked in Port Sudan, which Sudanese officials characterized as a solid show of political and diplomatic cooperation between the two nations.

The kidnapping of foreigners for ransom in Darfur continued in 2012, though no U.S. citizens were kidnapped during the year. These kidnappings have hindered humanitarian operations in Darfur. Abductees have been released unharmed amid rumors of ransoms having been paid.

In June 2010, four Sudanese men sentenced to death for the January 1, 2008 killing of a U.S. diplomat assigned to the Embassy, as well as a locally employed U.S. Embassy staff member, escaped from Khartoum's maximum security Kober prison. That same month Sudanese authorities confirmed that they recaptured one of the four convicts, and a second escapee was reported killed in Somalia in May

2011. The whereabouts of the other two convicts remained unknown at year's end.

Two cases that stemmed from the murder of the two U.S. Embassy employees remained active in 2012. In the first, the Sudanese Supreme Court is deliberating on an appeal filed by defense attorneys of the three men remaining alive who were convicted of the two murders, requesting that their death sentences be commuted. In the second, in April, a Sudanese court reduced the sentence of five men involved in facilitating the 2010 prison escape of all four convicted killers, including Abdul Raouf Abu Zaid, the murderer who was recaptured shortly after his escape. In November, an appeals court threw out the conviction of one man accused of being involved in the escape attempt, though it upheld the convictions of the other four, including Abu Zaid. The Government of Sudan has been active in continuing the investigations but the unusual circumstances surrounding the escape raised widespread concerns of involvement by Sudanese authorities.

Sudan is a member of the Middle East and North Africa Financial Action Task Force (MENAFATF), a Financial Action Task Force (FATF)-style regional body. Since February 2010, Sudan has been publicly identified by the FATF as a jurisdiction with strategic anti-money laundering/combating the financing of terrorism (AML/CFT) deficiencies, for which it has developed an action plan with the FATF to address these weaknesses. Since that time, the Government of Sudan continued to cooperate with the FATF and has taken steps to meet international standards in AML/CTF, but still has strategic deficiencies to address. Sudan was subject to a mutual evaluation conducted by the MENAFATF; this report was adopted by the MENAFATF in November 2012. Sudan continued to cooperate with the United States in investigating financial crimes related to terrorism.

Syria

Designated in 1979 as a State Sponsor of Terrorism, Syria continued its political support to a variety of terrorist groups affecting the stability of the region and beyond, even amid significant internal unrest. Syria provided political and weapons support to Lebanese Hizballah and continued to allow Iran to re-arm the terrorist organization. The Syrian regime's relationship with Hizballah and Iran appears to have gotten stronger over the course of the conflict in Syria. President Bashar al-Asad continued to be a staunch defender of Iran's policies while Iran exhibited equally energetic support for Syrian regime efforts to put down the growing protest movement within Syria. Statements supporting terrorist groups, particularly Hizballah, were often in Syrian government speeches and press statements.

President Asad continued to express public support for Palestinian terrorist groups as elements of the resistance against Israel. Damascus provided safe haven in Syria for exiled individuals, although the Palestinian groups were subject to the same level of insecurity as the rest of the Syrian population and fighting has fractured their alliances with the Syrian regime. As part of a broader strategy during the year, the regime has attempted to portray Syria itself as a victim of terrorism, characterizing all its armed opponents as "terrorists."

Syria continued to generate significant concern regarding the role it plays in terrorist financing.

Industry experts reported that 60 percent of all business transactions were conducted in cash and that nearly 80 percent of all Syrians did not use formal banking services. Despite Syrian legislation that required money-changers to be licensed by the end of 2007, many money-changers continued to operate illegally in Syria's vast black market, estimated to be as large as Syria's formal economy. Regional *hawala* networks remained intertwined with smuggling and trade-based money laundering and were facilitated by notoriously corrupt customs and immigration officials. This raised significant concerns that some members of the Syrian government and the business elite were complicit in terrorist finance schemes conducted through these institutions.

Syria is a member of the Middle East and North Africa Financial Action Task Force (MENAFATF), a Financial Action Task Force (FATF)-style regional body. Since February 2010, Syria has been publicly identified by the FATF as a jurisdiction with strategic anti-money laundering/combating the financing of terrorism (AML/CFT) deficiencies for which it has developed an action plan with the FATF to address these weaknesses. Since then, Syria has made limited progress on its AML/CFT regime. In February 2012, Syria was named in the FATF Public Statement for its lack of progress in implementing its action plan, including its need to address the deficiencies by providing sufficient legal basis for implementing its S/RES/1373 obligations and implementing adequate procedures for identifying and freezing terrorist assets, and ensuring that appropriate laws and procedures are in place to provide mutual legal assistance.

In 2012, we continued to closely monitor Syria's proliferation-sensitive materials and facilities, including Syria's significant stockpile of chemical weapons, which we assess remains under the Asad regime's control. There is significant concern, given the instability in Syria, that these materials could find their way to terrorist organizations. We are coordinating closely with a number of like-minded nations and partners to prevent Syria's stockpiles of chemical and advanced conventional weapons from falling into the hands of violent extremists.[11]

---

11   US Department of State: Chapter 3: State Sponsors of Terrorism Overview, 2013 http://www.state.gov/j/ct/rls/crt/2012/209985.htm

BOX 5.4: ENHANCED DUE DILIGENCE (3)

Although Risk factor 3 has no direct link with customers who do not sponsor terrorism, Risk factor 3 does have a direct link with customers determined to be among those sponsoring terrorism.

Standard due diligence would enable a financial institution/DNFBP determine if a customer is among those sponsoring terrorism in a country designated by the US Secretary of State as a state sponsor of terrorism.

Questions like what you do for a living would assist the financial institution/DNFBP in determining if the customer is a top government official in the country concerned.

Financial institutions/DNFBPs must therefore obtain additional information from such customers, to determine if such customers also finance terrorist activities.

5.4 COUNTRIES IDENTIFIED BY CREDIBLE SOURCES AS HAVING SIGNIFICANT LEVELS OF CORRUPTION, OR OTHER CRIMINAL ACTIVITY

First launched in 1995, the Corruption Perceptions Index has been widely credited with putting the issue of corruption on the international policy agenda.[12]

Corruption is the abuse of entrusted power for private gain. It hurts everyone who depends on the integrity of people in a position of authority.[13]

---

12 Transparency International http://www.transparency.org/research/cpi/overview Accessed 6th April 2015

13 Transparency International http://www.transparency.org/whatwedo/ Accessed 6th April 2015

Poorly equipped schools, counterfeit medicine and elections decided by money are just some of the consequences of public sector corruption. Bribes and backroom deals don't just steal resources from the most vulnerable – they undermine justice and economic development, and destroy public trust in government and leaders.

Based on expert opinion from around the world, the Corruption Perceptions Index put together by Transparency International, measures the perceived levels of public sector corruption worldwide, and it paints an alarming picture. Not one single country gets a perfect score and more than two-thirds score below 50, on a scale from 0 (highly corrupt) to 100 (very clean).

Corruption is a problem for all countries. A poor score is likely a sign of widespread bribery, lack of punishment for corruption and public institutions that don't respond to citizens' needs. Countries at the top of the index also need to act. Leading financial centres in the EU and US need to join with fast-growing economies to stop the corrupt from getting away with it. The G20 needs to prove its global leadership role and prevent money laundering and stop secret companies from masking corruption.

The Corruption Perceptions Index ranks countries and territories based on how corrupt their public sector is perceived to be. A country or territory's score indicates the perceived level of public sector corruption on a scale of 0 (highly corrupt) to 100 (very clean). A country or territory's rank indicates its position relative to the other countries and territories in the index. The 2014 index includes 175 countries and territories. Note that N/A means a country was not included in the index during a particular year.

Below is the Corruption Perceptions Index for 2014. Financial institutions/DNFBPs are however advised to check the 'Transparency International' Website on the last month of every year, for the latest version of the Index.

1	Denmark	92		29	Saint Vincent and the Grenadines	67
2	New Zealand	91				
3	Finland	89		30	Bhutan	65
4	Sweden	87		31	Botswana	63
5	Norway	86		31	Cyprus	63
5	Switzerland	86		31	Portugal	63
7	Singapore	84		31	Puerto Rico	63
8	Netherlands	83		35	Poland	61
9	Luxembourg	82		35	Taiwan	61
10	Canada	81		37	Israel	60
11	Australia	80		37	Spain	60
12	Germany	79		39	Dominica	58
12	Iceland	79		39	Lithuania	58
14	United Kingdom	78		39	Slovenia	58
15	Belgium	76		42	Cape Verde	57
15	Japan	76		43	Korea (South)	55
17	Barbados	74		43	Latvia	55
17	Hong Kong	74		43	Malta	55
17	Ireland	74		43	Seychelles	55
17	United States	74		47	Costa Rica	54
21	Chile	73		47	Hungary	54
21	Uruguay	73		47	Mauritius	54
23	Austria	72		50	Georgia	52
24	Bahamas	71		50	Malaysia	52
25	United Arab Emirates	70		50	Samoa	52
26	Estonia	69		53	Czech Republic	51
26	France	69		54	Slovakia	50
26	Qatar	69		55	Bahrain	49

55	Jordan	49	85	Philippines	38
55	Lesotho	49	85	Sri Lanka	38
55	Namibia	49	85	Thailand	38
55	Rwanda	49	85	Trinidad and Tobago	38
55	Saudi Arabia	49	85	Zambia	38
61	Croatia	48	94	Armenia	37
61	Ghana	48	94	Colombia	37
63	Cuba	46	94	Egypt	37
64	Oman	45	94	Gabon	37
64	The FYR of Macedonia	45	94	Liberia	37
64	Turkey	45	94	Panama	37
67	Kuwait	44	100	Algeria	36
67	South Africa	44	100	China	36
69	Brazil	43	100	Suriname	36
69	Bulgaria	43	103	Bolivia	35
69	Greece	43	103	Mexico	35
69	Italy	43	103	Moldova	35
69	Romania	43	103	Niger	35
69	Senegal	43	107	Argentina	34
69	Swaziland	43	107	Djibouti	34
76	Montenegro	42	107	Indonesia	34
76	Sao Tome and Principe	42	110	Albania	33
78	Serbia	41	110	Ecuador	33
79	Tunisia	40	110	Ethiopia	33
80	Benin	39	110	Kosovo	33
80	Bosnia and Herzegovina	39	110	Malawi	33
80	El Salvador	39	115	Côte d'Ivoire	32
80	Mongolia	39	115	Dominican Republic	32
80	Morocco	39	115	Guatemala	32
85	Burkina Faso	38	115	Mali	32
85	India	38	119	Belarus	31
85	Jamaica	38	119	Mozambique	31
85	Peru	38	119	Sierra Leone	31

119	Tanzania	31	
119	Vietnam	31	
124	Guyana	30	
124	Mauritania	30	
126	Azerbaijan	29	
126	Gambia	29	
126	Honduras	29	
126	Kazakhstan	29	
126	Nepal	29	
126	Pakistan	29	
126	Togo	29	
133	Madagascar	28	
133	Nicaragua	28	
133	Timor-Leste	28	
136	Cameroon	27	
136	Iran	27	
136	Kyrgyzstan	27	
136	Lebanon	27	
136	Nigeria	27	
136	Russia	27	
142	Comoros	26	
142	Uganda	26	
142	Ukraine	26	
145	Bangladesh	25	
145	Guinea	25	
145	Kenya	25	
145	Laos	25	
145	Papua New Guinea	25	
150	Central African Republic	24	
150	Paraguay	24	

152	Congo, Republic of	23
152	Tajikistan	23
154	Chad	22
154	Congo, Democratic Republic of	22
156	Cambodia	21
156	Myanmar	21
156	Zimbabwe	21
159	Burundi	20
159	Syria	20
161	Angola	19
161	Guinea-Bissau	19
161	Haiti	19
161	Venezuela	19
161	Yemen	19
166	Eritrea	18
166	Libya	18
166	Uzbekistan	18
169	Turkmenistan	17
170	Iraq	16
171	South Sudan	15
172	Afghanistan	12
173	Sudan	11
174	Korea (North)	8
174	Somalia	8[14]

---

14 Transparency International: Corruption Perceptions Index 2014: Results https://www.transparency.org/cpi2014/results

BOX 5.5: ENHANCED DUE DILIGENCE (4)

Individuals holding prominent public positions in a government body or an international organization have been known to be the most corrupt.

Standard due diligence would enable a financial institution/DNFBP determine if a customer holds a prominent public position or function in a government body or an international organisation.

Questions like where do you work, would assist the financial institution in determining if the customer holds either one of the following positions:

(a) Head of State or head of a country or government; or

(b) government minister or equivalent senior politician; or

(c) senior government official; or

(d) Judge of the High Court of a country, the Federal Court of a country or a Supreme Court of a State or Territory, or a Judge of a court of equivalent seniority in a foreign country or international organisation; or

(e) governor of a central bank or any other position that has comparable influence to the Governor of an Apex Bank or

(f) senior foreign representative, ambassador, or high commissioner; or

(g) high-ranking member of the armed forces; or

(h) board chair, chief executive, or chief financial officer of, or any other position that has comparable influence in, any State enterprise or international organisation; and

Financial institutions would also have to find out, who an immediate family member of a PEP is? Including:

(a) a spouse; or

(b) a de facto partner; or

(c) a child and a child's spouse or de facto partner; or

(d) a parent; and

Who is a close associate of a PEP, which means any individual who is known (having regard to information that is public or readily available) to have:

(a) joint beneficial ownership of a legal entity or legal arrangement with a PEP; or

(b) sole beneficial ownership of a legal entity or legal arrangement that is known to exist for the benefit of a PEP.

Financial institutions/DNFBPs must therefore obtain additional information to establish the source of income and source of wealth from customers designated as Politically Exposed Persons.

CHAPTER 6

INTERNAL CONTROLS

In order for financial institutions/DNFBPs to have effective risk-based approaches, the risk-based process must be imbedded within the internal controls of financial Institutions. The board of directors, acting through senior management, is ultimately responsible for the approval of Anti-Money Laundering/Countering the Financing of Terrorism (AML/CFT) Programme and ensuring that the financial institution/DNFBP maintains an effective AML/CFT internal control structure, including suspicious activity monitoring and reporting. The board of directors and management should create a culture of compliance to ensure staff adherence to the financial institution's AML/CFT policies, procedures and processes.[1]

Internal controls are the institution's policies, procedures and processes designed to limit and control risks and to achieve compliance with the Financial Action Task Force (FATF) Recommendations.

The level of sophistication of the internal controls should be commensurate with the size, structure, risks and complexity of the financial

---

1 FATF Guidance on the Risk Based Approach to combating money laundering and terrorist financing, (High Level principles and procedures) 2007, paragraph 3.20

institution. Large complex financial institutions are more likely to implement departmental internal controls for AML/CFT compliance.

Departmental internal controls typically address risks and compliance requirements unique to a particular line of business or department and are part of a comprehensive AML/CFT Compliance Programme.

Internal controls should:

(i) Identify financial institution's operations (i.e. products, services, customers, entities and geographic locations) that are more vulnerable to abuse by money launderers and criminals. They should ensure that the institution provides for periodic updates to its risk profile and has AML/CFT Compliance Programme that is tailored to manage risks;

(ii) Be such that the board of directors or its committee thereof and senior management are informed of AML/CFT compliance initiatives, identified compliance deficiencies and corrective action taken, and the directors and senior management should be notified of returns rendered to the regulatory authorities;

(iii) Identify a person or persons responsible for AML/CFT compliance;

(iv) Provide for Programme continuity by way of back-up in personnel and information storage and retrieval in cases of changes in management or employee composition or structure;

(v) Provide for meeting all regulatory record-keeping and reporting requirements, implement all recommendations for

AML/CFT compliance and provide for timely updates in response to changes in regulations;

(vi) Cover the implementation of risk-based Customer Due Diligence (CDD) policies, procedures and processes;

(vii) Identify reportable transactions and that all the required reports are accurately rendered promptly and these include Suspicious Transaction Reports (STRs) and Currency Transaction Reports (CTRs). Financial institutions are required to centralize their review and report-rendition functions within a unit in the branches and head-offices;

(viii) Provide for dual controls and the segregation of duties as much as possible. For example, employees that complete the reporting forms (such as STRs and CTRs generally should not also be responsible for taking the decision to file the reports);

(ix) Provide sufficient controls and systems for rendering CTRs;

(x) Provide sufficient controls and systems of monitoring timely detection and reporting of suspicious activity;

(xi) Provide for adequate supervision of employees that handle currency transactions, complete reporting formats, grant exemptions, monitor suspicious activity or engage in any other activity covered by the FATF Recommendations;

(xii) Incorporate AML/CFT Regulation-compliance into the job descriptions and performance evaluations of financial institution personnel, as appropriate; and

(xiii) Provide for the training of employees to be aware of their responsibilities under the AML/CFT Regulations and internal policy guidelines.[2]

The nature and extent of AML/CFT controls will depend upon a number of factors, including:

- The nature, scale and complexity of a financial institution's business.

- The diversity of a financial institution's operations, including geographical diversity.

- The financial institution's customer, product and activity profile.

- The distribution channels used.

- The volume and size of the transactions.

- The degree of risk associated with each area of the financial institution's operation.

- The extent to which the financial institution is dealing directly with the customer or is dealing through intermediaries, third parties, correspondents, or non-face-to-face access.[3]

---

2 Central Bank of Nigeria's Anti-Money Laundering/Combating the Financing of Terrorism (AML/CFT) Risk Based Supervision (RBS) Framework, 2011, paragraph 5.1

3 FATF Guidance on the Risk Based Approach to combating money laundering and terrorist financing, (High Level principles and procedures) 2007, paragraph 3.21

Case 6.1: Financial Crimes Enforcement Network v. Pamrapo Savings Bank, S.L.A. Number 2010-3

Pamrapo failed to establish adequate policies, procedures and internal controls reasonably designed to ensure compliance with the Bank Secrecy Act (BSA). The Bank conducted business without implementing adequate procedures and internal controls, as appropriate and practical, to detect and timely report suspicious activity and large currency transactions.

The Bank's Bank Secrecy Act/Anti-Money Laundering risk assessment process was flawed and did not adequately evaluate and distinguish customers with heightened BSA/AML risks, including money services businesses ("MSBs"). The Bank did not assess its risk exposure within the context of products, services, customers, transaction types or geographical reach of the institution. The Bank's risk assessment inaccurately stated that none of the Bank's branches were in High Intensity Financial Crime Areas (HIFCAs) or High Intensity Drug Trafficking Areas (HIDTAs). In addition, the Bank's due diligence procedures lacked the scope and specificity necessary to adequately evaluate risk, thereby disabling its ability to identify potential suspicious activity. Moreover, even those inadequate due diligence procedures were never implemented by the Bank.

The Bank did not develop AML policies, procedures and controls related to maintaining accounts of MSBs because of a standing practice not to open accounts for check cashing businesses. However, the Bank failed to realize that the definition of an MSB extends beyond check cashers. Even after identification of two money transmitter accounts by regulators in 2007, the Bank did not assess risk in this area or review its customer base. Afterwards, an additional 37 MSB accounts were identified by regulators in 2008, for which the Bank had not obtained proper documentation, conducted proper risks assessments, or conducted proper account monitoring as detailed in the Interagency Interpretive Guidance on Providing Banking Services to Money Services Businesses Operating in the United States, issued on April 26, 2005.

Through April 2009, the Bank routinely conducted cash transactions utilizing a particular transaction code which would not identify the transactor or affiliated account. This transaction code was originally intended to process employee transactions. However, over time this code was routinely used throughout the Bank's branch network to process employee, customer and non-customer transactions without accompanying systems and controls to ensure compliance with the recordkeeping and reporting requirements of the BSA. With the use of this transaction code, the Bank could not capture customer identification information such as name or account number. Therefore, the Bank had no way to determine which customer or individual was conducting cash transactions (e.g., purchasing monetary instruments with cash or cashing checks) and no way to track cash transaction activity. Transactions processed using this code would not appear on the Bank's Large Cash Transaction Report ("LCTR") which was the only report used to file currency transaction reports. In addition, Bank employees were aware that transactions processed using this code would not appear on the LCTR, thus enabling customers and non-customers to structure cash transactions without any risk of detection. Despite this knowledge, Bank employees continued to use the code for at least four years and thereby prevented those transactions from being reported in violation of the currency transaction reporting requirements.

Furthermore, even when proper codes were used, the Bank's systems did not always aggregate cash activity between accounts belonging to one customer. As a result of the coding procedure and processing system errors, Pamrapo failed to aggregate multiple transactions amounting to over ten thousand dollars for individual customers in a single business day. Even after these deficiencies were brought to Bank management's attention, as early as 2005, Bank management failed to take any steps to correct this problem for several years. As a result, the Bank knowingly failed to file numerous currency transaction reports and failed to file accurate and complete currency transaction reports.

The Bank's Suspicious Activity Reporting (SAR) monitoring program was one-dimensional and only included weekly reviews of the LCTR without any regard toward other types of transactions for suspicious or unusual activity. Furthermore, the Bank's manual cash transaction monitoring for unusual activity was ineffective and not commensurate with the size of the institution, volume of transactions, customer base, or geographic footprint. The Bank did not employ automated systems to detect and monitor for suspicious activity. The Bank's suspicious activity monitoring process was primitive and relied solely on verbalizing and/or documenting observed singular events of unusual customer activity by front-line personnel without any enterprise-wide systems in place to determine patterns of potentially suspicious transaction activity within customer accounts. The BSA officer also manually reviewed the LCTR for potential structuring activity. However, as noted previously, this report not only failed to capture numerous transactions, but until 2006 did not include any transactions below ten thousand dollars, rendering it useless for monitoring for patterns of structuring.

In addition, the Bank failed to understand the significance of subpoenas received from law enforcement. The receipt of a grand jury subpoena should cause a financial institution to conduct a risk assessment and account review of the subject customer. The Bank had no procedures in place to evaluate information concerning transactions and accounts subject to a subpoena, so that a determination could be made as to whether additional account monitoring should be implemented or a suspicious activity report should be filed.

After considering the seriousness of the violations and the financial resources available to Pamrapo, the Financial Crimes Enforcement Network has determined that the appropriate penalty in this matter is one million dollars.

6.1 INDEPENDENT TESTING

Senior management will need to have a means of independently validating the development and operation of the risk assessment and management processes and related internal controls, and obtaining appropriate comfort that the adopted risk-based methodology reflects the risk profile of the financial institution/DNFBP. This independent testing and reporting should be conducted by, for example, the internal audit department, external auditors, specialist consultants or other qualified parties who are not involved in the implementation or operation of the financial institution's AML/CFT compliance programme. The testing should be risk-based (focusing attention on higher-risk customers, products and services); should evaluate the adequacy of the financial institution's overall AML/CFT programme; and the quality of risk management for the financial institution's operations, departments and subsidiaries; include comprehensive procedures and testing; and cover all activities.

While the frequency of audit is not specifically defined in any statute, a sound practice is for the financial institution/DNFBP to conduct independent testing generally every 12 to 18 months or commensurate with the Money Laundering/Financing of Terrorism ML/FT risk profile of the institution.

Financial institutions/DNFBPs that do not employ outside auditors, consultants or have internal audit departments may comply with this requirement by using qualified persons who are not involved in the function that is tested.

The persons conducting the AML/CFT testing should report directly to the board of directors or to a designated board committee consisting primarily or completely of outside directors.

Those persons responsible for conducting an objective independent evaluation of the written AML/CFT Compliance Programme should perform testing for specific compliance with the FATF Recommendations (Recommendation 1). They are required to also evaluate pertinent management information systems (MIS). The audit has to be risk-based and must evaluate the quality of risk management for all the financial institution's operations, departments and subsidiaries.

Risk-based Audit Programmes will vary depending on the institution's size, complexity, scope of activities, risk profile, quality of control functions, geographic diversity and use of technology. An effective risk-based auditing Programme will cover all of the institution's activities. The frequency and depth of each audit activity will vary according to the activity's risk assessment.

It should be noted that the risk-based auditing will enable the board of directors and auditors to use the financial institution's risk assessment to focus its scope of audit on the areas of greatest concern. The testing should assist the board of directors and management in identifying areas of weakness or areas where there is a need for enhancements or stronger controls.

Independent testing should (at a minimum) include:

- The evaluation of the overall adequacy and effectiveness of the AML/CFT Compliance Programme, including policies, procedures and processes. This evaluation will contain an explicit statement about the AML/CFT compliance programme's overall adequacy and effectiveness and compliance with applicable regulatory requirements. At the very least, the audit should contain sufficient information for the reviewer (e.g. an Examiner, review auditor or Financial Intelligence Unit officer) to reach a conclusion about the overall quality of the AML/CFT Compliance Programme;

- A review of the financial institution's risk assessment for reasonableness given the institution's risk profile (products, services, customers, entities and geographic locations);

- Appropriate risk-based transaction testing to verify the financial institution's adherence to the Financial Action Task Force record keeping and rendition of returns requirements on Politically Exposed Persons (PEPs), STRs and CTRs information sharing requests;

- An evaluation of management's efforts to resolve violations and deficiencies noted in previous audits and regulatory examinations, including progress in addressing outstanding supervisory actions (if applicable);

- A review of staff training for adequacy, accuracy and completeness ;

- A review of the effectiveness of the suspicious transaction monitoring systems (are they manual, automated or a combination?) used for AML/CFT compliance. Related reports may include, but are not limited to :

- Suspicious transaction monitoring reports ;

- Large currency aggregation reports ;

- Monetary instrument records ;

- Funds transfer records ;

- Non-sufficient funds (NSF) reports ;

- Large balance fluctuation reports ;

- Account relationship reports ;

- An assessment of the overall process for identifying and reporting suspicious transaction, including a review of filed or prepared STRs to determine their accuracy, timeliness, completeness and effectiveness of the institution's policy ; and

- An assessment of the integrity and accuracy of MIS used in the AML/ CFT Compliance Programme. MIS includes reports used to identify and extract data on the large currency transactions, aggregate daily currency transactions, funds-transfer transactions, monetary instrument sales transactions and analytical and trend reports.

The auditors' reports should include their documentation on the scope of the audit, procedures performed, transaction testing completed and findings of the review.

All audit documentation and work-papers should be made available for the Examiner to review. Any violations, policy and/or procedures exceptions or other deficiencies noted during the audit should be included in the audit report and reported to the board of directors or its designated committee in a timely manner.

The board or designated committee and the audit staff are required to track the deficiencies observed in the auditors' report and document the corrective actions recommended and taken.[4]

Case 6.2: Financial Crimes Enforcement Network v. BPI, Inc. Number 2014-06

BPI failed to conduct an independent test of its Anti-Money Laundering (AML) program for a period of more than three years. BPI arranged for an independent review in November 2007. BPI did not arrange for another such independent test until November 2011, and did so only after its initial meeting with the Department of the Treasury Internal Revenue Service-Small Business/Self-Employed Division (IRS-SB/SE) commencing the 2011 Bank Secrecy Act/Anti-Money Laundering (BSA/AML) examination. Moreover, BPI failed to conduct independent testing even though its own policies required such testing to be conducted at least annually, and its independent auditor recommended in 2008 that such testing be conducted at least every 18 months. BPI had been cited for failure to provide for an independent review by the New Jersey Department of Banking and Insurance (NJDBI) in 2005 and 2006, and also by the IRS SB/SE in 2006. Thus, as with the other BSA violations discussed above, BPI was on notice of this deficiency in its independent testing.

FinCEN determined that the penalty in this matter will be one hundred and twenty five thousand dollars.

---

4 Central Bank of Nigeria's Anti-Money Laundering/Combating the Financing of Terrorism (AML/CFT) Risk Based Supervision (RBS) Framework, 2011, paragraph 5.1

6.2 CHIEF COMPLIANCE OFFICER

The institution's board of directors is required to designate a qualified individual that must not be less than a General Manager to serve as the Chief Compliance Officer (CCO). The individual is to ensure that the firm has effective internal controls. The CCO is responsible for the coordinating and monitoring of day-to-day AML/CFT compliance by the institution. The CCO is also charged with managing all aspects of the AML/CFT Compliance Programme and with managing the institution's adherence to AML/CFT Requirements. However, it is the board of directors that is ultimately responsible for the institution's AML/CFT compliance.

As the title of the individual responsible for overall AML/CFT compliance is of importance, his/her level of authority and responsibility within the financial institution/DNFBP is also critical. Though the CCO may delegate the AML/CFT duties to other employees, he/she will be held responsible for the overall AML/CFT compliance by the institution. The board of directors is responsible for ensuring that the CCO has sufficient authority and resources (monetary, physical and personnel) to administer an effective AML/CFT Compliance Programme based on the institution's risk profile.

The CCO should be fully knowledgeable of AML/CFT requirements. The CCO should also understand the institution's products, services, customers, entities, geographic locations and the potential money laundering and terrorist financing risks associated with these activities.

The appointment of a CCO is not sufficient to meet the regulatory requirement if that person does not have the expertise, authority or time to satisfactorily carry out the job efficiently and effectively.

Confirm that the line of communication allows the CCO to regularly apprise the board of directors and senior management of ongoing compliance with AML/CFT regime of the institution. Ensure that pertinent AML/CFT-related information, including the reporting of STRs rendered to the Financial Intelligence Unit are reported to the board of directors or an appropriate board committee so that these individuals can make informed decisions about the overall AML/CFT compliance of the institution.

Ensure also that the CCO is responsible for carrying out the directives of the board and ensuring that employees adhere to the institution's AML/CFT policies, procedures and processes.[5]

Case 6.3: Financial Crimes Enforcement Network v. North Dade Community Development. Number 2014-07

A federally chartered credit union is required to designate a person responsible for ensuring day to day compliance with Bank Secrecy Act (BSA) requirements. 31 C.F.R. § 1020.210; 12 C.F.R. § 748.2(c). North Dade failed to designate a person responsible to oversee BSA compliance, and no staff member was otherwise assigned or technically competent to oversee ongoing compliance efforts. This compliance violation was highlighted during an independent testing review conducted in 2011. While North Dade repeatedly indicated that it would correct this issue, it failed to designate a compliance officer until January 2014, three years later.

FinCEN determined that the penalty in this matter will be three hundred thousand dollars.

---

5 Central Bank of Nigeria's Anti-Money Laundering/Combating the Financing of Terrorism (AML/CFT) Risk Based Supervision (RBS) Framework, 2011, paragraph 5.1

CHAPTER 7

TRAINING AND AWARENESS

Financial institutions/DNFBPs are required to provide their employees with Anti-Money Laundering/Countering the Financing of Terrorism (AML/CFT) training, and it is important that financial institution/DNFBP employees receive appropriate and proportional training with regard to money laundering and terrorist financing.

A financial institution's commitment to having successful controls relies on both training and awareness. This requires an enterprise-wide effort to provide all relevant employees with at least general information on AML/CFT laws, regulations and internal policies.[1]

Financial institutions/DNFBPs are required to ensure that appropriate personnel are trained in applicable aspects of the Money Laundering Laws/Regulations in the country concerned. The training should cover the regulatory requirements and the institution's internal AML/CFT policies, procedures and processes.

---

1 FATF Guidance on the Risk Based Approach to combating money laundering and terrorist financing, (High Level principles and procedures) 2007, paragraph 3.18

At a minimum, the financial institution's training Programme must provide training for all personnel and particularly for those whose duties require knowledge of the FATF Recommendations (Recommendation 1). The training should be tailored to the person's specific responsibilities. In addition, an overview of the AML/CFT requirements typically should be given to new staff during employee orientation. Training should encompass information related to applicable business lines such as trust services, international and private banking.

The Chief Compliance Officer (CCO) should receive periodic training that is relevant and appropriate given changes to regulatory requirements as well as the activities and overall ML/FT risk profile of the institution.

The board of directors and senior management should be informed of changes and new developments in the Money Laundering Laws/ Regulations of the country concerned, other guidelines and directives, and regulations by other agencies. While the board of directors may not require the same degree of training as the institution operations personnel, they need to understand the importance of AML/ CFT regulatory requirements, the ramifications of non-compliance and the risks posed to the institution. Without a general understanding of the FATF Recommendations/Guidelines, the board of directors cannot adequately provide AML/CFT oversight, approve AML/ CFT policies, procedures and processes or provide sufficient AML/ CFT resources.

Training should be on-going and incorporate current developments and changes to the FATF Recommendations and other related guidelines. Changes to internal policies, procedures, processes and monitoring systems should also be covered during training. The training Programme should reinforce the importance that the board and senior management place on the institution's compliance with the FATF Recommendations and ensure that all employees understand their roles in maintaining an effective AML/CFT Compliance Programme.

Examples of money laundering and suspicious transaction monitoring and reporting can and should be tailored to each individual audience. For example, training for tellers should focus on examples involving large currency transactions or other suspicious transactions while training for the loan department should provide examples involving money laundering through lending arrangements.

Financial institutions/DNFBPs are required to document their training Programmes. Training and testing materials, the dates of training sessions and attendance records should be maintained by the institution and be made available for Bank Examiners to review.[2]

It is important that financial institution/DNFBP employees receive appropriate and proportional training with regard to money laundering and terrorist financing. A financial institution's commitment to having successful controls relies on both training and awareness. This requires an enterprise-wide effort to provide all relevant employees with at least general information on AML/CFT laws, regulations and internal policies.

Applying a risk-based approach to the various methods available for training, however, gives each financial institution/DNFBP additional flexibility regarding the frequency, delivery mechanisms and focus of such training. A financial institution/DNFBP should review its own workforce and available resources and implement training programmes that provide appropriate AML/CFT information that is:

---

2 Central Bank of Nigeria's Anti-Money Laundering/Combating the Financing of Terrorism (AML/CFT) Risk Based Supervision (RBS) Framework, 2011, paragraph 5.1

- Tailored to the appropriate staff responsibility (e.g. customer contact or operations).

- At the appropriate level of detail (e.g. front-line personnel, complicated products or customer-managed products).

- At a frequency related to the risk level of the business line involved.

- Testing to assess knowledge commensurate with the detail of information provided.[3]

The following elements are to be adequately addressed in the training program and materials:

(i) The importance placed by the board of directors and senior management on on-going education, training and compliance;

(ii) Employees' accountability for ensuring compliance with the FATF Recommendations (Recommendation 1) and related requirements;

(iii) Comprehensiveness of the training, considering the specific risks of individual business lines;

(iv) Training of personnel from all applicable areas of the financial institution;

(v) Frequency of training;

---

3 FATF Guidance on the Risk Based Approach to combating money laundering and terrorist financing, (High Level principles and procedures) 2007, paragraph 3.19

(vi) Documentation of attendance records and training materials;

(vii) Coverage of the institution's policies, procedures, processes and new rules and regulations;

(viii) Coverage of different forms of money laundering and terrorist financing as it relates to identification and examples of suspicious transaction;

(ix) Penalties for non-compliance with internal policies and regulatory requirements; and

(x) AML/CFT training should be extended to all staff of financial institutions.[4]

7.1 TRAINING METHODS AND ASSESSMENT

There is no single solution when determining how to deliver training; a mix of training techniques may be appropriate. On-line learning systems can often provide an adequate solution for many employees, but there will be classes of employees for whom such an approach is not suitable. Focused classroom training for higher risk or minority areas can be more effective. Relevant videos always stimulate interest, but continually re-showing the same video may produce diminishing returns.[5]

Procedures manuals, whether paper or intranet based, are useful in raising staff awareness and in supplementing more dedicated forms of

---

4 Central Bank of Nigeria's Anti-Money Laundering/Combating the Financing of Terrorism (AML/CFT) Risk Based Supervision (RBS) Framework, 2011, paragraph 3.4

5 The Joint Money Laundering Steering Group JMLSG, Prevention of money laundering/combating terrorist financing 2014 Revised Version, Guidance for the UK financial s sector Part I, Amended November 2014, paragraph 7.35

training, but their main purpose is to provide ongoing reference and they are not generally written as training material.[6]

Ongoing training should be given at appropriate intervals to all relevant employees. Particularly in larger firms, this may take the form of a rolling programme.[7]

Whatever the approach to training, it is vital to establish comprehensive records to monitor who has been trained, when they received the training, the nature of the training given and its effectiveness.[8]

6 The Joint Money Laundering Steering Group JMLSG, Prevention of money laundering/combating terrorist financing 2014 Revised Version, Guidance for the UK financial s sector Part I, Amended November 2014, paragraph 7.36

7 The Joint Money Laundering Steering Group JMLSG, Prevention of money laundering/combating terrorist financing 2014 Revised Version, Guidance for the UK financial s sector Part I, Amended November 2014, paragraph 7.37

8 The Joint Money Laundering Steering Group JMLSG, Prevention of money laundering/combating terrorist financing 2014 Revised Version, Guidance for the UK financial s sector Part I, Amended November 2014, paragraph 7.38

CHAPTER 8

THE RULE BASED APPROACH

The Money Laundering Laws/Regulations of most countries around the world contain language that authorise financial institutions/ DNFBPs to adopt a rule-based approach to discharging certain of their anti-money laundering (AML) and countering the financing of terrorism (CFT) obligations.[1]

This chapter analyses those AML and CFT obligations.

---

1 Australia Anti-Money Laundering and Counter-Terrorism Financing Act 2006 (as amended), s 41, s106, Canada Proceeds of Crime (Money Laundering) and Terrorist Financing Act 2000 (as amended), s 6, 7, China Administrative Rules for Financial Institutions on Customer Identification and Record Keeping of Customer Identity and Transaction Information (2007), Article 29, Germany Money Laundering Act 2008 (as amended), s 8, s 11, Hong Kong, China Guideline on Anti-Money Laundering and Counter-Terrorist Financing 2015, paragraph 7.1, India Prevention of Money-Laundering (Maintenance of Records) Amendment Rules, 2013, rule 10, Nigeria Money Laundering Prohibition Act 2011 (as amended), s 6 (2), See Nigeria Special Control Unit against Money Laundering: Anti-Money Laundering/Combating the Financing of Terrorism Regulations for Designated Non-Financial Businesses and Professions in Nigeria 2013, Regulation 6, See Singapore Notice to Banks, Monetary Authority of Singapore Act, Cap.186, Prevention of Money Laundering and Countering the Financing of Terrorism 2007 (as amended), paragraph 10, 11, See South Africa Financial Intelligence Centre Act, 2001 (as amended), s 22, 23, 29, See also United Kingdom Proceeds of Crime Act 2002 (as amended), s 330, 331, See United Kingdom Money Laundering Regulations 2007, Regulation 19, See United States Codified Bank Secrecy Act Regulations 2010, s 1020.320 (a) (1)

BOX 8.1: THE DIFFERENCE BETWEEN A RISK-BASED APPROACH AND A RULE-BASED APPROACH

The Risk-Based Approach requires financial institutions/ DNFBPs to differentiate between high-risk, low-risk and medium-risk customers. The Rule-Based approach on the other hand requires equal treatment.

A risk based approach is applied to a firm's Customer Identification Program, its Monitoring Program and its Training Program. A rule based approach is applied to a firm's Suspicious Transaction Reporting Programme and Record Keeping Programme.

8.1 SUSPICIOUS TRANSACTION REPORTING

A financial institution/DNFBP is required to render a Suspicious Transaction Report (STR) to the Financial Intelligence Unit (FIU) only and inform the Unit of same whenever it detects a known or suspected criminal violation of the money laundering law of a particular country or a suspicious transaction related to money laundering and terrorism financing activities or a violation of other laws and regulations.[2]

---

2 Australia Anti-Money Laundering and Counter-Terrorism Financing Act 2006 (as amended), s 41, Canada Proceeds of Crime (Money Laundering) and Terrorist Financing Act 2000 (as amended), s 7, China Anti-Money Laundering Rules (2007), Article 11, Germany Money Laundering Act 2008 (as amended), s 11, Hong Kong, China Guideline on Anti-Money Laundering and Counter-Terrorist Financing 2015, paragraph 7.1, India Prevention of Money-Laundering (Maintenance of Records) Amendment Rules, 2013, rule 9 (12) (ii), Nigeria Money Laundering Prohibition Act 2011 (as amended), s 6, See Singapore Notice to Banks, Monetary Authority of Singapore Act, Cap.186, Prevention of Money Laundering and Countering the Financing of Terrorism 2007 (as amended), paragraph 11, See South Africa Financial Intelligence Centre Act, 2001 (as amended), s 29, See also United Kingdom Proceeds of Crime Act 2002 (as amended), s 330, 331, See United States Codified Bank Secrecy Act Regulations 2010, s 1020.320 (a) (1)

The reporting of suspicious transactions or activity is critical to a country's ability to utilize financial information to combat money laundering, terrorist financing and other financial crimes. Countries' reporting regimes are laid down in national law, requiring institutions to file reports when the threshold of suspicion is reached.[3]

Where a legal or regulatory requirement mandates the reporting of suspicious activity once a suspicion has been formed, a report must be made and, therefore, a risk-based approach for the reporting of suspicious activity under these circumstances is not applicable.[4]

A risk-based approach is, however, appropriate for the purpose of identifying suspicious activity, for example, by directing additional resources at those areas a financial institution/DNFBP has identified as higher risk. As part of a risk-based approach, it is also likely that a financial institution will utilize information provided by competent authorities to inform its approach for identifying suspicious activity. A financial institution/DNFBP should also periodically assess the adequacy of its system for identifying and reporting suspicious transactions.[5]

8.1.1 POTENTIALLY SUSPICIOUS ACTIVITY THAT MAY INDICATE MONEY LAUNDERING

The following are examples of potentially suspicious activities or red flags for both money laundering and terrorist financing. Although these lists are not all inclusive, they may help Accountable Institutions and Examiners to recognize possible money laundering and terrorist

---

3 FATF Guidance on the Risk Based Approach to combating money laundering and terrorist financing, (High Level principles and procedures) 2007, paragraph 3.15

4 FATF Guidance on the Risk Based Approach to combating money laundering and terrorist financing, (High Level principles and procedures) 2007, paragraph 3.16

5 FATF Guidance on the Risk Based Approach to combating money laundering and terrorist financing, (High Level principles and procedures) 2007, paragraph 3.17

financing schemes. Management's primary focus should be on reporting suspicious activities, rather than on determining whether the transactions are in fact linked to money laundering, terrorist financing or a particular crime.

The following examples are red flags that, when encountered, may warrant additional scrutiny. The mere presence of a red flag is not by itself evidence of criminal activity. Closer scrutiny should help to determine whether the activity is suspicious or one for which there does not appear to be a reasonable business or legal purpose.

1. Customers Who Provide Insufficient or Suspicious Information—

    (i)   A customer uses unusual or suspicious identification documents that cannot be readily verified.

    (ii) A customer provides an individual tax identification number after having previously used a Social Security number.

    (iii) A customer uses different tax identification numbers with variations of his or her name.

    (iv) A business is reluctant when establishing a new account to provide complete information about the nature and purpose of its business, anticipated account activity, prior banking relationships, the names of its officers and directors or information on its business location.

    (v) A customer's home or business telephone is disconnected.

(vi) The customer's background differs from that which would be expected on the basis of his or her business activities.

(vii) A customer makes frequent or large transactions and has no record of past or present employment experience.

(viii) A customer is a trust, shell company or Private Investment Company that is reluctant to provide information on controlling parties and underlying beneficiaries. Beneficial owners may hire nominee incorporation services to establish shell companies and open bank accounts for those shell companies while shielding the owner's identity.

2. Efforts to Avoid Reporting or Record-keeping Requirement—

(i) A customer or group tries to persuade a bank employee not to file required reports or maintain required records.

(ii) A customer is reluctant to provide information needed to file a mandatory report, to have the report filed or to proceed with a transaction after being informed that the report must be filed.

(iii) A customer is reluctant to furnish identification when purchasing negotiable instruments in recordable amounts.

(iv) A business or customer asks to be exempted from reporting or recordkeeping requirements.

(v) A person customarily uses the automated teller machine to make several bank deposits below a specified threshold.

(vi) A customer deposits funds into several accounts, usually in amounts of less than ten thousand US dollars, which are subsequently consolidated into a master account and transferred outside of the country, particularly to or through a location of specific concern (e.g., countries designated by national authorities and Financial Action Task Force on Money Laundering (FATF) as non-cooperative countries and territories).

(vii) A customer accesses a safe deposit box after completing a transaction involving a large withdrawal of currency or accesses a safe deposit box before making currency deposits structured at or just under ten thousand US dollars, to evade Currency Transaction Report (CTR) filing requirements.

3. Funds Transfers—

(i) Many funds transfers are sent in large and rounded amounts.

(ii) Funds transfer activity occurs to or from a financial secrecy haven, or to or from a higher-risk geographic location without an apparent business reason or when the activity is inconsistent with the customer's business or history.

(iii) Many small, incoming transfers of funds are received, or deposits are made using cheques and money orders. Almost immediately, all or most of the transfers or deposits are wired to another city or country in a manner inconsistent with the customer's business or history.

(iv) Large, incoming funds transfers are received on behalf of a foreign client with little or no explicit reason.

(v) Funds transfer activity is unexplained, repetitive or shows unusual patterns.

(vi) Payments or receipts with no apparent links to legitimate contracts, goods or services are received.

(vii) Funds transfers are sent or received from the same person to or from different accounts.

(viii) Funds transfers contain limited content and lack related party information.

4. Activity Inconsistent with the Customer's Business—

(i) The currency transaction patterns of a business show a sudden change inconsistent with normal activities.

(ii) A large volume of cashier's cheques, money orders, or funds transfers is deposited into or purchased through an account when the nature of the accountholder's business would not appear to justify such activity.

(iii) A retail business has dramatically different patterns of currency deposits from similar businesses in the same general location.

(iv) Unusual transfers of funds occur among related accounts or among accounts that involve the same or related principals.

(v) The owner of both retail business and a cheque-cashing service does not ask for currency when depositing cheques, possibly indicating the availability of another source of currency.

(vi) Goods or services purchased by the business do not match the customer's stated line of business.

(vii) Payments for goods or services are made by cheques, money orders, or bank drafts not drawn from the account of the entity that made the purchase.

5. Lending Activity—

(i) Loans secured by pledged assets are held by third parties unrelated to the borrower.

(ii) Loan secured by deposits or other readily marketable assets, such as securities, particularly when owned by apparently unrelated third parties.

(iii) Borrower defaults on a cash-secured loan or any loan that is secured by assets which are readily convertible into currency.

(iv) Loans are made for or are paid on behalf of a third party with no reasonable explanation.

(v) To secure a loan, the customer purchases a certificate of deposit using an unknown source of funds, particularly when funds are provided via currency or multiple monetary instruments.

(vi) Loans that lack a legitimate business purpose, provide the bank with significant fees for assuming little or no risk, or tend to obscure the movement of funds (e.g., loans made to a borrower and immediately sold to an entity related to the borrower).

6. Changes in Bank-to-Bank Transactions—

   (i) The size and frequency of currency deposits increase rapidly with no corresponding increase in non-currency deposits.

   (ii) A bank is unable to track the true account-holder of correspondent or concentration account transactions.

   (iii) The turnover in large-denomination bills is significant and appears uncharacteristic, given the bank's location.

   (iv) Changes in currency-shipment patterns between correspondent banks are significant.

7. Trade Finance—

   (i) Items shipped that are inconsistent with the nature of the customer's business (e.g., a steel company that starts dealing in paper products, or an information technology company that starts dealing in bulk pharmaceuticals).

(ii) Customers conducting business in higher-risk jurisdictions.

(iii) Customers shipping items through higher-risk jurisdictions, including transit through non-cooperative countries.

(iv) Customers involved in potentially higher-risk activities, including activities that may be subject to export/import restrictions (e.g., equipment for military or police organizations of foreign governments, weapons, ammunition, chemical mixtures, classified defense articles, sensitive technical data, nuclear materials, precious gems, or certain natural resources such as metals, ore and crude oil).

(v) Obvious over or under-pricing of goods and services.

(vi) Obvious misrepresentation of quantity or type of goods imported or exported.

(vii) Transaction structure appears unnecessarily complex and designed to obscure the true nature of the transaction.

(viii) Customer requests payment of proceeds to an unrelated third party.

(ix) Shipment locations or description of goods not consistent with letter of credit.

(x) Significantly amended letters of credit without reasonable justification or changes to the beneficiary or location of payment. Any changes in the names of parties should prompt additional review.

8. Privately Owned Automated Teller Machines—

    (i) Automated teller machine (ATM) activity levels are high in comparison with other privately owned or bank-owned ATMs in comparable geographic and demographic locations.

    (ii) Sources of currency for the ATM cannot be identified or confirmed through withdrawals from account, armoured car contracts, lending arrangements, or other appropriate documentation.

9. Insurance—

    (i) A customer purchases products with termination features without concern for the product's investment performance.

    (ii) A customer purchases insurance products using a single, large premium payment, particularly when payment is made through unusual methods such as currency or currency equivalents.

    (iii) A customer purchases a product that appears outside the customer's normal range of financial wealth or estate planning needs.

(iv) A customer borrows against the cash surrender value of permanent life insurance policies, particularly when payments are made to apparently unrelated third parties.

(v) Policies are purchased that allow for the transfer of beneficial ownership interests without the knowledge and consent of the insurance issuer. This would include second-hand endowment and bearer insurance policies.

(vi) A customer is known to purchase several insurance products and uses the proceeds from an early policy surrender to purchase other financial assets.

(vii) A customer uses multiple currency equivalents (e.g., cashier's cheques and money orders) from different banks and money services businesses to make insurance policy or annuity payments.

10. Shell Company Activity—

(i) A bank is unable to obtain sufficient information or information is unavailable to positively identify originators or beneficiaries of accounts or other banking activity (using internet, commercial database searches or direct inquiries to a respondent bank).

(ii) Payments to or from the company have no stated purpose, do not reference goods or services or identify only a contract or invoice number.

(iii) Goods or services, if identified, do not match profile of company provided by respondent bank or character of the financial activity; a company references remarkably dissimilar goods and services in related funds transfers; explanation given by foreign respondent bank is inconsistent with observed funds transfer activity.

(iv) Transacting businesses share the same address, provide only a registered agent's address or have other address inconsistencies.

(v) Unusually large number and variety of beneficiaries are receiving funds transfers from one company.

(vi) Frequent involvement of multiple jurisdictions or beneficiaries located in higher-risk offshore financial centres.

(vii) A foreign correspondent bank exceeds the expected volume in its client profile for funds transfers, or an individual company exhibits a high volume and pattern of funds transfers that is inconsistent with its normal business activity.

(viii) Multiple high-value payments or transfers between shell companies with no apparent legitimate business purpose.

(ix) Purpose of the shell company is unknown or unclear.

11. Embassy and Foreign Consulate Accounts—

(i) Official embassy business is conducted through personal accounts.

    (ii) Account activity is not consistent with the purpose of the account, such as pouch activity or payable upon proper identification transactions.

    (iii) Accounts are funded through substantial currency transactions.

    (iv) Accounts directly fund personal expenses of foreign nationals without appropriate controls, including, but not limited to, expenses for college students.

12. Employees—

    (i) Employee exhibits a lavish lifestyle that cannot be supported by his or her salary.

    (ii) Employee fails to conform to recognized policies, procedures and processes, particularly in private banking.

    (iii) Employee is reluctant to take a vacation.

13. Other Unusual or Suspicious Customer Activity—

    (i) Customer frequently exchanges small-dollar denominations for large-dollar denominations.

    (ii) Customer frequently deposits currency wrapped in currency straps or currency wrapped in rubber bands that is disorganized and does not balance when counted.

    (iii) Customer purchases a number of cashier's cheques, money orders, or traveller's cheques for large amounts under a specified threshold.

(iv) Customer purchases a number of open-end prepaid cards for large amounts. Purchases of prepaid cards are not commensurate with normal business activities.

(v) Customer receives large and frequent deposits from online payments systems yet has no apparent online or auction business.

(vi) Monetary instruments deposited by mail are numbered sequentially or have unusual symbols or stamps on them.

(vii) Suspicious movements of funds occur from one bank to another, and then funds are moved back to the first bank.

(viii) Deposits are structured through multiple branches of the same bank or by groups of people who enter a single branch at the same time.

(ix) Currency is deposited or withdrawn in amounts just below identification or reporting thresholds.

(x) Customer visits a safe deposit box or uses a safe custody account on an unusually frequent basis.

(xi) Safe deposit boxes or safe custody accounts opened by individuals who do not reside or work in the institution's service area, despite the availability of such services at an institution closer to them.

(xii) Customer repeatedly uses a bank or branch location that is geographically distant from the customer's home or office without sufficient business purpose.

(xiii) Customer exhibits unusual traffic patterns in the safe deposit box area or unusual use of safe custody accounts. For example, several individuals arrive together, enter frequently, or carry bags or other containers that could conceal large amounts of currency, monetary instruments, or small valuable items.

(xiv) Customer rents multiple safe deposit boxes to store large amounts of currency, monetary instruments, or high-value assets awaiting conversion to currency, for placement into the banking system. Similarly, a customer establishes multiple safe custody accounts to park large amounts of securities awaiting sale and conversion into currency, monetary instruments, outgoing funds transfers, or a combination thereof, for placement into the banking system.

(xv) Unusual use of trust funds in business transactions or other financial activity.

(xvi) Customer uses a personal account for business purposes.

(xvii)Customer has established multiple accounts in various corporate or individual names that lack sufficient business purpose for the account complexities or appear to be an effort to hide the beneficial ownership from the bank.

(xviii)Customer makes multiple and frequent currency deposits to various accounts that are purportedly unrelated.

(xix) Customer conducts large deposits and withdrawals during a short time period after opening and then subsequently closes the account or the account becomes dormant. Conversely, an account with little activity may suddenly experience large deposit and withdrawal activity.

(xx) Customer makes high-value transactions not commensurate with the customer's known incomes.

14. Potentially Suspicious Activity That May Indicate Terrorist Financing—

The following examples of potentially suspicious activity that may indicate terrorist financing are primarily based on guidance provided by the Financial Action Task Force (FATF). FATF is an inter-governmental body whose purpose is the development and promotion of policies, both at national and international levels to combat money laundering and terrorist financing.

15. Activity Inconsistent with the Customer's Business—

(i) Funds are generated by a business owned by persons of the same origin or by a business that involves persons of the same origin from higher-risk countries (e.g., countries designated by national authorities and FATF as non-cooperative countries and territories).

(ii) The stated occupation of the customer is not commensurate with the type or level of activity.

(iii) Persons involved in currency transactions share an address or phone number, particularly when the address is also a business location or does not seem to correspond to the stated occupation (e.g., student, unemployed or self-employed).

(iv) Regarding non-profit or charitable organizations, financial transactions occur for which there appears to be no logical economic purpose or in which there appears to be no link between the stated activity of the organization and the other parties in the transaction.

(v) A safe deposit box opened on behalf of a commercial entity when the business activity of the customer is unknown or such activity does not appear to justify the use of a safe deposit box.

16. Funds Transfers—

(i) A large number of incoming or outgoing funds transfers take place through a business account and there appears to be no logical business or other economic purpose for the transfers, particularly when this activity involves higher-risk locations.

(ii) Funds transfers are ordered in small amounts in an apparent effort to avoid triggering identification or reporting requirements.

(iii) Funds transfers do not include information on the originator, or the person on whose behalf the transaction is conducted, when the inclusion of such information would be expected.

(iv) Multiple personal and business accounts or the accounts of non-profit organizations or charities are used to collect and funnel funds to a small number of foreign beneficiaries.

(v) Foreign exchange transactions are performed on behalf of a customer by a third party, followed by funds transfers to locations having no apparent business connection with the customer or to higher-risk countries.

17. Other Transactions That Appear Unusual or Suspicious—

(i) Transactions involving foreign currency exchanges are followed within a short time by funds transfers to higher-risk locations.

(ii) Multiple accounts are used to collect and funnel funds to a small number of foreign beneficiaries, both persons and businesses, particularly in higher risk locations.

(iii) A customer obtains a credit instrument or engages in commercial financial transactions involving the movement of funds to or from higher-risk locations when there appear to be no logical business reasons for dealing with those locations.

(iv) Banks from higher-risk locations open accounts.

(v) Funds are sent or received via international transfers from or to higher risk locations.

(vi) Insurance policy loans or policy surrender values that are subject to a substantial surrender charge.[6]

---

6 Central Bank of Nigeria (Anti-Money Laundering and Combating the Financing of Terrorism in Banks and Other Financial Institutions in Nigeria) Regulations, 2013, Schedule III

8.1.2 CONFIDENTIALITY OF STRS

A financial institution/DNFBP must not disclose to any person other than the Financial Intelligence Unit or the institution's primary regulator the fact that the Financial Intelligence Unit (FIU) has requested or obtained information. A financial institution should designate one or more points of contact for receiving information-requests. An affiliated group of financial institutions may establish one point of contact to distribute the subject-list to respond to requests. However, the subject-lists cannot be shared with any foreign office, branch or affiliate (unless the request specifically states otherwise). The lists cannot be shared with affiliates or subsidiaries of financial institutions' holding companies, if the affiliates or subsidiaries are not financial institutions.

Each financial institution/DNFBP must maintain adequate procedures to protect the security and confidentiality of requests from the FIU. The procedures to ensure confidentiality will be considered adequate if the financial institution/DNFBP applies procedures similar to those it has established to comply with regulatory requirements in order to protect its customers' non-public personal information.

Financial institutions/DNFBPs may keep a log of all requests received and of any positive matches identified and reported to the FIU.

BOX 8.2: THE RISK-BASED APPROACH TO SUSPICIOUS ACTIVITY REPORTING

The Rule-Based Approach requires financial institutions/DNFBPs to report every transaction that is deemed suspicious. This approach could end up flooding the Financial Intelligence Unit internal database

(ELMER)[7] which as a result would lead to the Law Enforcement Agents (the Investigators) system being flooded with reports, and the higher the volume of reports the Investigators have to process within the timelines, the higher the risk that valid reports will slip through the system.[8] It could also be damaging to the client relationships as such reports could cause delay in the processing of transactions.

A risk-based approach would have allowed firms to only report a suspicious activity when it involves a high-risk customer or when the transaction involves a very large amount. This therefore makes the risk-based approach with regards to suspicious transaction reporting, a preferable approach.

8.2 AML/CFT RECORD RETENTION REQUIREMENTS

The Anti-Money Laundering/Countering the Financing of Terrorism (AML/CFT) regime establishes record-keeping requirements related to all types of records including customer accounts (e.g., loan, deposit or trust), AML/CFT filing requirements and records that document

---

7   See National Crime Agency 'The SARs regime' (http://www.nationalcrimeagency.gov.uk 2015),http://www.nationalcrimeagency.gov.uk/about-us/what-we-do/specialist-capabilities/ukfiu/ the-sars-regime   accessed 21st April 2014, which states that SARs are logged onto the UKFIU internal database (ELMER) for information, evaluation and analysis and all SARs are made available to Law Enforcement Agents (those who investigate) with the exception of certain sensitive SARs. ELMER database is the existing IT system in which NCA stores all SARs submitted by the reporting sector. See also China Anti-Money Laundering Rules (2007), Article 6 which states that: The China Anti-Money Laundering Monitoring and Analysis Centre established by the People's Bank of China, shall perform the responsibility of receiving and analysing large-value and suspicious transaction reports in RMB or foreign currencies

8   See Financial Markets Law Committee Issue 69 – Proceeds of Crime Act 2002: Analysis of whether and if so, of what nature there is legal uncertainty in relation to part 7 of the Proceeds of Crime Act 2002

a financial institution's compliance with the AML/CFT regulations.[9] In general, the AML/CFT requires that a financial institution/DNFBP maintains most records for at least five years.[10] These records can be maintained in many forms including original, microfilm, electronic, copy or a reproduction. A financial institution/DNFBP is not required to keep a separate system of records for each of the AML/CFT requirements. However, a financial institution/DNFBP must maintain all records in a way that makes them accessible in a reasonable period of time.

8.2.1 PRESERVATION OF RECORDS

The records related to the transactions discussed below must be retained by a financial institution/DNFBP for at least five years. However, as noted below, the records related to the identity of a financial institution customer must be maintained for five years after the account (e.g., loan, deposit or trust) is closed. Additionally, on a case-by-case basis, a financial institution/DNFBP may be ordered or requested to maintain some of these records for longer periods.

---

9 Australia Anti-Money Laundering and Counter-Terrorism Financing Act 2006 (as amended), s 106-114, Canada Proceeds of Crime (Money Laundering) and Terrorist Financing Act 2000 (as amended), s 6, China Anti-Money Laundering Rules (2007), Article 10, Germany Money Laundering Act 2008 (as amended), s 8, Hong Kong, China Guideline on Anti-Money Laundering and Counter-Terrorist Financing 2015, paragraph 8.1, India Prevention of Money-Laundering (Maintenance of Records) Amendment Rules, 2013, rule 10, Nigeria Money Laundering Prohibition Act 2011 (as amended), s 7, See Singapore Notice to Banks, Monetary Authority of Singapore Act, Cap.186, Prevention of Money Laundering and Countering the Financing of Terrorism 2007 (as amended), paragraph 10, See South Africa Financial Intelligence Centre Act, 2001 (as amended), s 22, 23, See also United Kingdom Money Laundering Regulations 2007, Regulation 19, See United States Federal Financial Institutions Examination Council: Bank Secrecy Act/Anti-Money Laundering Examination Manual 2014, 101-102.

10 Although most jurisdictions require financial institutions to keep records for a minimum period of 5 years, Australia and Hong Kong require financial institutions to keep records for longer periods. Australia requires financial institutions to keep records for 7 years while Hong Kong requires financial institutions to keep records for 6 years. See Australia Anti-Money Laundering and Counter-Terrorism Financing Act 2006 (as amended), s 107 and Hong Kong, China Guideline on Anti-Money Laundering and Counter-Terrorist Financing 2015, paragraph 8.6 for more info.

1. International Transactions in Excess of the Designated Threshold

Financial institutions are required to maintain records of requests made or instructions received or given regarding transfers of currency or other monetary instruments, cheques, funds, investment securities or credit greater than the designated threshold to or from any person, account or place outside the country concerned.

2. Signature Cards

Financial institutions are required to keep records of each grant of signature authority over each deposit account.

3. Account Statements

Financial institutions are also required to keep statements, ledger cards or other records on each deposit account showing each transaction in or with respect to that account.

4. Cheques

Each cheque, draft or money order drawn on the financial institution or issued and payable by it must be kept.

5. Deposits

Each deposit slip or credit ticket reflecting a transaction, record for direct deposit or other funds transfer deposit transactions are required to be kept. The slip or ticket must record the amount of any currency involved.

6. Records to Reconstruct Demand Deposit Accounts

To be kept are the records prepared or received by the financial institution in the ordinary course of business which would be needed to reconstruct a transaction account and to trace a cheque deposited in a demand deposit account through its domestic processing system or to supply a description of a deposited cheque.

7. Certificates of Deposit Purchased or Presented

This record which contained the following will be kept:

(i)   Name of customer (purchaser or presenter).

(ii) Address of customer.

(iii) Tax Identification Number (TIN) of customer.

(iv) Description of the certificate of deposit.

(v)   Notation of the method of payment if purchased.

(vi) Date of transaction.

8. Purchase of Monetary Instruments

A financial institution must maintain records of each of its cheques/draft, cashier's cheque, money order or traveler's cheque.

If the purchaser has a deposit account with the financial institution, this record shall contain:

(i)   Name of purchaser.

(ii) Date of purchase

(iii) Type(s) of instrument purchased.

(iv) Amount of each of the instrument(s) purchased.

(v) Serial number(s) of the instrument(s) purchased.

If the purchaser does not have a deposit account with the bank, this record shall contain:

(i) Name of purchaser.

(ii) Address of purchasers.

(iii) Social security number of purchaser or alien identification number.

(iv) Date of birth of purchaser.

(v) Date of purchase

(vi) Type(s) of instrument purchased.

(vii) Amount of each of the instrument(s) purchased.

(viii) Serial number(s) of the instrument(s) purchased.

(ix) Description of document or method used to verify the name and address of the purchaser (e.g., state of issuance and number driver's licence).

Funds Transfers

A financial institution's AML/CFT record-keeping requirements with respect to funds transfer vary based upon its role with respect to the funds transfer.

Financial institution acting as an originator

For each payment order that the financial institution accepts as the originator, it must obtain and retain records of the following information:

(i) Name and address of originator.

(ii) Amount of the payment order.

(iii) Execution date of the payment order.

(iv) Any payment instruction received from the originator with the payment order.

(v) Identity of the beneficiary's financial institution.

(vi) As many of the following items as are received with the payment order:

(a) Name and address of the beneficiary

(b) Account number of the beneficiary.

(c) Any other specific identifier of the beneficiary.

(d) For each payment order that a financial institution accepts for an originator that is not its established customer, it (in addition to the information listed above) must obtain appropriate extra information as may be required.

Bank acting as an intermediary or a beneficiary's bank

For each payment order that a bank accepts as an intermediary bank or a beneficiary's financial institution, it must retain a record of the payment order.

For each payment order that a financial institution accepts for a beneficiary that is not its established customer, the financial institution must also obtain additional information as required.

9. Tax Identification Number (TIN)

The institution is required to keep the record of the TIN of any customer opening an account.

In cases of joint accounts, information on a person with a financial interest must be maintained.

10. Exceptions in respect of TIN

A financial institution does not need to maintain TIN for accounts or transactions with the following:

(i) Agencies and instrumentalities of federal, state, local or foreign governments.

(ii) Judges, public officials or clerks of courts of record as custodians of funds in controversy or under the control of the court.

(iii) Certain aliens.

(iv) Certain tax exempt organizations and units of tax-exempt organizations.

(v) A person under 18 years of age with respect to an account opened as a part of a school thrift savings Programme.

11. Suspicious Transaction Report and Supporting Documentation

A financial institution must maintain a record of any STR filed and the original or business record equivalent of any supporting documentation for a period of five years from the date of filing.

12. Currency Transaction Report

A financial institution must maintain a record of all Currency Transaction Reports (CTR) for a period of five years from the date of filing.

Customer Identification Programme

A financial institution must maintain a record of all information it obtains under its procedures for implementing its CIP. At a minimum, these records must include the following:

(i) All identifying information about a customer (e.g., name, date of birth, address and TIN).

(ii) A description of the document that the bank/other financial institution relied upon to identity of the customer.

(iii) A description of the non-documentary methods and results of any measures the financial institution took to verify the identity of the customer.

(iv) A description of the financial institution's resolution of any substantive discrepancy discovered when verifying the identifying information obtained.

A financial institution must retain the identifying information about a customer for a period of five years after the date the account is closed or in the case of credit card accounts, five years after the account becomes closed or dormant.

A financial institution must retain the information relied on, methods used to verify identity and resolution of discrepancies for a period of five years after the record is made.

These AML/CFT record-keeping requirements are independent of and in addition to requirements to file and retain reports imposed by other laws.[11]

BOX 8.3: THE RISK-BASED APPROACH TO RECORD-KEEPING REQUIREMENTS

The Financial Action Task Force requires financial institutions to apply a rule-based approach to record-keeping requirements. In other words, financial institutions are required by law to maintain records on transactions and

11 Central Bank of Nigeria's Anti-Money Laundering/Combating the Financing of Terrorism (AML/CFT) Risk Based Supervision (RBS) Framework, 2011

information obtained through the CDD measures for a minimum period of five years.

A risk-based approach may be a preferable option to a rule-based approach.

A risk-based approach is designed to make it more difficult for money launderers and terrorist organizations to make use of financial institutions due to the increased focus on the identified higher-risk activities that are undertaken by these criminal elements.[12]

Countries should not be allowed to stipulate a minimum time frame for financial institutions to maintain records. Rather, the period should depend on whether or not the customer is high risk.

For customers who have been designated as higher risk by a firm, financial institutions should be allowed to keep records of information obtained through CDD measures for ten years or more. For customers designated as lower risk, financial institutions should be allowed to keep records of information obtained through CDD measures for as little as two years.

Keeping information for five years may lead to an unnecessary interference with a person's right to a private life, and such interference cannot be justified.

---

12 FATFGuidanceontheRiskBasedApproachtoCombatingMoneyLaunderingandTerroristFinancing, (HighLevelPrinciplesandProcedures)(2007), paragraph 1.17.

CHAPTER 9

HUMAN RIGHTS

The previous chapters gave a thorough analysis of the risk-based approach. This chapter determines the level of impact the risk-based approach has on the human rights of certain clients or customers of financial institutions/designated non-financial institutions.

9.1 RIGHT TO RESPECT FOR PRIVATE AND FAMILY LIFE

Article 8 of the European Convention on Human Rights (the convention) protects an interesting set of rights. According to **Article 8 (1)**, everyone has the right to respect for his private and family life.[1] The jurisprudence of the convention confirms that private and family life, are distinct although often overlapping interests.[2]

This section would determine if the risk-based approach interferes with the private and family life of an individual.

---

1   European Convention on Human Rights 1950 as amended, Article 8 (1)

2   J Rehman, 'International Human Rights Law' (2nd Edition Pearson Education Limited 2010) 205.

9.1.1 PRIVATE LIFE

Respect for private life comprises to a certain degree the right to establish and develop relationships with other human beings.[3]Such right can be violated where there is an interference with a person's relationship.[4] The interference could be with the relationship of a person with his lover or business partner.

Such interference may amount to a violation of a person's right when it is not justified.[5]

An interference comes into play where a law that exists directly affects the private life of an individual, in such a way that such an individual would have to respect the law and be mandated to do something which may prevent him from developing his relationship with some people and if he does not do it, he or she could be liable to criminal prosecution.[6]

The designation of certain customers as high-risk customers could interfere with the personal relationship of the individual concerned. Certain institutions/individuals may not want to form relationships with persons determined to be of high-risk.

For example, In May 2014, one of the four largest financial institutions in Australia closed accounts held by customers trading in Bitcoin, citing reputational risk. Likewise, the largest U.S. bank in

---

3 See Niemietz v. Germany (1993) 16 EHRR 97, Para 27. See also Evans V United Kingdom (2008) 46 EHRR 34, Para 71.

4 Dudgeon v. United Kingdom (1982) 4 EHRR 149, Para 43

5 See Dudgeon v. United Kingdom (1982) 4 EHRR 149,Para 43 which is to the effect that an interference will not be justified unless it is in accordance with the law, has an aim or aims that is or are legitimate and is necessary in a democratic society for the aforesaid aim or aims.

6 See Dudgeon v. United Kingdom (1982) 4 EHRR 149, Para 41

assets scaled back lending to pawn shops, payday lenders, check cashers and car dealerships.[7]

In the United Kingdom, the Financial Conduct Authority observed a recent trend for Banks to remove banking services from their money services businesses (MSB) customers because of the money laundering and terrorist financing risks posed by the sector.[8]

Although the actions taking by financial institutions in Australia, the United States and the United Kingdom amounts to an unjustifiable interference with a person's private life, such interference could be directly linked to the 'de-risking approach' adopted by those financial institutions and not the risk-based approach.

The FATF Recommendations only require financial institutions to terminate customer relationships, on a case-by-case basis, where the money laundering and terrorist financing risks cannot be mitigated. This is fully in line with AML/CFT objectives. What is not in line with the FATF standards is the wholesale cutting loose of entire classes of customer, without taking into account, seriously and comprehensively, their level of risk or risk mitigation measures for individual customers within a particular sector.[9]

9.1.2 FAMILY LIFE

Family Life encompasses marriage-based relationships and other de facto 'family ties' where parties are living together outside marriage.

---

7 ACAMS TODAY: De-Risking: Does one bad apple spoil the bunch? September-November 2014 Vol.13 No.4

8 Financial Conduct Authority: Anti-money laundering annual report 2012/13, paragraph 7.9

9 Financial Action Task Force: FATF clarifies risk-based approach: case-by-case, not wholesale de-risking: http://www.fatf-gafi.org/documents/documents/rba-and-de-risking.html

A child born out of such a relationship is ipso jure part of that 'family unit' from the moment of its birth and by the very fact of it.[10]

Such right can be violated where there is an interference with a person's relationship.[11] The interference could be with the relationship of a person with his wife or his child.

Such interference may amount to a violation of a person's right when it is not justified.[12]

The designation of an individual as a politically exposed person (PEP) may interfere with the marriage of high-risk customers. Non-high-risk customers may decide to annul the marriage between themselves and their partners, so as to prevent firms from designating them as PEPs also.

The above interference could be justified on the basis that the enhanced measures adopted by firms does mitigate money laundering and terrorist financing risks effectively.

9.2 DIRECT DISCRIMINATION

Article 14 of the Convention provides for the universally recognised norm of non-discrimination. However Article 14 was restricted to protecting persons against discrimination only in respect of rights contained in the convention,[13] but that has now been redressed by the

---

10   See Kroon and Others v. the Netherlands [1994] ECHR 18535/91, Para 30, See also Keegan v. Ireland [1994] ECHR 16969/90, Para 44, See also Mikulic v. Croatia [2002] ECHR 53176/99, Para 51

11   Dudgeon v. United Kingdom (1982) 4 EHRR 149, Para 43

12   See Dudgeon v. United Kingdom (1982) 4 EHRR 149,Para 43 which is to the effect that an interference will not be justified unless it is in accordance with the law, has an aim or aims that is or are legitimate and is necessary in a democratic society for the aforesaid aim or aims.

13   European Convention on Human Rights 1950 as amended, Article 14. See also J Rehman, 'International Human Rights Law' (2nd Edition Pearson Education Limited 2010) 214.

adoption of Protocol 12, which extends beyond the rights provided in the Convention to 'any right set forth by the law.'[14]

This section aims to determine if the risk-based approach directly discriminates against the different human rights of high-risk customers. It would determine this by looking into the conditions which must be cumulatively met in order for direct discrimination to occur. These conditions include differential treatment, prohibited grounds, without objective and reasonable justification and no reasonable relationship of proportionality.[15]

9.2.1 DIFFERENTIAL TREATMENT

One of the conditions that must exist before direct discrimination can occur is that there must be a given difference in treatment, which may concern the exercise of any right set forth by law.[16]

The risk-based approach does create a difference in treatment, concerning the exercise of the right for a person to develop a relationship, marry and found a family and even enjoy a property.

The risk-based approach requires that firms apply enhanced due diligence measures to customers determined to be high risk. Customers who are found to be low risk would be subjected to simplified due diligence measures.

---

14 See Protocol No 12 to the European Convention On Human Rights, Article 1, See also J Rehman, 'International Human Rights Law' (2nd Edition Pearson Education Limited 2010) 214

15 See Belgian Linguistic Case,(1979 -80) 1 EHRR 252, Para 10, See also Swedish Engine Driver's Union v. Sweden (1979-80) 1 EHRR, 617, Para's 45, 47, 48, , See also National Union of Belgian Police v. Belgium (1979 -80) 1 EHRR 578, Para 44, 46, See also Engel and Others v. The Netherlands (No.1) (1979-80) 1 EHRR 647, Para 72, See also The Republic of Ireland v. The United Kingdom (1979-80) 2 EHRR 25, Para 226

16 See Belgian Linguistic Case (1979 -80) 1 EHRR 252, Para 10, See also National Union of Belgian Police v. Belgium (1979 -80) 1 EHRR 578 Para's 44, 46

This therefore creates a difference in treatment with regards to the right to private life of an individual.

9.2.2 PROHIBITED GROUNDS

Article 14 of the Convention provides that discrimination could be on the ground of sex, race, colour, national or social origin, property, birth or other status.[17]

Discrimination with regards to high-risk customers is on the ground of the place of work and the amount of money earned by an individual.

Customers who work in top government positions would be designated as Politically Exposed Persons and in the event, be subject to enhanced due diligence measures.

9.2.3 NO OBJECTIVE AND REASONABLE JUSTIFICATION

The third condition for a direct discrimination to occur is that the distinction or difference in treatment would have no objective and reasonable justification. The existence of such a justification must be assessed in relation to the aim and effects of the measure under consideration.[18] So this means that in order to determine if the risk-based approach has no reasonable justification, one has to look at what its aims and objectives are.

The enhanced due diligence measures embedded within the risk assessment process does assist firms in adequately assessing the money laundering and terrorist financing risks associated with certain

---

17   European Convention on Human Rights 1950 as amended, Article 14
18   See Belgian Linguistic Case (1979 -80) 1 EHRR 252, Para 10, See also National Union of Belgian Police v. Belgium (1979 -80) 1 EHRR 578, Para 46

customers. The enhanced on-going monitoring measure enables firms to effectively detect suspicious transactions in accounts maintained by high-risk customers.

In view of the above facts, the risk-based approach does have a legitimate aim.[19]

9.2.4 NO REASONABLE RELATIONSHIP OF PROPORTIONALITY

Article 14 is likewise violated when it is clearly established that there is no reasonable relationship of proportionality between the means employed and the aim sought to be realised.[20] In other words, the State must strike a fair balance between the protection of the interests of the community, and respect for the rights and freedoms safeguarded by the convention.[21] Hence if the measure in question creates no impediment to the exercise of the individual rights enshrined in the Convention, then it would be a fair balance.[22]

The risk-based approach does not interfere with the individual rights of high-risk customers.

The risk-based approach has proved to be the most effective approach in combating money laundering and terrorist financing. The approach ensures that measures applied to mitigate money laundering and terrorist financing risks, are proportionate to the risks identified.

---

19 See Belgian Linguistic Case (1979 -80) 1 EHRR 252, Para 7 which is to the effect that the European Convention on Human Rights Article 14 does not prohibit distinctions in treatment based on public interest.

20 See Belgian Linguistic Case (1979 -80) 1 EHRR 252, Para 10, See also National Union of Belgian Police v. Belgium (1979 -80) 1 EHRR 578, Para 46

21 See Belgian Linguistic Case (1979 -80) 1 EHRR 252, Para 7

22 See Belgian Linguistic Case (1979 -80) 1 EHRR 252, Para 13

On this note it can be said that the risk-based approach does not directly discriminate against the different human rights of high-risk customers.

HIGH RISK CUSTOMERS

(A) MONEY SERVICE BUSINESSES (MSB)

The MSB industry is extremely diverse, ranging from large international companies with numerous outlets worldwide to small, independent convenience stores in communities with population concentrations that do not necessarily have access to traditional banking services or in areas where English is rarely spoken.

The range of products and services offered, and the customer bases served by MSBs, are equally diverse. Indeed, while they all fall under the definition of a money services business, the types of businesses are quite distinct. Some MSBs offer a variety of services, whilst others only offer money services as an ancillary component to their primary business, such as a convenience store that cashes cheques or a hotel that provides currency exchange.

MSB services can include one or more of the following activities:

- Currency dealing/exchanging;

- Cheque cashing;

- Money remitting; and

- Issuing, selling and redeeming stored value and monetary instruments, such as money orders and traveller's cheques.

Risk Factors

Several features of the MSB sector make it an attractive vehicle
through which criminal and terrorist funds can enter the financial
system, such as the simplicity and certainty of MSB transactions,
worldwide reach (in case of money remitters), the cash character of
transactions, low thresholds, the often less stringent customer identification rules that are applied to low value transactions compared
with opening bank accounts and reduced possibilities for verification
of the customer's identification than in credit or other financial institutions. The nature of the underlying customer's relationship with
the MSB and a low frequency of contact with them can also be a significant vulnerability.

Generally, MSBs can be used for money laundering and terrorist financing in two ways: either by wittingly or unwittingly performing
relevant transactions for their customers without knowledge of the illegal origin or destination of the funds concerned, or by a direct involvement of the staff/management of the provider through complicity or
through the ownership of such businesses by a criminal organisation.

MSBs can be used at all stages of the money laundering process.
Currency exchanges specifically are an important link in the money
laundering chain. Once the money has been exchanged, it is difficult

to trace its origin. Also, considering that many are small businesses, currency exchanges can be more easily prone to takeover by criminals and used to launder money.

Obtaining ownership of an MSB either directly or via sub-agent relationships provides criminals a perfect tool to manipulate the money transfer system and to launder money. Detecting such cases depends, to a certain extent, on the firm applying Customer Due Diligence (CDD) measures and monitoring/reporting obligations effectively.

The following indicators could be relevant in this context:

- Reluctance by the MSB to provide information about the identity of their customers when requested by the bank;

- Use of false identification and fictitious names for customers;

- Turnover of the MSB exceeding, to a large extent, the cash flows of other comparable businesses in the sector;

- Suspicious connections of the MSB owner;

- Suspicious transactions performed on the bank accounts of the MSB or its owner;

- Suspicion that a business (such as a travel agent or corner shop) is actually providing MSB services to the customers of its primary business, or leveraging another business name/type to cover up unregistered activity;

- Overly complicated agent/principal networks (e.g. multiple principals for one agent, agents with their own agents etc.) with inadequate oversight by principal.

- A survey carried out by FATF suggests the most important factors that may indicate possible misuse of MSBs include:

- Use of underground remittance systems;

- Mismatch between the economic activity, country of origin, or person and the money remittances received;

- Periodic transfers made by several people to the same beneficiary or related persons;

- Transfers over a short period of time of low amounts that together represent a large sum of money;

- Transfers from one or more senders in different countries to a local beneficiary.

- Sudden inflow of funds in cash followed by sudden outflow through financial instruments such as drafts and cheques;

- Structuring of transactions and/or changing of MSB for subsequent orders to keep a low profile; and

- False information during the customer identification procedure/lack of co-operation.

Many reported cases of abuse involve small value wire transfers (although some involve high-value amounts), but the total value of funds involved in these cases can be quite significant, raising the possible involvement of organised criminal activity.[1]

---

1 JMLSG: Guidance in respect of Money Service Businesses 2014

Risk Assessment

An effective risk assessment should be a composite of multiple factors and depending upon the circumstances, certain factors may be given more weight than others. The following factors may be used to help identify the level of risk presented by each MSB customer:

(i) Purpose of the account;

(ii) Anticipated account activity (type and volume);

(iii) Types of products and services offered by the MSB; and

(iv) Locations and markets served by the MSB.

Financial institution management may tailor these factors based on their customer base or the geographic locations in which the financial institution operates. Management should weigh and evaluate each risk assessment factor to arrive at a risk determination for each customer. A bank's due diligence should be commensurate with the level of risk assigned to the MSB customer, after consideration of these factors. If a bank's risk assessment indicates potential for a heightened risk of money laundering or terrorist financing, the bank will be expected to conduct further due diligence in a manner commensurate with the heightened risk.

Risk Mitigation

A financial institution's policies, procedures and processes should provide for sound due diligence and verification practices, adequate risk assessment of MSB accounts and ongoing monitoring and reporting of unusual or suspicious transactions. A financial institution that establishes and maintains accounts for MSBs should apply appropriate, specific risk-based and where necessary, EDD policies, procedures, and controls.

The factors below, while not all inclusive may reduce or mitigate the risk in some MSB accounts:

(i) MSB is registered and licensed;

(ii) MSB confirms it is subject to examination for AML compliance;

(iii) MSB affirms the existence of a written AML/CFT Programme and provides its CCO's name and contact information;

(iv) MSB has an established banking relationship and/or account activity consistent with expectations;

(v) MSB is an established business with an operating history;

(vi) MSB is a principal with one or few agents, or is acting as an agent for one principal;

(vii) MSB provides services only to local residents;

(viii) Most of the MSB's customers conduct routine transactions in not too much amounts;

(ix) The expected (lower-risk) transaction activity for the MSB's business operations is consistent with information obtained by the financial institution at account opening. Examples include the following:

    a. Cheque-cashing activity is limited to payroll or government cheques; And

    b. Cheque-cashing service is not offered for third-party or out-of-state cheques.

(x) Money-transmitting activities are limited to domestic entities (e.g., domestic bill payments).

Given the importance of licensing and registration requirements, a financial institution should file a Suspicious Transaction Report if it becomes aware that a customer is operating in violation of the registration or licensing requirements. The decision to maintain or close an account should be made by financial institution senior management under standards and guidelines approved by its board of directors.

The extent to which the financial institution should perform further due diligence beyond the minimum due diligence obligations set forth below will be dictated by the level of risk posed by the individual MSB customer. Because not all MSBs present the same level of risk, not all MSBs will require further due diligence. For example, a local grocer that also cashes payroll cheques for customers purchasing groceries may not present the same level of risk as a money transmitter specializing in cross-border funds transfers. Therefore, the customer due diligence requirements will differ based on the risk posed by each MSB customer. Based on existing AML/CFT Regulation requirements applicable to financial institutions, the minimum due diligence expectations associated with opening and maintaining accounts for any MSB are:

(i) Apply the financial institution's Customer Identification Program (CIP).

(ii) Confirm registration renewal.

(iii) Confirm compliance with licensing requirements, if applicable.

(iv) Confirm agent status, if applicable.

(v)   Conduct a basic ML/FT risk assessment to determine the level of risk associated with the account and whether further due diligence is necessary.

If the institution determines that the MSB customer presents a higher level of money laundering or terrorist financing risk, EDD measures should be conducted in addition to the minimum due diligence procedures. Depending on the level of perceived risk, the size and sophistication of the particular MSB, banking organizations may pursue some or all of the following actions as part of an appropriate EDD review:

(i)   Review the MSB's AML/CFT Programme.

(ii)   Review results of the MSB's independent testing of its AMLCFT Programme.

(iii) Review written procedures for the operation of the MSB.

(iv) Conduct on-site visits.

(v)   Review list of agents, including locations within or outside the country concerned which will be receiving services directly or indirectly through the MSB account.

(vi) Review written agent management and termination practices for the MSB.

(vii) Review written employee screening practices for the MSB.

(B) NON-RESIDENT ALIENS AND FOREIGN INDIVIDUALS

The financial institution's systems to manage the risks associated with transactions involving accounts held by non-resident aliens (NRA) and foreign individuals should be adequate and the management should have the ability to implement its due diligence, monitoring and reporting systems effectively.

Foreign individuals maintaining relationships with Nigeria/United States financial institutions can be divided into two categories of resident aliens and non-resident aliens.

For definitional purposes, a NRA is a non-American citizen who:

(i) is not a lawful permanent resident of Nigeria/United States during the calendar year and who does not meet the substantial presence test or

(ii) has not been issued an alien registration permit. The Federal Inland Revenue Service (FIRS) determines the tax liabilities of a foreign person and officially defines the person as a resident or non-resident.

Although NRAs are not permanent residents, they may have a legitimate need to establish an account relationship with a Nigeria/United States financial institution.

NRAs can use bank products and services for asset preservation (e.g., mitigating losses due to exchange rates), business expansion and investments.

Risk Factors

Financial institutions may find it more difficult to verify and authenticate an NRA accountholder's identification, source of funds and source of wealth which may result in ML/FT risks. The NRA's home country may also heighten the account risk, depending on the secrecy laws of that country. Because the NRA is expected to reside outside of Nigeria, funds transfers or the use of foreign automated teller machines (ATM) may be more frequent. The ML/FT risk may be further heightened if the NRA is a Politically Exposed Person (PEP).

Risk Mitigation

Financial institutions should establish policies, procedures and processes that provide for sound due diligence and verification practices, adequate risk assessment of NRA accounts, ongoing monitoring and reporting of unusual or suspicious activities. The following factors are to be considered when determining the risk level of an NRA account:

(i)   Account-holder's home country;

(ii) Types of products and services used;

(iii) Forms of identification;

(iv) Source of wealth and funds; and

(v)   Unusual account activity.

The financial institution's Customer Identification Programme should detail the identification requirements for opening an account for a non-United States person, including a NRA. The Programme should include the use of documentary and non-documentary methods to verify a customer. In addition, financial institutions must maintain due diligence procedures for private banking accounts for non-American persons, including those held for PEPs or senior foreign political figures.

In accepting business from non-face-to-face customers: banks should apply equally effective customer identification procedures for non-face-to-face customers as for those available for interview; and there must be specific and adequate measures to mitigate the higher risk.

Examples of measures to mitigate risk include:

- certification of documents presented;

- requisition of additional documents to complement those which are required for face-to-face customers;

- independent contact with the customer by the bank;

- third party introduction, e.g. by an introducer subject to the criteria established by the bank; or

- requiring the first payment to be carried out through an account in the customer's name with another bank subject to similar customer due diligence standards.

Source: Central Bank of Nigeria's Anti-Money Laundering/ Combating the Financing of Terrorism (AML/CFT) Risk Based Supervision (RBS) Framework, 2011

(C) POLITICALLY EXPOSED PERSONS

The amount of corruption and abuse of public funds by some government leaders and public officials over recent years have given great cause for concern both internationally as well as in countries involved. Those people are collectively known as politically exposed persons (PEPs).[2] PEPs are individuals who are or have been entrusted with

---

2 D Hopton, Money Laundering A Concise Guide For All Business (2nd Edition Gower 2009) 108

prominent public functions and an immediate family member or a known close associate of such a person.[3]

There are special challenges in entering into financial transactions and business relationships with PEPs. Typical customer due diligence (CDD) measures may prove insufficient for PEPs as financial transactions and business relationships with these individuals present a higher money laundering risk and hence require greater scrutiny than "normal" financial transactions and business accounts. To reduce the money laundering risk associated with PEPs, international conventions and national laws require that firms apply a risk based approach to their compliance programmes.[4]

Adopting a risk-based approach implies the adoption of a risk management process for dealing with money laundering and terrorist financing. This process encompasses recognising the existence of the risk at the Customer Due Diligence stage, undertaking an assessment of the risks at the Enhanced Due Diligence stage and developing strategies

---

3 The Financial Action Task Force (FATF): International Standards on Combating Money Laundering and the financing of terrorism and proliferation, (The FATF Recommendations) 2012, Recommendation 12.
See also Directive 2005/60/EC of the European Parliament and of the council of 26th October 2005 on the prevention of the use of the financial system for the purpose of money laundering and terrorist financing Article 3 (8). See also Money Laundering Regulations 2007/2157 Regulation 14 (5). See also the Joint Money Laundering Steering Group Guidance for the UK Financial Sector Part 1, Paragraph 5.5.19.
4 KKR Choo, 'Politically exposed persons (PEPs): risk and mitigation 2008, 11 (4) JMLC, 371 – 387'

to manage and mitigate the identified risks at the Enhanced on-going monitoring stage.[5]

Customer Due Diligence

Customer Due Diligence/know your customer is intended to enable a financial institution to form a reasonable belief that it knows the true identity of each customer and, with an appropriate degree of confidence, knows the type of transactions the customer is likely to undertake.[6]

Failure of firms taking adequate steps to identify PEPs may lead to corrupt PEPs opening accounts without being detected and in the process avoiding enhanced due diligence and ongoing monitoring. For example in the late 1980's a large multinational bank in London opened accounts for Ibrahim and Mohamed Sani Abacha, who represented themselves as "Commodity and Oil dealers" The bank failed to make note of the Father's position at the time as a General in the Army. By the late 1990's it was discovered that the two brothers had amassed and deposited, either for themselves or on behalf of others, approximately six hundred and sixty million dollars with the London bank. It was later revealed that Sani Abacha brothers and

---

5 FATF Guidance on the Risk Based Approach to combating money laundering and terrorist financing, (High Level principles and procedures) 2007, paragraph 1.8. See also The Financial Action Task Force (FATF): International Standards On Combating Money Laundering and the financing of terrorism and proliferation,(The FATF Recommendations) 2012, Recommendation 12,See also Basel Committee on Banking Supervision, core principles for effective banking supervision 2012, principle 15, see also Directive 2005/60/EC of the European Parliament and of the council of 26th October 2005 on the prevention of the use of the financial system for the purpose of money laundering and terrorist financing Article 13 (4), see also Money Laundering Regulations 2007/2157 Regulation 20, see also Financial Services Authority (FSA) Handbook Senior Management Arrangements, Systems and Controls SYSC 3.2.6 AR, 6.3.1 R, See also the Joint Money Laundering Steering Group Guidance for the UK Financial Sector Part 1, Paragraph 4.18, see also United Nations Convention Against Corruption 2004 Article 52

6 FATF Guidance on the Risk Based Approach to combating money laundering and terrorist financing, (High Level principles and procedures) 2007, paragraph 3.10.

other members of the Abacha circle had allegedly stolen an estimated four billion three hundred million dollars over a number of years.[7]

Another example is the Abubakar Atiku, s case. According to the US subcommittee on investigations (2010) report, Abubakar used a variety of schemes through wire transfers to launder suspected funds into the United States of America. In many cases, these accounts were disguised by using the variant of his wife, s name (Ms Douglas). The bank, s profile did not identify Ms Douglas as a PEP.[8]

In situations where the money-laundering risk associated with the business relationship is increased, for example where the customer is a PEP, banks must carry out additional enhanced due diligence.[9]

Enhanced Due Diligence

The Enhanced Due Diligence (EDD) should give firms a greater understanding of the customer and their associated risk than standard due diligence. It should provide more certainty that the customer and/or beneficial owner is who they say they are and that the purposes of the business relationship are legitimate; as well as

---

7   OJ Otusanya: 'The Role of offshore financial centres in elite money laundering practices: evidence from Nigeria. 2012,15(3) JMLC, 336 – 361'

8   OJ Otusanya: 'The Role of offshore financial centres in elite money laundering practices: evidence from Nigeria. 2012,15(3) JMLC, 336 – 361'

9   The Financial Action Task Force (FATF): International Standards On Combating Money Laundering and the financing of terrorism and proliferation,(The FATF Recommendations) 2012, Recommendation 12, See also Directive 2005/60/EC of the European Parliament and of the council of 26th October 2005 on the prevention of the use of the financial system for the purpose of money laundering and terrorist financing Article 13 (1), See also Money Laundering Regulations 2007/2157 Regulation 14 (1), see also Uniting and Strengthening America by Providing Appropriate Tools Required to Intercept and Obstruct Terrorism Act 2001 S 312 (1)

increasing opportunities to identify and deal with concerns that they are not.[10]

It is for each firm to decide the steps it takes to determine whether a PEP is seeking to establish a business relationship for legitimate reasons. Firms should in any case take adequate meaningful measures to establish the source of funds and source of wealth. Firms may wish to refer to information sources such as asset and income declarations, which some jurisdictions expect certain senior public officials to file and which often include information about an official's source of wealth and current business interests. Firms should note that not all declarations are publicly available and that a PEP customer may have a legitimate reason for not providing a copy.[11] It is the opinion of the author that in countries where the declarations ought to be publicly available and are not still available for example countries like Nigeria who just signed an agreement committing to publication of asset declaration with the United States Government,[12] firms should insist that they see the declaration and if they are not given the declaration they should not open the account. It is worth noting that despite the agreement being signed, President Goodluck Jonathan has refused to publicly declare his assets.[13] This poses problems for firms.

Once the source of wealth and source of funds are established banks will need to analyse the information for "red flag" for corrupt PEP

---

10 Financial crime: a guide for firms part 1: A firm's guide to preventing financial crime by the Financial Services Authority 2012 Box 3.7. See also Uniting and Strengthening America by Providing Appropriate Tools Required to Intercept and Obstruct Terrorism Act 2001 S 312 (2) (B) I, ii which states that the enhanced due diligence policies and procedures enables firms in the United States to ascertain for any such foreign bank, the shares of which are not publicly traded, the identity of each owners of the foreign bank and the nature and extent of the ownership interest of each such owner.

11 Joint Money Laundering Steering Group Guidance for the UK Financial Sector Part 1, Paragraph 5.5.29.

12 O Aigbovo: Nigerian anti-corruption statutes: an impact assessment 2013 16 (1) JMLC 62 – 78.

13 O Aigbovo: Nigerian anti-corruption statutes: an impact assessment 2013 16 (1) JMLC 62 – 78.

activity.[14] In all cases if a bank suspects that the funds are proceeds of criminal activity, the bank is required to file a Suspicious Transaction Report with the Financial Intelligence Unit.[15] A risk based approach for the reporting of suspicious activity under these circumstances is not applicable.[16] A risk based approach is however appropriate for the purpose of identifying suspicious activity, for example by directing additional resources at those areas a financial institution has identified as higher risk and in this case to customers who are identified as PEPs.[17]

Senior Management Approval

The FATF standard requires banks to obtain senior management approval for establishing a business relationship with PEPs and continuing a business relationship with a customer who is subsequently found to be a PEP or becomes a PEP.[18] The group AML/CTF officer should be involved in the PEP approval process since he is in the best position to say that a person should not be accepted regardless of the size of the account.[19]

---

14   T S Greenberg: Stolen Asset Recovery, Politically Exposed Persons, A policy paper on strengthening preventive measures

15   T S Greenberg: Stolen Asset Recovery, Politically Exposed Persons, A policy paper on strengthening preventive measures

16   FATF Guidance on the Risk Based Approach to combating money laundering and terrorist financing, (High Level principles and procedures) 2007, paragraph 3.16.

17   FATF Guidance on the Risk Based Approach to combating money laundering and terrorist financing, (High Level principles and procedures) 2007, paragraph 3.17.

18   The Financial Action Task Force (FATF): International Standards On Combating Money Laundering and the financing of terrorism and proliferation,(The FATF Recommendations) 2012, Recommendation 12, See also Directive 2005/60/EC of the European Parliament and of the council of 26th October 2005 on the prevention of the use of the financial system for the purpose of money laundering and terrorist financing Article 13 (4) (b), See also Money Laundering Regulations 2007/2157 Regulation 14 (4) (a).

19   T S Greenberg: Stolen Asset Recovery, Politically Exposed Persons, A policy paper on strengthening preventive measures

Enhanced On Going Monitoring

Once a business relationship has been established with a PEP, banks must conduct enhanced on-going monitoring of the business relationship. [20]

The principle aim of monitoring in a risk based system is to respond to enterprise wide issues based on each financial institution, s analysis of major risks and in this case the major risks are PEPs.[21]

(D) EMBASSY AND FOREIGN CONSULATE ACCOUNTS

Embassies contain the offices of the foreign ambassador, the diplomatic representative and their staff. The embassy, led by the ambassador, is a foreign government's official representation in the United States (or other countries).

Foreign consulate offices act as branches of the embassy and perform various administrative and governmental functions (e.g., issuing visas and handling immigration matters). Foreign consulate offices are typically located in major metropolitan areas. In addition, foreign ambassadors' diplomatic representatives, their families and associates may be considered politically exposed persons (PEP) in certain circumstances.

Embassies and foreign consulates require access to the banking system to meet many of their day-to-day financial responsibilities.

---

20 The Financial Action Task Force (FATF): International Standards On Combating Money Laundering and the financing of terrorism and proliferation, (The FATF Recommendations) 2012, Recommendation 12, See also Directive 2005/60/EC of the European Parliament and of the council of 26th October 2005 on the prevention of the use of the financial system for the purpose of money laundering and terrorist financing Article 13 (4) (d), See also Money Laundering Regulations 2007/2157 Regulation 14 (4) (c).

21 FATF Guidance on the Risk Based Approach to combating money laundering and terrorist financing, (High Level principles and procedures) 2007, paragraph 3.13.

Such services can range from account relationships for operational expenses (e.g., payroll, rent and utilities) to inter and intra-governmental transactions (e.g., commercial and military purchases). In addition to official embassy accounts, some financial institutions provide ancillary services or accounts to embassy staff, families and current or prior foreign government officials. Each of these relationships poses different levels of risk to the financial institution.

Embassy accounts, including those accounts for a specific embassy office such as a cultural or education ministry, a defence attaché or ministry, or any other account should have a specific operating purpose, stating the official function of the foreign government office. Consistent with established practices for business relationships, these embassy accounts should have written authorization by the foreign government.

Risk Factors

To provide embassy and foreign consulate services, a financial institution may need to maintain a foreign correspondent relationship with the embassy's or foreign consulate's financial institution. Financial institutions conducting business with foreign embassies or consulates should assess and understand the potential risks of these accounts and should develop appropriate policies, procedures and processes. Embassy or foreign consulate accounts may pose a higher risk in the following circumstances:

(i) Accounts are from countries that have been designated as higher risk;

(ii) Substantial currency transactions take place in the accounts;

(iii) Account activity is not consistent with the purpose of the account (e.g., pouch activity or payable upon proper identification transactions);

(iv) Accounts directly fund personal expenses of foreign nationals including but not limited to expenses for college students; and

(v) Official embassy business is conducted through personal accounts.

Risk Mitigation

Financial institutions should obtain comprehensive due diligence information on embassy and foreign consulate account relationships. For private banking accounts for non-American persons specifically, financial institutions must obtain due diligence information. The financial institution's due diligence related to embassy and foreign consulate account relationships should be commensurate with the risk levels presented. In addition, financial institutions are expected to establish policies, procedures and processes that provide for greater scrutiny and monitoring of all embassy and foreign consulate account relationships. Management should fully understand the purpose of the account and the expected volume and nature of account activity. On-going monitoring of embassy and foreign consulate account relationships is critical to ensuring that the account relationships are being used as anticipated.

(E) DESIGNATED NON-FINANCIAL INSTITUTIONS

The financial institution's systems to manage the risks associated with accounts of designated non- financial institutions (DNFI) should be adequate and the management should have the ability to implement its monitoring and reporting systems effectively.

Common examples of DNFIs include but not limited to:

(i)   Casinos, hotels, supermarkets and card clubs;

(ii) Dealers in cars, luxury goods, chartered accountants, audit firms, clearing and settlement companies, legal practitioners; and

(iii) Dealers in precious metals, stones or jewellery.

Some DNFIs are currently required to develop an AML/CFT Programme, comply with the reporting and recordkeeping requirements of the relevant Money Laundering Laws/Regulations and report suspicious activity to the relevant regulatory authority. DNFIs typically need access to banking services in order to operate.

While financial institutions are expected to manage risk associated with all accounts including DNFI accounts, the institution will not be held responsible for their customers' non-compliance with the Money Laundering Laws in force in that country and other relevant laws and regulations.

Risk Factors

DNFI industries are extremely diverse, ranging from large multinational corporations to small, independent businesses that offer financial services only as an ancillary component to their primary business (e.g., grocery store that offers cheque- cashing). The range of products and services offered and the customer bases served by DNFIs are equally diverse. As a result of this diversity, some DNFIs may be of lower risk and some may be of higher risk for money laundering. Financial institutions that maintain account relationships with DNFIs may be exposed to a higher risk for potential money laundering activities because many DNFIs:

(i) Lack ongoing customer relationships and require minimal or no identification by customers;

(ii) Maintain limited or inconsistent record-keeping on customers and transactions;

(iii) Engage in frequent currency transactions;

(iv) Are subject to varying levels of regulatory requirements and oversight;

(v) Can quickly change their product mix or location and quickly enter or exit an operation; and

(vi) Sometimes operate without proper registration or licensing.

Risk Mitigation

Financial institutions that maintain account relationships with DNFIs should develop policies, procedures and processes to:

(i) Identify DNFI relationships;

(ii) Assess the potential risks posed by the DNFI relationships;

(iii) Conduct adequate and ongoing due diligence on the DNFI relationships when necessary; and

(iv) Ensure DNFI relationships are appropriately considered within the financial institution's suspicious activity monitoring and reporting systems.

Risk assessment factors of financial institutions assess the risks posed by their DNFI customers and direct their resources most appropriately to those accounts that pose a more significant money laundering risk.

Risk factors may be used to help identify the relative risks within the DNFI portfolio. Nevertheless, management should weigh and evaluate each risk assessment factor to arrive at a risk determination for each customer and to prioritize oversight resources. Relevant risk factors include:

(i) Types of products and services offered by the DNFI;

(ii) Locations and markets served by the DNFI;

(iii) Anticipated account activity; and

(iv) Purpose of the account.

A financial institution's due diligence should be commensurate with the level of risk of the DNFI customer identified through its risk assessment. If a financial institution's risk assessment indicates potential for a heightened risk of money laundering or terrorist financing, it will be expected to conduct further due diligence in a manner commensurate with the heightened risk.

(F) PROFESSIONAL SERVICE PROVIDERS

The financial institution's systems to manage the risks associated with professional service provider relationships should be adequate and the management should have the ability to implement its due diligence, monitoring and reporting systems effectively.

A professional service provider acts as an intermediary between its client and the financial institution. Professional service providers include lawyers, accountants, investment brokers and other third parties that act as financial liaisons for their clients. These providers may conduct financial dealings for their clients.

For example, an attorney may perform services for a client or arrange for services to be performed on the client's behalf. Such services include settlement of real estate transactions, asset transfers, management of client monies, investment services and trust arrangements.

Risk Factors

In contrast to escrow accounts that are set up to serve individual clients, professional service provider accounts allow for ongoing business transactions with multiple clients. Generally, a financial institution has no direct relationship with or knowledge of the beneficial owners of these accounts who may be a constantly changing group of individuals and legal entities.

As with any account that presents third-party risk, the financial institution could be more vulnerable to potential money laundering abuse. Some potential examples of abuse could include:

(i)   Laundering illicit currency;

(ii) Structuring currency deposits and withdrawals; and

(iii) Opening any third-party account for the primary purpose of masking the underlying client's identity.

As such, the financial institution should establish an effective due diligence Programme for the professional service provider.

Risk Mitigation

When establishing and maintaining relationships with professional service providers, financial institutions should adequately assess account risk and monitor the relationship for suspicious or unusual activity. At account opening, the financial institution should have an understanding of the intended use of the account, including anticipated transaction volume, products and services used, and geographic locations involved in the relationship.

(G) NON-GOVERNMENTAL ORGANIZATIONS AND CHARITIES

The financial institution's systems to manage the risks associated with accounts of non-governmental organizations (NGO) should be adequate and charities and the management should have the ability to implement its due diligence, monitoring and reporting systems effectively.

NGOs are private non-profit organizations that pursue activities intended to serve the public good. NGOs may provide basic social services work to relieve suffering, promote the interests of the poor, bring citizen concerns to governments, encourage political participation, protect the environment, or undertake community development to serve the needs of citizens, organizations or groups in one or more of the communities that the NGO operates. An NGO can be any non-profit organization that is independent from government.

NGOs can range from large regional, national or international charities to community-based self-help groups. NGOs may also include research institutes, churches, professional associations and lobby groups. NGOs typically depend (in whole or in part) on charitable donations and voluntary service for support.

Risk Factors

Because NGOs can be used to obtain funds for charitable organizations, the flow of funds both into and out of the NGO can be complex, making them susceptible to abuse by money launderers and terrorists. Guidelines will be issued to assist charities in adopting practices to reduce the risk of terrorist financing or abuse.

Risk Mitigation

To assess the risk of NGO customers, a financial institution should conduct adequate due diligence on the organization. In addition to required Customer Identification Program (CIP) information, due diligence for NGOs should focus on other aspects of the organization, such as the following:

(i) Purpose and objectives of their stated activities;

(ii) Geographic locations served including headquarters and operational areas;

(iii) Organizational structure;

(iv) Donor and volunteer base;

(v) Funding and disbursement criteria including basic beneficiary information;

(vi) Record keeping requirements;

(vii) Its affiliation with other NGOs, governments or groups; and

(viii) Internal controls and audits.

For accounts that financial institution management considers to be higher risk, stringent documentation, verification and transaction monitoring procedures should be established. NGO accounts that are at higher risk for ML/FT concerns include those operating or providing services internationally, conducting unusual or suspicious activities or lacking proper documentation. EDD for these accounts should include:

(i)   Evaluating the principals;

(ii)   Obtaining and reviewing the financial statements and audits;

(iii) Verifying the source and use of funds; and

(iv)   Evaluating large contributors or grantors to the NGO.

(H) BUSINESS ENTITIES (DOMESTIC AND FOREIGN)

The financial institution's systems to manage the risks associated with transactions involving domestic and foreign business entities should be adequate and the management should have the ability to implement its due diligence, monitoring and reporting systems effectively.

The term business entities refers to limited liability companies, corporations, trusts, and other entities that may be used for many purposes such as tax and estate planning. Business entities are relatively easy to establish. Individuals, partnerships and existing corporations establish business entities for legitimate reasons but the entities may be abused for money laundering and terrorist financing.

Shell companies are a type of domestic business entity that may pose heightened risks. Shell companies can be used for money laundering and other crimes because they are easy and inexpensive to form and operate. In addition, ownership and transactional information can be concealed from regulatory agencies and law enforcement in large part because it requires minimal disclosures of such information during the formation process.

The term domestic refers to entities formed or organized in the United States. These entities may have no other connection to the United States and ownership and management of the entities may reside abroad.

The term shell company generally refers to an entity without a physical presence in any country.

Shares of shell companies can be publicly traded or privately held. Although publicly traded shell companies can be used for illicit purposes, the vulnerability of the shell company is compounded when it is privately held and beneficial ownership can more easily be obscured or hidden. Lack of transparency of beneficial ownership can be a desirable characteristic for some legitimate uses of shell companies, but it is also a serious vulnerability that can make some shell companies ideal vehicles for money laundering and other illicit financial activity.

In some, only minimal information is required to register articles of incorporation or to establish and maintain good standing for business entities - increasing the potential for their abuse by criminal and terrorist organizations.

Frequently used foreign entities include trusts, investment funds and insurance companies. Two foreign entities that can pose particular money laundering risk are International Business Corporations

(IBC) and Private Investment Companies (PIC) opened in Offshore Financial Centres (OFCs). Many OFCs have limited organizational disclosure and record-keeping requirements for establishing foreign business entities, creating an opportune environment for money laundering.

Risk Factors

Money laundering and terrorist financing risks arise because business entities can hide the true owner of assets or property derived from or associated with criminal activity. The privacy and confidentiality surrounding some business entities may be exploited by criminals, money launderers and terrorists. Verifying the grantors and beneficial owner(s) of some business entities may be extremely difficult, as the characteristics of these entities shield the legal identity of the owner. Few public records will disclose true ownership. Overall, the lack of ownership transparency; minimal or no record-keeping requirements, financial disclosures and supervision; and the range of permissible activities all increase money laundering risk.

While business entities can be established in most international jurisdictions, many are incorporated in OFCs that provide ownership privacy and impose few or no tax obligations. To maintain anonymity, many business entities are formed with nominee directors, officeholders and shareholders. In certain jurisdictions, business entities can also be established using bearer shares; ownership records are not maintained, rather ownership is based on physical possession of the stock certificates. Revocable trusts are another method used to insulate the grantor and beneficial owner and can be designed to own and manage the business entity, presenting significant barriers to law enforcement.

The following indicators of potentially suspicious activity may be commonly associated with shell company activity:

(i) Insufficient or no information available to positively identify originators or beneficiaries of funds transfers (using internet, commercial database searches or direct inquiries to a respondent bank);

(ii) Payments have no stated purpose, do not reference goods or services. They identify only a contract or invoice number;

(iii) Goods or services, if identified, do not match profile of company provided by respondent bank or character of the financial activity; a company references remarkably dissimilar goods and services in related funds transfers; explanation given by foreign respondent bank is inconsistent with observed funds transfer activity;

(iv) Transacting businesses share the same address, provide only a registered agent's address or other inconsistent addresses;

(v) Many or all of the funds transfers are sent in large, round amounts;

(vi) Unusually large number and variety of beneficiaries receiving funds transfers from one company;

(vii) Frequent involvement of multiple jurisdictions or beneficiaries located in higher-risk OFCs;

(viii) A foreign correspondent bank exceeds the expected volume in its client profile for funds transfers, or an individual company exhibits a high volume and pattern of funds transfers that is inconsistent with its normal business activity;

(ix) Multiple high-value payments or transfers between shell companies with no apparent legitimate business purpose; and

(x) Purpose of the shell company is unknown or unclear.

Risk Mitigation

Management should develop policies, procedures and processes that enable the financial institution to identify account relationships in particular deposit accounts, with business entities and monitor the risks associated with these accounts in all the financial institution's departments. Business entity customers may open accounts within the private banking department, within the trust department, or at local branches. Management should establish appropriate due diligence at account opening and during the life of the relationship to manage risk in these accounts. The financial institution should gather sufficient information on the business entities and their beneficial owners to understand and assess the risks of the account relationship. Important information for determining the valid use of these entities includes the type of business, the purpose of the account, the source of funds and the source of wealth of the owner or beneficial owner.

The financial institution's CIP should detail the identification requirements for opening an account for a business entity. When opening an account for a customer that is not an individual, financial institution should obtain information about the individuals who have authority and control over such accounts in order to verify the customer's identity (the customer being the business entity). Required account opening information may include articles of incorporation, a corporate resolution by the directors authorizing the opening of the account, or the appointment of a person to act as a signatory for the entity on the account.

Particular attention should be paid to articles of association that allow for nominee shareholders, board members and bearer shares.

If the financial institution, through its trust or private banking departments, is facilitating the establishment of a business entity for a new or existing customer, the money laundering risk to the financial statement is typically mitigated. Because the financial institution is aware of the parties (e.g., grantors, beneficiaries and shareholders) involved in the business entity, initial due diligence and verification is easier to obtain. Furthermore, in such cases, the financial institution frequently has ongoing relationships with the customers initiating the establishment of a business entity.

Risk assessments may include a review of the domestic or international jurisdiction where the business entity was established, the type of account (or accounts) and expected versus actual transaction activities, the types of products that will be used, and whether the business entity was created in-house or externally. If ownership is held in bearer share form, financial institution should assess the risks these relationships pose and determine the appropriate controls.

In most cases, financial institutions should choose to maintain (or have an independent third party maintain) bearer shares for customers. In rare cases involving lower-risk, well-known, established customers, financial institutions may find that periodically re-certifying beneficial ownership is effective. The financial institution's risk assessment of a business entity customer becomes more important in complex corporate formations. For example, a foreign IBC may establish a series of layered business entities with each entity naming its parent as its beneficiary.

On-going account monitoring is critical to ensure that the accounts are reviewed for unusual and suspicious activity. The financial institution should be aware of higher-risk transactions in these accounts, such as activity that has no business or apparent lawful purpose, funds transfer activity to and from higher-risk jurisdictions, currency intensive transactions and frequent changes in the ownership or control of the non-public business entity.

(I) CASH INTENSIVE BUSINESSES

The financial institution's systems to manage the risks associated with cash-intensive businesses and entities should be adequate and the management should have the ability to implement its due diligence, monitoring and reporting systems effectively.

Cash-intensive businesses and entities cover various industry sectors. Most of these outfits conduct legitimate business. However, some aspects of these businesses may be susceptible to money laundering or terrorist financing. Common examples include but are not limited to, the following:

(i)   Convenience stores;

(ii) Restaurants;

(iii) Retail stores;

(iv) Liquor stores;

(v)   Cigarette distributors;

(vi) Privately owned automated teller machines (ATM;

(vii) Vending machine operators; and

(viii) Parking garages.

Risk Factors

Some businesses and entities may be misused by money launderers to legitimize their illicit proceeds. For example, a criminal may own a cash-intensive business such as a restaurant and use it to launder currency from illicit criminal activities. The restaurant's currency deposits with its bank do not, on the surface, appear unusual because the business is legitimately a cash-generating entity.

However, the volume of currency in a restaurant used to launder money will most likely be higher in comparison with similar restaurants in the area. The nature of cash-intensive businesses and the difficulty in identifying unusual activity may cause these businesses to be considered higher risk.

Risk Mitigation

When establishing and maintaining relationships with cash-intensive businesses, financial institution should establish policies, procedures and processes to identify higher-risk relationships; assess ML/FT risks; complete due diligence at account opening and periodically throughout the relationship; and include such relationships in appropriate monitoring for unusual or suspicious activity. At the time of account opening, the financial institution should have an understanding of the customer's business operations; the intended use of the account including anticipated transaction volume, products and services used; and the geographic locations involved in the relationship.

When conducting a risk assessment of cash-intensive businesses, financial institution should direct their resources to those accounts that pose the greatest risk of money laundering or terrorist financing. The following factors may be used to identify the risks:

(i) Purpose of the account;

(ii) Volume, frequency and nature of currency transactions;

(iii) Customer history (e.g., length of relationship, CTR and STR filings);

(iv) Primary business activity, products and services offered;

(v) Business or business structure;

(vi) Geographic locations and jurisdictions of operations; and

(vii) Availability of information and cooperation of the business in providing information. For those customers deemed to be particularly higher risk management may consider implementing sound practices such as periodic on-site visits, interviews with the business's management or closer reviews of transactional activity.

(J) THIRD PARTY PAYMENT PROCESSORS

The financial institution's systems should be adequate to manage the risks associated with its relationships with third-party payment processors and the management should have the ability to implement its monitoring and reporting systems effectively.

Non-bank or third-party payment processors (processors) are bank or other financial institution customers that provide payment-processing services to merchants and other business entities. Traditionally, processors primarily contract with retailers that have physical locations in order to process the retailers' transactions.

These merchant transactions primarily included credit card payments but also covered automated clearing house (ACH) transactions, Remotely Created Cheques (RCCs), debit and prepaid cards transactions. With the expansion of the internet, retail borders have been eliminated. Processors now provide services to a variety of merchant accounts, including conventional retail and internet-based establishments, prepaid travel, telemarketers and internet gaming enterprises.

Third-party payment processors often use their commercial bank accounts to conduct payment processing for their merchant clients. For example, the processor may deposit into its account RCCs generated on behalf of a merchant client, or act as a third-party sender of ACH transactions. In either case, the financial institution does not have a direct relationship with the merchant. The increased use by processor customers, particularly telemarketers of RCCs also raises the risk of fraudulent payments being processed through the processor's bank account.

Risk Factors

Processors generally are not subject to AML/CFT compliance and regulatory requirements. As a result, some processors may be vulnerable to money laundering, identity theft, fraud schemes and illicit transactions or transactions prohibited by the FATF Recommendations.

The financial institution's ML/FT risks when dealing with a processor account are similar to risks from other activities in which the financial institution's customer conducts transactions through the bank on behalf of the customer's clients. When the financial institution is unable to identify and understand the nature and source of the transactions processed through an account, the risks to the financial institution and the likelihood of suspicious activity can increase. If a financial institution has not implemented an adequate processor-approval Programme that goes beyond credit risk management, it could be vulnerable to processing illicit or sanction-able transactions.

Risk Mitigation

Financial institutions offering account services to processors should develop and maintain adequate policies, procedures and processes to address risks related to these relationships. At a minimum, these policies should authenticate the processor's business operations and assess their risk level. A financial institution may assess the risks associated with payment processors by considering the following:

(i) Implementing a policy that requires an initial background check of the processor (using for example, state incorporation departments, internet searches and other investigative processes) and of the processor's underlying merchants on a risk-adjusted basis in order to verify their creditworthiness and general business practices;

(ii) Reviewing the processor's promotional materials, including its Web site to determine the target clientele. A financial institution may develop policies, procedures and processes that restrict the types of entities for which it will allow processing services. These entities may include higher risk entities such as offshore companies, online gambling-related operations, telemarketers and online pay lenders. These restrictions should be clearly communicated to the processor at account opening stage;

(iii) Determining whether the processor re-sells its services to a third party who may be referred to as an agent or provider of independent sales institution opportunities or internet service provider (gateway) arrangements;

(iv) Reviewing the processor's policies, procedures and processes to determine the adequacy of its due diligence standards for new merchants;

(v) Requiring the processor to identify its major customers by providing information such as the merchant's name, principal business activity and geographic location;

(vi) Verifying directly or through the processor that the merchant is operating a legitimate business by comparing the merchant's identifying information against public record databases, fraud and financial institution check databases;

(vii) Reviewing corporate documentation including independent reporting services and, if applicable, documentation on principal owners; and

(viii) Visiting the processor's business operations centre.

Financial institutions which provide account services to third-party payment processors should monitor their processor relationships for any significant changes in the processor's business strategies that may affect their risk profile. Financial institutions should periodically re-verify and update the processors' profiles to ensure the risk assessment is appropriate.

In addition to adequate and effective account opening and due diligence procedures for processor accounts, management should monitor these relationships for unusual and suspicious activities. To effectively monitor these accounts, the financial institution should have an understanding of the following processor information:

(i) Merchant base;

(ii) Merchant activities;

(iii) Average number of dollar volume and number of transactions;

(iv) Swiping versus keying volume for credit card transactions;

(v) Charge-back history, including rates of return for ACH debit transactions and Remotely Created Cheques (RCCs); and

(vi) Consumer complaints that suggest a payment processor's merchant clients are inappropriately obtaining personal account information and using it to create unauthorized RCCs or ACH debits.

With respect to account monitoring, a financial institution should thoroughly investigate high levels of returns and should not accept high levels of returns on the basis that the processor has provided collateral or other security to the financial institution. A financial institution should implement appropriate policies, procedures and processes that address compliance and fraud risks. High levels of RCCs or ACH debits returned for insufficient funds or as unauthorized can be an indication of fraud or suspicious activity.

Source: Central Bank of Nigeria's Anti-Money Laundering/ Combating the Financing of Terrorism (AML/CFT) Risk Based Supervision (RBS) Framework, 2011

APPENDIX 2

HIGH RISK PRODUCTS/SERVICES

(A) PARALLEL BANKING

The financial institution's systems are required to be adequate to manage the risks associated with parallel banking relationships and the management should have the ability to implement its due diligence, monitoring and reporting systems effectively.

A parallel financial institution exists when at least one Canadian financial institution and one foreign financial institution are controlled either directly or indirectly by the same person or group of persons who are closely associated in their business dealings or otherwise acting together, but are not subject to consolidated supervision by a single home country supervisor.

The foreign financial institution will be subject to different money laundering rules and regulations and a different supervisory oversight structure, both of which may be less stringent than Canada. The regulatory and supervisory differences heighten the ML/FT risk associated with parallel banking organizations.

Risk Factors

Parallel banking organizations may have common management, share policies and procedures, cross-sell products, or generally be linked to a foreign parallel financial institution in a number of ways. The key money laundering concern regarding parallel banking organizations is that the Canadian financial institution may be exposed to greater risk through transactions with the foreign parallel financial institution. Transactions may be facilitated and risks heightened because of the lack of arm's length dealing or reduced controls on transactions between financial institutions that are linked or closely associated. For example, officers or directors may be common to both entities or may be different but nonetheless work together.

Risk Mitigation

The financial institution's policies, procedures and processes for parallel banking relationships should be consistent with those of other foreign correspondent bank relationships. In addition, parallel financial institutions should:

(i) Provide for independent lines of decision-making authority;

(ii) Guard against conflicts of interest; and

(iii) Ensure independent and arm's-length dealings between related entities.

(B) CORRESPONDENT ACCOUNTS (DOMESTIC)

The financial institution's systems are to be adequate to manage the ML/FT risks associated with offering of domestic correspondent account relationships, and the management must have the ability to implement its monitoring and reporting systems effectively.

Financial institutions maintain correspondent relationships at other domestic financial institutions to provide certain services that can be performed more economically or efficiently because of the other financial institution's size, expertise in a specific line of business or geographic location. Such services may include:

(i)   Deposit accounts — Assets known as due from financial institution deposits or correspondent financial institution balances may represent the financial institution's primary operating account;

(ii) Funds transfers — A transfer of funds between financial institutions may result from the collection of cheques or other cash items, transfer and settlement of securities transactions, transfer of participating loan funds, purchase or sale of government funds, or processing of customer transactions; and

(iii) Other services — Services include processing of loan participations, facilitating secondary market loan sales, performing data processing and payroll services and exchanging foreign currency.

Risk Factors

Because domestic financial institutions must follow the same regulatory requirements, ML/FT risks in domestic correspondent banking are minimal in comparison to other types of financial services, especially for proprietary accounts (i.e., the domestic financial institution is using the correspondent account for its own transactions). Each financial institution, however, has its own approach for conducting its AML/CFT Compliance Programme, including customer due diligence, MIS, account monitoring, and reporting suspicious transactions.

Furthermore, while a domestic correspondent account may not be considered higher risk, transactions through the account, which may be conducted on behalf of the respondent's customer, may be higher risk. ML/FT risks can be heightened when a respondent financial institution allows its customers to direct or execute transactions through the correspondent account, especially when such transactions are directed or executed through an ostensibly proprietary account.

The correspondent financial institution also faces heightened risks when providing direct currency shipments for customers of respondent financial institution. This is not to imply that such activities necessarily entail money laundering, but these direct currency shipments should be appropriately monitored for unusual and suspicious activity. Without such a monitoring system, the correspondent bank is essentially providing these direct services to an unknown customer.

Risk Mitigation

Financial institutions that offer correspondent bank services to respondent banks should have policies, procedures and processes to manage the ML/FT risks involved in these correspondent relationships and to detect and report suspicious activities. Financial institution should ascertain whether domestic correspondent accounts are proprietary or allow third-party transactions. When the respondent financial institution allows third-party customers to transact business through the correspondent account, the correspondent financial institution should ensure that it puts the necessary steps in understanding the due diligence and procedures of the monitoring applied by the respondent on its customers that will be utilizing the account.

The level of risk varies depending on the services provided and the types of transactions conducted through the account and the respondent financial institution's AML/CFT Compliance Programme, products, services, customers, entities and geographic locations. Each financial institution should appropriately monitor transactions of domestic correspondent accounts relative to the level of assessed risk.

(C) CORRESPONDENT ACCOUNTS (FOREIGN)

The financial institution's systems are required to be adequate to manage the ML/FT risks associated with foreign correspondent banking and the management should have the ability to implement its due diligence, monitoring and reporting systems effectively.

Foreign financial institutions maintain accounts at domestic financial institutions to gain access to the country's financial system and to take advantage of services and products that may not be available in the foreign financial institution's jurisdiction. These services may be performed more economically or efficiently by the domestic financial institutions or may be necessary for other reasons, such as the facilitation of international trade. Services may include:

(i) Cash management services, including deposit accounts;

(ii) International funds transfers;

(iii) Check clearing;

(iv) Payable through accounts;

(v) Pouch activities;

(vi) Foreign exchange services;

(vii) Overnight investment accounts (sweep accounts); and

(viii) Loans and letters of credit.

Each relationship that a domestic financial institution has with a foreign correspondent financial institution should be governed by an agreement or a contract describing each party's responsibilities and other relationship details (e.g., products and services provided, acceptance of deposits, clearing of items, forms of payment and acceptable forms of endorsement). The agreement or contract should also consider the foreign financial institution's AML/CFT regulatory requirements, customer-base, due diligence procedures and permitted third-party usage of the correspondent account.

Risk Factors

Some foreign financial institutions are not subject to the same or similar regulatory guidelines as domestic financial institutions; therefore, these foreign institutions may pose a higher money laundering and financing terrorists risk to their respective domestic financial institutions correspondent(s). Investigations have disclosed that in the past, foreign correspondent accounts were used to launder funds.

Shell companies are sometimes used in the layering process to hide the true ownership of accounts at foreign correspondent financial institutions. Because of the large amount of funds, multiple transactions, and the domestic financial institution's potential lack of familiarity with the foreign correspondent financial institution's customer, criminals and terrorists can more easily conceal the source and use of illicit funds. Consequently, each domestic financial institution, including all overseas branches, offices and subsidiaries should closely monitor transactions related to foreign correspondent accounts.

Risk Mitigation

Financial institutions that offer foreign correspondent financial institution services should have policies, procedure, and processes to manage the ML/FT risks inherent with these relationships and should closely monitor transactions related to these accounts to detect and report suspicious transactions.

The level of risk varies depending on the foreign financial institution's products, services, customers and geographic locations. Financial institutions' policies, procedures and processes should:

(i) Specify appropriate account-opening procedures and KYC requirements, which may include minimum levels of documentation to be obtained from prospective customers; an account approval process independent of the correspondent account business line for potential higher-risk customers; and a description of circumstances when the financial institution will not open an account;

(ii) Assess the risks posed by a prospective foreign correspondent customer relationship utilizing consistent, well-documented risk-rating methodologies, and incorporate that risk determination into the financial institution's suspicious transaction monitoring system;

(iii) Understand the intended use of the accounts and expected account activity (e.g., determine whether the relationship will serve as a payable through account);

(iv) Understand the foreign correspondent financial institution's other correspondent relationships (e.g., determine whether nested accounts will be utilized);

(v)   Conduct adequate and ongoing due diligence on the foreign correspondent financial institution relationships, which may include periodic visits;

(vi) Establish a formalized process for escalating suspicious information on potential and existing customers to an appropriate management level for review;

(vii) Ensure that foreign correspondent financial institution relationships are appropriately included within the domestic financial institution's suspicious transaction monitoring and reporting systems;

(viii) Ensure that appropriate due diligence standards are applied to those accounts determined to be higher risk; and

(ix) Establish criteria for closing the foreign correspondent financial institution account.

As a sound practice, financial institutions are encouraged to communicate their AML/CFT-related expectations to their foreign correspondent financial institutions' customers. Moreover, the financial institutions should generally understand the AML/CFT controls at the foreign correspondent financial institution, including customer due diligence practices and record keeping documentation.

(D) BULK SHIPMENTS OF CURRENCY

Financial institution's systems are required to be adequate to manage the risks associated with receiving bulk shipments of currency and management should have the ability to implement effective monitoring and reporting systems.

Bulk shipments of currency entail the use of common, independent, or Postal Service's air/land/sea carriers to transport large volumes of bank notes (local or foreign) from sources either inside or outside the country concerned to a bank in the country concerned. Often, but not always, shipments take the form of containerized cargo.

Shippers may be Currency Originators i.e., individuals or businesses that generate currency from cash sales of commodities or other products or services (including monetary instruments or exchanges of currency).

Shippers also may be intermediaries that ship currency gathered from their customers who are Currency Originators. Intermediaries may also ship currency gathered from other intermediaries. Intermediaries may be other financial institutions, central banks, non-deposit financial institutions or agents of these entities.

Financial institutions receive bulk shipments of currency directly when they take possession of an actual shipment. Financial institutions receive bulk shipments of currency indirectly when they take possession of the economic equivalent of a currency shipment, such as through a cash letter notification.

Risk Factors

Bulk shipments of currency to financial institutions from shippers that are presumed to be reputable may nevertheless originate from illicit activity. The monetary proceeds of criminal activities, for example, often reappear in the financial system as seemingly legitimate funds that have been placed and finally integrated by flowing through numerous intermediaries and layered transactions that disguise the origin of the funds. Layering can include shipments to or through other jurisdictions. Accordingly, financial institutions that receive direct or indirect bulk shipments of currency risk becoming complicit in money laundering or terrorist financing schemes.

In recent years, the smuggling of bulk currency has become a preferred method for moving illicit funds across borders. However, the activity of shipping currency in bulk is not necessarily indicative of criminal or terrorist activity.

Many individuals and businesses, both domestic and foreign, generate currency from legitimate cash sales of commodities or other products or services. Also, intermediaries gather and ship currency from single or multiple currency originators whose activities are legitimate. Financial institutions may legitimately offer services to receive such shipments. However, financial institutions should be aware of the potential misuse of their services by shippers of bulk currency. Financial institutions also should guard against introducing the monetary proceeds of criminal or terrorist activity into the financial system.

Risk Mitigation

Financial institutions that offer services to receive bulk shipments of currency should have policies, procedures and processes in place that mitigate and manage the ML/FT risks associated with the receipt of bulk currency shipments. Financial institutions should also closely monitor bulk currency shipment transactions to detect and report suspicious transaction, with particular emphasis on the source of funds and the reasonableness of transaction volumes from currency originators and intermediaries.

ML/FT risk mitigation begins with an effective risk assessment process that distinguishes relationships and transactions that present a higher risk of money laundering or terrorist financing. Risk assessment processes should consider currency originator's and intermediary's ownership, geographies and the nature, source, location and control of bulk currency.

Financial institution's policies, procedures and processes should:

(i) Specify appropriate ML/FT risk-based relationship and account opening procedures which may include minimum levels of documentation to be obtained from prospective currency originators and intermediaries;

(ii) Specify relationship approval process that, for potential higher-risk relationships, is independent of the business line and may include a visit to the prospective shipper or shipping-preparation sites;

(iii) Describe the circumstances under which the financial institution will not open a relationship;

(iv) Determine the intended use of the relationship, the expected volumes, frequency of activity arising from transactions, sources of funds, reasonableness of volumes based on originators and shippers and any reporting requirements (CTRs, STRs, PEPs, etc);

(v) Identify the characteristics of acceptable and unacceptable transactions, including circumstances when the bank will or will not accept bulk currency shipments;

(vi) Assess the risks posed by a prospective shipping relationship using consistent and well-documented risk-rating methodologies;

(vii) Incorporate risk assessments, as appropriate, into the financial institution's customer due diligence, EDD and suspicious transaction monitoring systems;

(viii) Once the relationship is established, require adequate and ongoing due diligence which, as appropriate, may include periodic visits to the shipper and to shipping-preparation sites and as necessary, scrutinize for legitimacy the root source of cash shipments, using risk-based processes;

(ix) Ensure that appropriate due diligence standards are applied to relationships determined to be higher risk;

(x) Include procedures for processing shipments, including employees' responsibilities, controls, reconciliation and documentation requirements, and employee/management authorizations;

(xi) Establish a process for escalating suspicious information on potential and existing currency originator and intermediary relationships and transactions to an appropriate management level for review;

(xii) Refuse shipments that have questionable or suspicious origins;

(xiii) Ensure that shipping relationships and comparisons of expected and actual shipping volumes are included, as appropriate, within the financial institution's systems for monitoring and reporting suspicious transaction; and

(xiv) Establish criteria for terminating a shipment relationship.

As a sound practice, financial institutions should inform currency originators and intermediaries of the AML/CFT-related requirements and expectations that apply to financial institutions. The financial institutions also should understand the AML/CFT controls that apply to or are otherwise adopted by the currency originator or intermediary, including any customer due diligence and recordkeeping requirements or practices.

Other financial institutions' controls may also prove useful in protecting financial institution against illicit bulk shipments of currency. These may include effective controls over foreign correspondent banking activity, pouch activity, funds transfers, international automated clearing house transactions and remote deposit capture.

(E) FOREIGN CURRENCY DENOMINATED DRAFTS

The financial institution's systems are required to be adequate to manage the ML/FT risks associated with foreign currency denominated drafts and the management should have the ability to implement its monitoring and reporting systems effectively.

A foreign currency draft is a financial institution's drafts or cheque denominated in foreign currency and made available at foreign financial institution.

These drafts are drawn on a correspondent account by a foreign financial institution. Such drafts are frequently purchased to pay for commercial or personal transactions and to settle overseas obligations.

Risk Factors

Most foreign currency denominated drafts could be legitimate. However, such drafts have proven to be vulnerable to money laundering abuse. Schemes involving foreign currency drafts could involve the smuggling of currency to a foreign financial institution for the purchase of a cheque or draft denominated in another foreign currency. The foreign financial institution accepts the draft denominated in a particular foreign currency and issues another draft denominated in a different foreign currency. Once the currency is in the form of a bank draft, the money launderer can more easily conceal the source of funds. The ability to convert illicit proceeds to a bank draft at a foreign financial institution makes it easier for a money launderer to transport the instrument either back into the originating country or to endorse it to a third party in a jurisdiction where money laundering laws or compliance are lax. In any case, when the individual has succeeded in laundering his illicit proceeds, the draft or cheque would be returned ultimately for processing in the originating country.

Risk Mitigation

The financial institution's policies, procedures and processes should:

(i) Outline criteria for opening a foreign currency denominated draft relationship with a foreign financial institution or entity (e.g., jurisdiction, products, services, target market, purpose of account and anticipated activity or customer history);

(ii) Detail acceptable and unacceptable transactions (e.g., structuring transactions or the purchase of multiple sequentially numbered drafts for the same payee);

(iii) Detail the monitoring and reporting of suspicious transaction associated with foreign currency denominated drafts; and

(iv) Discuss criteria for closing a foreign currency denominated draft relationships.

(F) PAYABLE THROUGH ACCOUNTS

The financial institution's systems are required to be adequate to manage the risks associated with payable through accounts (PTA), and the management should have the ability to implement its monitoring and reporting systems effectively.

Foreign financial institutions use PTAs, also known as pass-through or pass-by accounts to provide their customers with access to the Australian financial system. Some financial institutions in Australia also offer payable through accounts as a service to foreign financial institutions. The risk associated with money laundering/ financing of terrorism and other illicit activities is higher in PTAs that are not adequately controlled.

Generally, a foreign financial institution requests a PTA for its customers that want to conduct banking transactions in Australia through the foreign financial institution's account at financial institution in Australia. The foreign financial institution provides its customers, commonly referred to as sub account holders, with cheques that allow them to draw funds from the foreign financial institution's account from an Australian financial institution. The sub accountholders, which may number several hundred or in the thousands for one PTA, all become signatories on the foreign financial institution's account in an Australian financial institution. While payable through customers are able to write cheques and make deposits at a financial institution in Australia like any other accountholder, they might not be directly subject to the financial institution's account opening requirements in Australia.

PTA activities should not be confused with traditional international correspondent banking relationships in which a foreign financial institution enters into an agreement with an Australian financial institution to process and complete transactions on behalf of the foreign financial institution and its customers. Under the latter correspondent arrangement, the foreign financial institution's customers do not have direct access to the correspondent account at the Australian financial institution, but they do transact business through the Australian financial institution.

This arrangement differs significantly from a PTA with sub accountholders who have direct access to the Australian financial system by virtue of their independent ability to conduct transactions with the Australian financial system through the PTA.

Risk Factors

PTAs may be prone to higher risk because Australian financial institutions do not typically implement the same due diligence requirements for PTAs that they require of domestic customers who want to open current and other accounts.

Foreign financial institutions use of PTAs, coupled with inadequate oversight by Australian financial institutions, may facilitate unsound banking practices, including money laundering/financing of terrorism and other related criminal activities. The potential for facilitating money laundering or terrorist financing, and other serious crimes increases when an Australian financial institution is unable to identify and adequately understand the transactions of the ultimate users (all or most of whom are outside of Australia) of its account with a foreign correspondent.

PTAs used for illegal purposes can cause financial institutions serious financial losses in criminal and civil fines and penalties, seizure or forfeiture of collateral and reputation damage.

Risk Mitigation

Financial institutions offering PTA services should develop and maintain adequate policies, procedures and processes to guard against possible illicit use of these accounts. At a minimum, policies, procedures and processes should enable each Australian financial institution to identify the ultimate users of its foreign financial institution's PTA. This should include the financial institution's obtaining (or having the ability to obtain through a trusted third-party arrangement) substantially the same information on the ultimate PTA users as it obtains on its direct customers.

Policies, procedures and processes should include a review of the foreign financial institution's processes to identify and monitor the transactions of its sub-account holders and to comply with any AML/CFT statutory and regulatory requirements existing in Australia (as the host country). It should also review the foreign financial institution's master agreement with the Australian financial institutions on the PTAs. In addition, Australian financial institutions should have procedures for monitoring transactions conducted in the foreign financial institutions' PTAs.

In an effort to address the risk inherent in PTAs, financial institutions in Australia should have a signed contract (i.e., master agreement) that includes:

(i)   Roles and responsibilities of each party;

(ii) Limits or restrictions on transaction types and amounts (e.g., currency deposits, funds transfers, cheque cashing);

(iii) Restrictions on some types of sub account holders (e.g., finance companies, funds remitters or other non-bank financial institutions);

(iv) Prohibitions or restrictions on multi-tier sub accountholders; and

(v) Access to the foreign financial institution's internal documents and audits that pertain to its PTA activity.

Financial institutions should consider closing the PTA in the following circumstances:

(i) Insufficient information on the ultimate PTA users;

(ii) Evidence of substantive or ongoing suspicious activity; and

(iii) Inability to ensure that the PTAs are not being used for money laundering or other illicit purposes.

(G) POUCH ACTIVITIES

The financial institution's systems are required to be adequate to manage the ML/FT risks associated with pouch activities and the management should have the ability to implement its monitoring and reporting systems effectively.

Pouch activity entails the use of a carrier, courier (either independent or common) or a referral agent employed by the courier to transport currency, monetary instruments and other documents from foreign countries to financial institutions in Germany.

Pouches can be sent by financial institution or individuals. Pouch services are commonly offered in conjunction with foreign correspondent banking services.

Pouches can contain loan repayments, transactions for demand deposit accounts or other types of transactions.

Risk Factors

Financial institutions should be aware that bulk amounts of monetary instruments purchased in Germany that appear to have been structured to avoid the AML/CFT-reporting requirements often have been found in pouches or cash letters received from foreign financial institutions. The monetary instruments involved are frequently traveller's cheques and bank cheques that usually have one or more of the following characteristics in common:

(i) The instruments purchased on the same or consecutive days at different locations;

(ii) The payee lines are left blank or made out to the same person (or to only a few people);

(iii) They contain little or no purchaser information;

(iv) They bear the same stamp, symbol or initials;

(v) They are purchased in round denominations or repetitive amounts; and

(vi) The depositing of the instruments is followed soon after by a funds transfer out in the same dollar amount.

Risk Mitigation

Financial institutions should have policies, procedures and processes related to pouch activity that should:

(i) Outline criteria for opening a pouch relationship with an individual or a foreign financial institution (e.g., customer due diligence requirements, type of institution or person, acceptable purpose of the relationship);

(ii) Detail acceptable and unacceptable transactions (e.g., monetary instruments with blank payees, unsigned monetary instruments and a large number of consecutively numbered monetary instruments);

(iii) Detail procedures for processing the pouch including employee responsibilities, dual control, reconciliation, documentation requirements, and employee sign off;

(iv) Detail procedures for reviewing of unusual or suspicious transaction including elevating concerns to management. Contents of pouches may be subject to CTR, Report of International Transportation of Currency or Monetary Instruments (CMIR); and

(v) Discuss criteria for closing pouch relationships.

The above factors should be included within an agreement or contract between the financial institution and the courier that details the services to be provided and the responsibilities of both parties.

(H) ELECTRONIC BANKING

The financial institution's systems should be adequate to manage the risks associated with electronic banking (e-banking) customers including Remote Deposit Capture (RDC) activity and the management should have the ability to implement its monitoring and reporting systems effectively.

E-banking systems which provide electronic delivery of banking products to customers include automated teller machine (ATM) transactions; online account opening; internet banking transactions; and telephone banking. For example, credit cards, deposit accounts, mortgage loans and funds transfers can all be initiated online without face-to-face contact. Management needs to recognize this as a potentially higher-risk area and develop adequate policies, procedures and processes for customer identification and monitoring for specific areas of banking.

Risk Factors

Financial institutions should ensure that their monitoring systems adequately capture transactions conducted electronically. As with any account, they should be alert to anomalies in account behaviour. Red flags may include the velocity of funds in the account or in the case of ATMs, the number of debit cards associated with the account.

Accounts that are opened without face-to-face contact may be a higher risk for money laundering and terrorist financing for the following reasons:

(i) More difficult to positively verify the individual's identity;

(ii) Customer may be out of the financial institution's targeted geographic area or country;

(iii) Customer may perceive the transactions as less transparent;

(iv) Transactions are instantaneous; and

(v) May be used by a front company or unknown third party.

Risk Mitigation

Financial institutions should establish AML/CFT monitoring, identification and reporting for unusual and suspicious transactions occurring through e-banking systems. Useful MIS for detecting unusual transaction in higher-risk accounts include ATM activity reports, funds transfer reports, new account activity reports, change of internet address reports, Internet Protocol (IP) address reports and reports to identify related or linked accounts (e.g., common addresses, phone numbers, e-mail addresses and tax identification numbers).

In determining the level of monitoring required for an account, financial institutions should include how the account was opened as a factor. Financial institutions engaging in transactional internet banking should have effective and reliable methods to authenticate a customer's identity when opening accounts online and should establish policies for when a customer should be required to open accounts on a face-to-face basis. Financial institutions may also institute other controls, such as establishing transaction dollar limits for large items that require manual intervention to exceed the preset limit.

(I) REMOTE DEPOSIT CAPTURE

Remote Deposit Capture (RDC) is a deposit transaction delivery system that has made cheque and monetary instrument processing (e.g., traveller's cheques) more efficient.

In broad terms, RDC allows a financial institution's customers to scan a cheque or monetary instrument and then transmit the scanned or digitized image to the institution.

It should be noted that scanning and transmission activities can take place at remote locations including the financial institution's branches, ATMs, domestic and foreign correspondents, and locations owned or controlled by commercial or retail customers. By eliminating face-to-face transactions, RDC decreases the cost and volume of paper associated with physically mailing or depositing items.

RDC also supports new and existing banking products and improves customers' access to their deposits.

Risk Factors

RDC may expose financial institutions to various risks including money laundering, financing of terrorists, fraud and information security. Fraudulent, sequentially numbered or physically altered documents, particularly money orders and traveler's cheques may be more difficult to detect when submitted by RDC and not inspected by a qualified person. Financial institutions may face challenges in controlling or knowing the location of RDC equipment because the equipment can be readily transported from one jurisdiction to another.

This challenge is increased as foreign correspondents and foreign money services businesses are increasingly using RDC services to replace pouch and certain instrument processing and clearing activities. Inadequate controls could result in intentional or unintentional alterations to deposit item data, re-submission of a data file, or duplicate presentment of cheques and images at one or multiple financial institutions. In addition, original deposit items are not typically forwarded to financial institutions, but instead the customer or the customer's service provider retains them. As a result, record keeping, data safety and integrity issues may increase.

Higher-risk customers may be defined by industry, incidence of fraud or other criteria. Examples of higher-risk parties include online payment processors, certain credit-repair services, certain mail order and telephone order companies, online gambling operations, businesses located offshore and adult entertainment businesses.

Risk Mitigation

Management should develop appropriate policies, procedures and processes to mitigate the risks associated with RDC services and to effectively monitor for unusual or suspicious transactions. Examples of risk mitigants include:

(i) Comprehensively identifying and assessing RDC risk prior to implementation. Senior management should identify AML/CFT operational, information security, compliance, legal, and reputation risks. Depending on the financial institution's size and complexity, this comprehensive risk assessment process should include staff from information technology and security, deposit operations, treasury or cash management sales, business continuity, audit, compliance, accounting and legal;

(ii) Conducting appropriate CDD and EDD;

(iii) Creating risk-based parameters that can be used to conduct Remote Deposit Capture (RDC) customer suitability reviews. Parameters may include a list of acceptable industries, standardized underwriting criteria (e.g., credit history, financial statements and ownership structure of business) and other risk factors. When the level of risk warrants, financial institutions' staff should consider visiting the customer's physical location as part of the suitability review. During these visits, the customer's operational controls and risk management processes should be evaluated;

(iv) Conducting vendor due diligence when financial institutions use a service provider for RDC activities. Management should ensure implementation of sound vendor management processes;

(v) Obtaining expected account activity from the RDC customer, such as the anticipated RDC transaction volume, and type (e.g., payroll cheques, third party cheques, or traveller's cheques), comparing it to actual transaction and resolving significant deviations;

(vi) Comparing expected activity to business type to ensure they are reasonable and consistent;

(vii) Establishing or modifying customer Remote Deposit Capture transaction limits;

(viii) Developing well-constructed contracts that clearly identify each party's role, responsibilities and liabilities, and detail record retention procedures for RDC data. These procedures should include physical and logical security expectations for access, transmission, storage and ultimate disposal of original documents. The contract should also address the customer's responsibility for properly securing RDC equipment and preventing inappropriate use, including establishing effective equipment security controls (e.g., passwords and dual control access). In addition, contracts should detail the RDC customer's obligation to provide original documents to the financial institution in order to facilitate investigations related to unusual transactions or poor quality transmissions, or to resolve disputes. Contracts should clearly detail the authority of the financial institution to mandate specific internal controls, conduct audits or terminate the RDC relationship. Implementing additional monitoring or review when significant changes occur in the type or volume of transactions, or when significant changes occur in the underwriting criteria, customer base, customer risk management processes or geographic location that the bank relied on when establishing RDC services;

(ix) Ensuring that RDC customers receive adequate training. The training should include documentation that addresses issues such as routine operations and procedures, duplication and problem resolution;

(x) Using improved aggregation and monitoring capabilities as facilitated by the digitized data; and

(xi) As appropriate, using technology to minimize errors (e.g., the use of franking to stamp or identify a deposit as being processed).

(J) INFORMAL VALUE TRANSFER SYSTEM

An Informal Value Transfer System (IVTS) is used to describe a currency or value transfer system that operates informally to transfer money as a business.

In countries lacking a stable financial sector or with large areas not served by formal financial institutions, IVTS may be the only method for conducting financial transactions. Persons living in Nigeria may use IVTS to transfer funds to their home countries.

Risk Factors

Funds transfers may present a heightened degree of ML/FT risk, depending on such factors as the number and Naira volume of transactions, geographic location of originators and beneficiaries, and whether the originator or beneficiary is a financial institution customer. The size and complexity of a financial institution's operation and the origin and destination of the funds being transferred will determine which type of funds transfer system the financial institution uses. The vast majority of funds transfer instructions are conducted electronically. However, Examiners need to be mindful that physical instructions may be transmitted by other informal methods, as described earlier.

Cover payments made through SWIFT pose additional risks for intermediary financial institutions that do not have facilities that identify the originator and beneficiary of the funds transfer. Without such facilities, the intermediary financial institution is unable to monitor or filter payment information. This lack of transparency limits the Nigerian intermediary financial institution's ability to appropriately assess and manage the risk associated with correspondent and clearing operations and monitor suspicious transaction.

The risks of PUPID transactions to the beneficiary financial institution are similar to other transactions in which the financial institution does business with non-customers. However, the risks are heightened in PUPID transactions if the financial institution allows a non-customer to access the funds transfer system by providing minimal or no identifying information. Financial institutions that allow non-customers to transfer funds using the PUPID service pose significant risk to both the originating and beneficiary financial institution. In these situations, both financial institutions have minimal or no identifying information on the originator or the beneficiary.

Risk Mitigation

Funds transfers can be used in the placement, layering and integration stages of money laundering. Funds transfers purchased with currency are an example of the placement stage. Detecting unusual transaction in the layering and integration stages is more difficult for a financial institution because transactions may appear legitimate. In many cases, a financial institution may not be involved in the placement of the funds or in the final integration, only the layering of transactions. Financial institutions should consider all three stages of money laundering when evaluating or assessing funds transfer risks.

Financial institutions need to have sound policies, procedures and processes to manage the ML/FT risks of its funds transfer activities. Funds transfer policies, procedures and processes should address all foreign correspondent banking transactions, including transactions in which Nigerian branches and agencies of foreign financial institutions are intermediaries for their head offices.

Obtaining CDD information is an important risk mitigant in providing funds transfer services. Because of the nature of funds transfers, adequate and effective CDD policies, procedures and processes are critical in detecting unusual and suspicious transactions. An effective risk-based suspicious transaction monitoring and reporting system is equally important. Whether this monitoring and reporting system is automated or manual, it should be sufficient to detect suspicious trends and patterns typically associated with money laundering.

Financial institutions involved in international payments transactions are encouraged to adhere to the following:

(i) Financial institutions should not omit, delete or alter information in payment messages or orders for the purpose of avoiding detection of that information by any other financial institution in the payment process;

(ii) Financial institutions should not use any particular payment message for the purpose of avoiding detection of information by any other financial institution in the payment process;

(iii) Subject to all applicable laws, financial institutions should cooperate as fully as practicable with other financial institutions in the payment process when requested to provide information about the parties involved; and

(iv) Financial institutions should strongly encourage their correspondent financial institutions to observe these principles.

In addition, effective monitoring processes for cover payments include:

(i) Monitoring funds transfers processed through automated systems in order to identify suspicious transaction. This monitoring may be conducted after the transfers are processed, on an automated basis, and may use a risk-based approach; and

(ii) Given the volume of messages and data for large Nigerian intermediary financial institutions, a manual review of every payment order may not be feasible or effective. However, intermediary financial institutions should have, as part of their monitoring processes, a risk-based method to identify incomplete fields or fields with meaningless data. Nigerian financial institutions engaged in processing cover payments should have policies to address such circumstances, including those that involve systems other than SWIFT.

Originating and beneficiary financial institutions should establish effective and appropriate policies, procedures and processes for PUPID transaction including:

(i) Specifying the type of identification that is acceptable;

(ii) Maintaining documentation of individuals consistent with the bank's recordkeeping policies;

(iii) Defining which financial institution employees may conduct PUPID transactions;

(iv) Establishing limits on the amount of funds that may be transferred to or from the financial institution for non-customers;

(v) Monitoring and reporting suspicious transactions;

(vi) Providing enhanced scrutiny for transfers to or from certain jurisdictions; and

(vii) Identifying disbursement method for proceeds from a beneficiary financial institution.

(K) AUTOMATED CLEARING HOUSE (ACH) TRANSACTIONS

The financial institution's systems should be adequate to manage the risks associated with automated clearing house (ACH) and international ACH transactions (IAT) and the management should have the ability to implement its monitoring and reporting systems effectively.

The use of the ACH has grown markedly over the last several years due to the increased volume of electronic cheque conversion and one-time ACH debits, reflecting the lower cost of ACH processing relative to cheque processing. Cheque conversion transactions as well as one-time ACH debits are primarily of low currency value used for consumer transactions for purchases of goods and services or payment of consumer bills. ACH is primarily used for domestic payments.

Risk Factors

The ACH system was designed to transfer a high volume of domestic currency transactions which pose lower ML/FT risks. Nevertheless, the ability to send high international currency transactions through the ACH may expose banks to higher ML/FT risks. Banks/Other financial institutions (OFIs) without a robust ML/FT monitoring system may be exposed to additional risk particularly when accounts are opened over the internet without face-to face contact.

ACH transactions that are originated through a TPSP (that is, when the originator is not a direct customer of the ODFI) may increase ML/FT risks, therefore, making it difficult for an ODFI to underwrite and review originator's transactions for compliance with AML/CFT rules. Risks are heightened when neither the TPSP nor the ODFI performs due diligence on the companies for whom they are originating payments.

Certain ACH transactions, such as those originated through the internet or the telephone may be susceptible to manipulation and fraudulent use. Certain practices associated with how the banking industry processes ACH transactions may expose banks/OFIs to ML/FT risks. These practices include:

(i)   An Originating Depository Financial Institution (ODFI) authorizing a Third Party Service Provider (TPSP) to send ACH files directly to an ACH Operator, in essence by-passing the ODFI;

(ii) ODFIs and Receiving Depository Financial Institutions (RDFIs) relying on each other to perform adequate due diligence on their customers;

(iii) Batch processing that obscures the identities of originators; and

(iv) Lack of sharing of information on or about originators and receivers inhibits a bank's/OFIs' ability to appropriately assess, monitor, control/manage and mitigate the risk associated with correspondent and ACH processing operations, monitor for suspicious activity and screen for AML compliance.

Risk Mitigation

Financial institutions are required to have AML/CFT Compliance Programmes and appropriate policies, procedures and processes in place to monitor and identify unusual activity, including ACH transactions. Obtaining CDD information in all operations is an important mitigant to ML/FT risk in ACH transactions. Because of the nature of ACH transactions and the reliance that ODFIs and RDFIs place on each other for regulatory reviews and other necessary due diligence information, it is essential that all parties have a strong CDD Programme for regular ACH customers. For relationships with TPSPs, CDD on the TPSP can be supplemented with due diligence on the principals associated with the TPSP and, as necessary, on the originators.

Adequate and effective CDD policies, procedures and processes are critical in detecting a pattern of unusual and suspicious activities because the individual ACH transactions are typically not reviewed. Equally important is an effective risk-based suspicious activity monitoring and reporting system. In cases where a financial institution is heavily reliant upon the TPSP, the financial institution may want to review the TPSP's suspicious activity monitoring and reporting Programme, either through its own or an independent inspection. The ODFI may establish an agreement with the TPSP, which delineates general TPSP guidelines, such as compliance with ACH operating requirements and responsibilities and meeting other applicable regulations. Financial institutions may need to consider controls to restrict or refuse ACH services to potential originators and receivers engaged in questionable or deceptive business practices.

ACH transactions can be used in the layering and integration stages of money laundering. Detecting unusual activity in the layering and integration stages can be a difficult task, because ACH may be used to legitimize frequent and recurring transactions. Financial institutions should consider the layering and integration stages of money laundering when evaluating or assessing the ACH transaction risks of a particular customer.

The ODFI should be aware of IAT activity and evaluate the activity using a risk-based approach in order to ensure that suspicious activity is identified and monitored. The ODFI, if frequently involved in international transfers, may develop a separate process which may be automated for reviewing international transfers that minimizes disruption to general ACH processing, reconciliation and settlement.

The potentially higher risk inherent in international transfers should be considered in the financial institution's ACH policies, procedures and processes.

The financial institution should consider its current, potential roles and responsibilities when developing internal controls to monitor and mitigate the risk associated with international transfers and to comply with the financial institution's suspicious activity reporting obligations.

In processing international transfers, financial institutions should consider the following:

(i) Customers and transaction types and volume.

(ii) Third-party payment processor relationships.

(iii) Responsibilities, obligations and risks of becoming a Gateway Operator(GO).

(iv) CIP, CDD and EDD standards and practices.

(v) Suspicious activity monitoring and reporting.

(vi) Appropriate MIS, including the potential necessity for systems upgrades or changes.

(vii) Processing procedures (e.g., identifying and handling international transfers and handling non-compliant and rejected messages).

(viii) Training Programmes for appropriate bank personnel (e.g., ACH personnel, operations, compliance audit, customer service, etc.).

(ix) Legal agreements, including those with customers, third-party processors and vendors, and whether those agreements need to be upgraded or modified.

Financial institutions that have relationships with third-party service providers should assess the nature of those relationships and their related ACH transactions to ascertain the financial institution's level of ML/FT risk and to develop appropriate policies, procedures and processes to mitigate that risk.

(L) ELECTRONIC CASH

The financial institution's systems should be adequate to manage the risks associated with electronic cash (e-cash) and the management should have the ability to implement its monitoring and reporting systems effectively.

E-cash (e-money) is a digital representation of money. E-cash comes in several forms including computer-based, mobile telephone-based and prepaid cards. Computer e-cash is accessed through personal computer hard disks via a modem or stored-in-an-online repository. Mobile telephone-based e-cash is accessed through an individual's mobile telephone. Prepaid cards are used to access funds generally held by issuing financial institutions in pooled accounts.

In the case of computer e-cash, monetary value is electronically deducted from the financial institution account when a purchase is made or funds are transferred to another person.

Risk Factors

Transactions using e-cash may pose the following unique risks to the financial institution:

(i)   Funds may be transferred to or from an unknown third party;

(ii) Customers may be able to avoid border restrictions as the transactions can become mobile and may not be subject to jurisdictional restrictions;

(iii) Transactions may be instantaneous;

(iv) Specific cardholder activity may be difficult to determine by reviewing activity through a pooled account; and

(v)   The customer may perceive the transactions as less transparent.

Risk Mitigation

Financial institutions should establish AML/CFT monitoring, identification and reporting for unusual and suspicious activities occurring through e-cash.

Useful MIS for detecting unusual activity on higher-risk accounts include ATM activity reports (focusing on foreign transactions), funds transfer reports, new account activity reports, change of internet address reports, internet protocol (IP) address reports and reports to identify related or linked accounts (e.g., common addresses, phone numbers, e-mail addresses and taxpayer identification numbers). The financial institution also may institute other controls, such as establishing transaction and account/currency limits that require manual intervention to exceed the pre-set limit.

(M) PURCHASE AND SALE OF MONETARY INSTRUMENTS

The financial institution's systems should be adequate to manage the risks associated with monetary instrument and the management should have the ability to implement its monitoring and reporting systems effectively.

Monetary instruments are products provided by financial institutions and include cashier's cheques, traveller's cheques, and money orders. Monetary instruments are typically purchased to pay for commercial or personal transactions and, in the case of traveller's cheques, as a form of stored value for future purchases.

Risk Factors

The purchase or exchange of monetary instruments at the placement and layering stages of money laundering can conceal the source of illicit proceeds. As a result, financial institutions have been major targets in laundering operations because they provide and process monetary instruments through deposits. For example, customers or non-customers have been known to purchase monetary instruments in amounts below the reportable currency threshold to avoid having to provide adequate identification. Subsequently, monetary instruments are then placed into deposit accounts to circumvent the CTR filing threshold.

Risk Mitigation

Financial institutions selling monetary instruments should have appropriate policies, procedures and processes in place to mitigate risk. Policies should define:

(i) Acceptable and unacceptable monetary instrument transactions (e.g., non-customer transactions, monetary instruments with blank payees, unsigned monetary instruments, identification requirements for structured transactions, or the purchase of multiple sequentially numbered monetary instruments for the same payee);

(ii) Procedures for reviewing for unusual or suspicious activity, including elevating concerns to management; and

(iii) Criteria for closing relationships or refusing to do business with noncustomers who have consistently or egregiously been involved in suspicious activity.

(N) BROKERED DEPOSIT

The financial institution's systems should be adequate to manage the risks associated with brokered deposit relationship and the management should have the ability to implement its due diligence, monitoring and reporting systems effectively.

The use of brokered deposits is a common funding source for many banks and other financial institutions. Recent technology developments allow brokers to provide bankers with increased access to a broad range of potential investors who have no relationship with the bank and/or other financial institutions. Deposits can be raised over the internet through certificates of deposit listing services or through other advertising methods.

Deposit brokers provide intermediary services for financial institutions and investors. This activity is considered higher risk because each deposit broker operates under its own guidelines for obtaining deposits. The level of regulatory oversight over deposit brokers varies, as the applicability of AML/CFT Regulatory requirements directly on the deposit broker varies. However, the deposit broker is subject to other statutory requirements regardless of its regulatory status.

Consequently, the deposit broker may not be performing adequate customer due diligence. The financial institution accepting brokered deposits depends on the deposit broker to sufficiently perform required account opening procedures and to follow applicable AML/CFT Compliance Programme requirements.

Risk Factors

Money laundering and terrorist financing risks arise because the financial institution may not know the ultimate beneficial owners or the source of funds.

The deposit broker could represent a range of clients that may be of higher risk for money laundering and terrorist financing (e.g., non-resident or offshore customers, Politically Exposed Persons (PEP) or foreign shell banks).

Risk Mitigation

Financial institutions which accept deposit broker accounts or funds should develop appropriate policies, procedures and processes that establish minimum CDD procedures for all deposit brokers providing deposits to the bank or other financial institution. The level of due diligence performed by a financial institution should be commensurate with its knowledge of the deposit broker and the deposit broker's known business practices and customer base.

In an effort to address the risk inherent in certain deposit broker relationships, financial institutions may want to consider having a signed contract that sets out the roles and responsibilities of each party and restrictions on types of customers (e.g., non-resident or offshore customers, PEPs or foreign shell banks). Financial institutions should conduct sufficient due diligence on deposit brokers, especially unknown, foreign, independent or unregulated deposit brokers.

To manage the ML/FT risks associated with brokered deposits, the financial institution should:

(i) Determine whether the deposit broker is a legitimate business in all operating locations where the business is conducted;

(ii) Review the deposit broker's business strategies, including targeted customer markets (e.g., foreign or domestic customers) and methods for soliciting clients;

(iii) Determine whether the deposit broker is subject to regulatory oversight;

(iv) Evaluate whether the deposit broker's AML/CFT compliance policies, procedures, and processes are adequate (e.g., ascertain whether the deposit broker performs sufficient CDD including CIP procedures); and

(v) Evaluate the adequacy of the deposit broker's AML/CFT audits and ensure that they address compliance with applicable regulations and requirements.

Financial institutions should take particular care in their oversight of deposit brokers who are not adequately regulated entities and:

(i) Are unknown to the financial institution;

(ii) Conduct business or obtain deposits primarily in other jurisdictions;

(iii) Use unknown businesses and financial institutions for references;

(iv) Provide other services that may be suspect, such as creating shell companies for foreign clients;

(v) Refuse to provide requested audit and due diligence information or insist on placing deposits before providing this information; and

(vi) Use technology that provides anonymity to customers.

Financial institutions should also monitor existing deposit broker relationships for any significant changes in business strategies that may influence the broker's risk profile. As such, financial institutions should periodically re-verify and update each deposit broker's profile to ensure an appropriate risk assessment.

(O) NON-DEPOSIT INVESTMENT PRODUCTS

The financial institution's systems should be adequate to manage the risks associated with both networking and in-house non-deposit investment products (NDIP) and the management should have the ability to implement its monitoring and reporting systems effectively.

NDIP include a wide array of investment products (e.g., securities, bonds and fixed or variable annuities). Sales Programmes may also include cash management sweep accounts to retail and commercial clients; these Programmes are offered by the bank directly. Banks and other financial institutions offer these investments to increase fee income and provide customers with additional products and services. The manner in which the NDIP relationship is structured and the methods with which the products are offered substantially affect the bank's/other financial institution's ML/FT risks and responsibilities.

Risk Factors

ML/FT risks arise because NDIP can involve complex legal arrangements, large amounts and the rapid movement of funds. NDIP portfolios managed and controlled directly by clients pose a greater money laundering risk than those managed by the bank or other financial services provider. Sophisticated clients may create ownership structures to obscure the ultimate control and ownership of these investments. For example, customers can retain a certain level of anonymity by creating Private Investment Companies (PIC), offshore trusts or other investment entities that hide the customer's ownership or beneficial interest.

Risk Mitigation

Management should develop risk-based policies, procedures and processes that enable the bank/other financial institution to identify unusual account relationships and circumstances, questionable assets and sources of funds and other potential areas of risk (e.g., offshore accounts, agency accounts and unidentified beneficiaries). Management should be alert to situations that need additional review or research.

(P) CONCENTRATION ACCOUNTS

The financial institution's systems should be adequate to manage the AML/CFT risks associated with concentration accounts and the management should have the ability to implement its monitoring and reporting systems effectively.

Concentration accounts are internal accounts established to facilitate the processing and settlement of multiple or individual customer transactions within the financial institution, usually on the same day. These accounts may also be known as special-use, omnibus, suspense, settlement, intra-day, sweep, or collection accounts. Concentration accounts are frequently used to facilitate transactions for private banking, trust and custody accounts, funds transfers and international affiliates.

Risk Factors

Money laundering risk can arise in concentration accounts if the customer identifying information such as name, transaction amount and account number is separated from the financial transaction. If separation occurs, the audit trail is lost and accounts may be misused or administered improperly. Financial institution that use concentration accounts should implement adequate policies, procedures and processes covering the operation and recordkeeping for these accounts. Policies should establish guidelines to identify, measure, monitor and control the risks.

Risk Mitigation

Because of the risks involved, management should be familiar with the nature of their customers' businesses and with the transactions flowing through the financial institution's concentration accounts. Additionally, the monitoring of concentration account transactions is necessary to identify and report unusual or suspicious transactions.

Internal controls are necessary to ensure that processed transactions include the identifying customer information. Retaining complete information is crucial for compliance with regulatory requirements as well as ensuring adequate transaction monitoring. Adequate internal controls may include:

(i) Maintaining a comprehensive system that identifies (institution-wide) the general ledger accounts used as concentration accounts, as well as the departments and individuals authorized to use those accounts;

(ii) Requiring dual signatures on general ledger tickets;

(iii) Prohibiting direct customer access to concentration accounts;

(iv) Capturing customer transactions in the customer's account statements;

(v) Prohibiting customer's knowledge of concentration accounts or their ability to direct employees to conduct transactions through the accounts;

(vi) Retaining appropriate transaction and customer identifying information;

(vii) Frequent reconciliation of the accounts by an individual who is independent from the transactions;

(viii) Establishing timely discrepancy resolution process; and

(ix) Identifying recurring customer names, institution's involvement in trade finance minimizes payment risk to importers and exporters.

(Q) TRADE FINANCE ACTIVITIES

The nature of trade finance activities, however, requires the active involvement of multiple parties on both sides of the transaction. In addition to the basic exporter or importer relationship at the center of any particular trade activity, relationships may exist between the exporter and its suppliers and between the importer and its customers.

Both the exporter and importer may also have other banking relationships.

Furthermore, many other intermediary financial and non-financial institutions may provide conduits and services to expedite the underlying documents and payment flows associated with trade transactions. Financial institutions can participate in trade financing by, among other things, providing pre-export financing, helping in the collection process, confirming or issuing letters of credit, discounting drafts and acceptances or offering fee-based services such as providing credit and country information on buyers. Although most trade financing is short-term and self-liquidating in nature, medium-term loans (one to five years) or long-term loans (more than five years) may be used to finance the import and export of capital goods such as machinery and equipment.

In transactions that are covered by letters of credit, financial institutions are required to take the following roles:

Applicant—The buyer or party who requests the issuance of a letter of credit.

Issuing Bank—The bank that issues the letter of credit on behalf of the applicant and advises it to the beneficiary either directly or through an advising financial institution. The applicant is the issuing bank's customer.

Confirming Bank—Typically, is in the home country of the beneficiary and at the request of the issuing bank. It is the financial institution that adds its commitment to honour draws made by the beneficiary, provided the terms and conditions of the letter of credit are met.

Advising Bank—The bank that advises the credit at the request of the issuing bank. The issuing bank sends the original credit to the advising bank for onward forwarding to the beneficiary. The advising bank authenticates the credit and advises it to the beneficiary. There may be more than one advising bank in a letter of credit transaction. The advising bank may also be a confirming bank.

Beneficiary—The seller or party to whom the letter of credit is addressed.

Negotiation—The purchase by the nominated bank of drafts (drawn on a bank other than the nominated bank) or documents under a complying presentation by advancing or agreeing to advance funds to the beneficiary on or before the banking day on which reimbursement is due to the nominated bank.

Nominated Bank—The bank with which the credit is available or any bank in which the credit is available.

Accepting Bank—The bank that accepts a draft, providing a draft is called for by the credit. Drafts are drawn on the accepting bank that dates and signs the instrument.

Discounting Bank—The bank that discounts a draft for the beneficiary after it has been accepted by the accepting bank. The discounting bank is often the accepting bank.

Reimbursing Bank—The bank authorized by the issuing bank to reimburse the paying bank submitting claims under the letter of credit.

Paying Bank—The bank that makes payment to the beneficiary of the letter of credit. As an example, in a letter of credit arrangement, a bank can serve as the issuing bank, allowing its customer (the buyer) to purchase goods locally or internationally, or the bank can act as an advising bank, enabling its customer (the exporter) to sell its goods locally or internationally. The relationship between any two banks may vary and could include any of the roles listed above.

Risk Factors

The international trade system is subject to a wide range of risks and vulnerabilities that provide criminal organizations with the opportunity to launder the proceeds of crime and move funds to terrorist organizations with a relatively low risk of detection. The involvement of multiple parties on both sides of any international trade transaction can make the process of due diligence more difficult.

Also, because trade finance can be more document-based than other banking activities, it can be susceptible to documentary fraud which can be linked to money laundering, terrorist financing or the circumvention of sanctions or other restrictions (such as export prohibitions, licensing requirements or controls).

While financial institutions should be alert to transactions involving higher-risk goods (e.g., trade in weapons or nuclear equipment), they need to be aware that goods may be over or undervalued in an effort to evade AML/CFT requirements or customs regulations, or to move funds or value across national borders. For example, an importer may pay a large sum of money from the proceeds of an illegal activity for goods that are essentially worthless and are subsequently discarded. Alternatively, trade documents such as invoices may be fraudulently altered to hide the scheme. Variations on this theme include inaccurate or double invoicing, partial shipment of goods (short shipping) and the use of fictitious goods. Illegal proceeds transferred in such transactions thereby appear sanitized and enter the realm of legitimate commerce. Moreover, many suspect trade finance transactions also involve collusion between buyers and sellers.

The applicant's true identity or ownership may be disguised by the use of certain corporate forms such as shell companies or offshore front companies.

The use of these types of entities results in a lack of transparency, effectively hiding the identity of the purchasing party and thus increasing the risk of money laundering and terrorist financing.

Risk Mitigation

Sound CDD procedures are needed to gain a thorough understanding of the customer's underlying business and locations served. The financial institutions in the letter of credit process need to undertake varying degrees of due diligence depending upon their role in the transaction. For example, issuing bank should conduct sufficient due diligence on a prospective customer before establishing the letter of credit. The due diligence should include gathering sufficient information on the applicants and beneficiaries including their identities, nature of business and sources of funding. This may require the use of background checks or investigations, particularly in higher-risk jurisdictions. As such, financial institutions should conduct a thorough review and reasonably know their customers prior to facilitating trade-related activity and should have a thorough understanding of trade finance documentation.

Likewise, guidance provided by the Financial Action Task Force (FATF) on money laundering has helped in setting important industry standards and is a resource for financial institutions that provide trade finance services. The Wolfsberg Group also has published suggested industry standards and guidance for financial institutions that provide trade finance services.

Financial institutions taking other roles in the letter of credit process should complete due diligence that is commensurate with their roles in each transaction.

Financial institutions need to be aware that because of the frequency of transactions in which multiple banks are involved, issuing banks may not always have correspondent relationships with the advising or confirming bank.

To the extent feasible, financial institutions should review documentation, not only for compliance with the terms of the letter of credit, but also for anomalies or red flags that could indicate unusual or suspicious transaction. Reliable documentation is critical in identifying potentially suspicious transaction. When analyzing trade transactions for unusual or suspicious transaction, financial institutions should consider obtaining copies of official government import and export forms to assess the reliability of documentation provided. These anomalies could appear in shipping documentation, obvious under or over-invoicing, government licences (when required) or discrepancies in the description of goods on various documents. Identification of these elements may not, in itself, require the filing of STRs, but may suggest the need for further research and verification. In circumstances where STRs are warranted, the financial institution is not expected to stop trade or discontinue processing the transaction.

However, stopping the trade may be required to avoid a potential violation of the Financial Action Task Force Recommendations.

Trade finance transactions frequently use Society for Worldwide Interbank Financial Telecommunication (SWIFT) messages. Financial institutions must comply with relevant regulations and when necessary, provide funding in advance of consummating the deal involved. Financial institutions should monitor the names of the parties contained in these messages and compare the names against terrorist lists. Financial institutions with a high volume of SWIFT messages should determine whether their monitoring efforts are adequate to detect suspicious transaction, particularly if the monitoring mechanism is not automated.

Policies, procedures and processes should also require a thorough review of all applicable trade documentation (e.g., customs declarations, trade documents, invoices, etc) to enable the financial institution to monitor and report unusual and suspicious transactions based on the role played by the financial institution in the letter of credit process. The sophistication of the documentation review process and MIS should be commensurate with the size and complexity of the financial institution's trade finance portfolio and its role in the letter of credit process. The monitoring process should give greater scrutiny to:

(i) Items shipped that are inconsistent with the nature of the customer's business (e.g., a steel company that starts dealing in paper products or an information technology company that starts dealing in bulk pharmaceuticals);

(ii) Customers conducting business in higher-risk jurisdictions;

(iii) Customers shipping items through higher-risk jurisdictions including transit through non-cooperative countries;

(iv) Customers involved in potentially higher-risk activities including activities that may be subject to export/import restrictions (e.g., equipment for military or police organizations of foreign governments, weapons, ammunition, chemical mixtures, classified defense articles, sensitive technical

data, nuclear materials, precious gems, or certain natural resources such as metals, ore and crude oil) ;

(v)   Obvious over or under-pricing of goods and services;

(vi) Obvious misrepresentation of quantity or type of goods im-
      ported or exported;

(vii) Transaction structure appears unnecessarily complex and de-
      signed to obscure the true nature of the transaction;

(viii) Customer directs payment of proceeds to an unrelated third
       party;

(ix) Shipment locations or description of goods not consistent
      with letter of credit; and

(x)   Significantly amended letters of credit without reasonable
      justification or changes to the beneficiary or location of
      payment.

Unless customer behaviour or transaction documentation appears
unusual, the financial institution should not be expected to spend
undue time or effort reviewing all information. The examples above,
particularly for an issuing bank, may be included as part of its routine
CDD process. Financial institution with robust CDD Programmes
may find that less focus is needed on individual transactions as a result of their comprehensive knowledge of the customer's activities.

(R) TRUST AND ASSET MANAGEMENT SERVICES

The financial institution's policies, procedures, processes and systems to manage the ML/FT risks associated with trust and asset

management services should be adequate and the management should have the ability to implement effective due diligence, monitoring and reporting systems effectively.

Trust accounts are generally defined as a legal arrangement in which one party (the trustor or grantor) transfers ownership of assets to a person or bank/other financial institution (the trustee) to be held or used for the benefit of others.

These arrangements include the broad categories of court-supervised accounts (e.g., executorships and guardianships), personal trusts (e.g., living trusts, trusts established under a will, charitable trusts) and corporate trusts (e.g., bond trusteeships).

Agency accounts are established by contract and governed by contract law. Assets are held under the terms of the contract and legal title or ownership does not transfer to the financial institution as agent. Agency accounts include custody, escrow, investment management and safekeeping relationships. Agency products and services may be offered in a traditional trust department or through other financial institution departments.

Risk Factors

Trust and asset management accounts including agency relationships present ML/FT concerns similar to those of deposit taking, lending and other traditional financial institution's activities. Concerns are primarily due to the unique relationship structures involved when the financial institution handles trust and agency activities, such as:

(i)   Personal and court-supervised accounts;

(ii) Trust accounts formed in the private banking department;

(iii) Asset management and investment advisory accounts;

(iv) Global and domestic custody accounts;

(v) Securities lending;

(vi) Employee benefit and retirement accounts;

(vii) Corporate trust accounts;

(viii) Transfer Agent Accounts; and

(ix) Other related business lines.

As in any account relationship, money laundering risk may arise from trust and asset management activities. When misused, trust and asset management accounts can conceal the sources and uses of funds as well as the identity of beneficial and legal owners. Customers and account beneficiaries may try to remain anonymous in order to move illicit funds or avoid scrutiny.

For example, customers may seek a certain level of anonymity by creating private investment companies offshore trusts or other investment entities that hide the true ownership or beneficial interest of the trust.

Risk Mitigation

Management should develop policies, procedures and processes that enable the financial institution to identify unusual account relationships and circumstances, questionable assets and sources of assets and other potential areas of ML/FT risk (e.g., Offshore Accounts, PICs, Asset Protection Trusts (APT), agency accounts and unidentified beneficiaries). While the majority of traditional trust and asset management accounts will not need EDD, management should be alert to those situations that need additional review or research.

The financial institution must maintain required CIP information and complete the required one-time check of trust account names against VIS search requests.

The financial institution should also be able to identify customers who may be politically exposed persons (PEP), doing business with or located in a jurisdiction designated as primary money laundering concern. The financial institution should also determine the identity of other parties that may have control over the account, such as grantors or co-trustees.

CIRCUMSTANCES WARRANTING ENHANCED DUE DILIGENCE.

(i) Management should assess account risk on the basis of a variety of factors which may include:

(a) Type of trust or agency account and its size;

(b) Types and frequency of transactions;

(c) Country of residence of the principals or beneficiaries or the country where established or source of funds;

(d) Accounts and transactions that are not usual and customary for the customer or for the financial institution; and

(e) Stringent documentation, verification and transaction monitoring procedures should be established for accounts that the management considers as higher risk, (typically, employee benefit accounts and court supervised accounts are among the lowest ML/FT risks).

(ii) Circumstance in which EDD may be appropriate:

The financial institution is entering into a relationship with a new customer.

(a) Account principals or beneficiaries reside in a foreign jurisdiction or the trust or its funding mechanisms are established offshore;

(b) Assets or transactions are not typical for the type and character of the customer;

(c) Account type, size, assets or transactions are atypical for the financial institution;

(d) International funds transfers are conducted particularly through offshore funding sources;

(e) Accounts are funded with easily transportable assets such as gemstones, precious metals, coins, artwork, rare stamps or negotiable instruments;

(f) Accounts or relationships are maintained in way that the identities of the principals, beneficiaries, sources of funds are unknown or cannot be easily determined;

(g) Accounts transactions are for the benefit of charitable organizations or other Non-Governmental Organizations (NGOs) that may be used as a conduit for illegal activities;

(h) Interest on Lawyers' Trust Accounts (IOLTA) holding are processing significant currency/dollar amounts;

(i) Account assets that include PICs; and

(j) PEPs are parties to the accounts or transactions.

Source: Central Bank of Nigeria's Anti-Money Laundering/ Combating the Financing of Terrorism (AML/CFT) Risk Based Supervision (RBS) Framework, 2011

GLOSSARY OF TERMINOLOGY

Accounts

'*Accounts*' means a facility or an arrangement by which a financial institution:

(a) accepts deposits of currency;

(b) allows withdrawals of currency or transfers into or out of the account;

(c) pays cheques or payment orders drawn on a financial institution or cash dealer by a person or collect cheques or payment orders on behalf of a person;

(d) supplies a facility or an arrangement for a safe deposits box;

Accountable institutions

'*Accountable institutions*' include:

1. A legal practitioner

2. A board of executors or a trust company or any other person that invests, keeps in safe custody, controls or administers trust property

3. An estate agent

4. An authorised user of an exchange

5. A person who carries on the 'business of a bank'

6. A mutual bank

7. A person who carries on a 'long-term insurance business'

8. A person who carries on the business of making available a gambling activity

9. A person who carries on the business of dealing in foreign exchange.

10. A person who carries on the business of lending money against the security of securities

11. A person who carries on the business of a financial services provider, to provide advice and intermediary services in respect of the investment of any financial product and a health service benefit provided by a medical scheme

12. A person who issues, sells or redeems travellers' cheques, money orders or similar instruments.

13. A person who carries on the business of a money remitter.

Beneficial owner

(a) in relation to a corporation—

   (i) means an individual who—

      (A) owns or controls, directly or indirectly, including through a trust or bearer share holding, not less than 10% of the issued share capital of the corporation;

      (B) is, directly or indirectly, entitled to exercise or control the exercise of not less than 10% of the voting rights at general meetings of the corporation; or

      (C) exercises ultimate control over the management of the corporation; or

   (ii) if the corporation is acting on behalf of another person, means the other person;

(b) in relation to a partnership—

   (i) means an individual who—

      (A) is entitled to or controls, directly or indirectly, not less than a 10% share of the capital or profits of the partnership;

      (B) is, directly or indirectly, entitled to exercise or control the exercise of not less than 10% of the voting rights in the partnership; or

(C) exercises ultimate control over the management of the partnership; or

(ii) if the partnership is acting on behalf of another person, means the other person;

(c) in relation to a trust, means—

(i) an individual who is entitled to a vested interest in not less than 10% of the capital of the trust property, whether the interest is in possession or in remainder or reversion and whether it is defeasible or not;

(ii) the settlor of the trust;

(iii) a protector or enforcer of the trust; or

(iv) an individual who has ultimate control over the trust; and

(d) in relation to a person not falling within paragraph (a), (b) or (c)—

(i) means an individual who ultimately owns or controls the person; or

(ii) if the person is acting on behalf of another person, means the other person;

Business Relationship

'Business relationship' as between a person and a financial institution, means a business, professional or commercial relationship—

(a) that has an element of duration; or

(b) that the financial institution, at the time the person first contacts the financial institution in the person's capacity as a potential customer of the financial institution, expects to have an element of duration;

Certified Copy

'Certified copy' means a document that has been certified as a true copy of an original document by one of the following persons:

(1) a person who, under a law in force in a State or Territory, is currently licensed or registered to practise in an occupation listed in Part 1 of Schedule 2 of the *Statutory Declarations Regulations 1993*;

(2) a person who is enrolled on the roll of the Supreme Court of a State or Territory, or the High Court of Australia, as a legal practitioner(however described);

(3) a person listed in Part 2 of Schedule 2 of the *Statutory Declarations Regulations 1993*. For the purposes of these Rules, where Part 2 uses the term _5 or more years of continuous service', this should be read as_2 or more years of continuous service';

(4) an officer with, or authorised representative of, a holder of an Australian financial services licence, having 2 or more years of continuous service with one or more licensees;

(5) an officer with, or a credit representative of, a holder of an Australian credit licence, having 2 or more years of continuous service with one or more licensees;

(6) a person authorised as a notary public in a foreign country.

Correspondent Account

It is an account established to receive deposits from, make payments on behalf of a foreign financial institution or handles other financial transactions that relate to such institution.

Correspondent Banking Relationship

'Correspondent banking relationship' means a relationship that involves the provision by a financial institution (the ***first financial institution***) of banking services to another financial institution, where:

(a) the first financial institution carries on an activity or business at or through a permanent establishment of the financial institution in a particular country; and

(b) the other financial institution carries on an activity or business at or through a permanent establishment of the other financial institution in another country; and

(c) the correspondent banking relationship relates, in whole or in part, to those permanent establishments; and

(d) the relationship is not of a kind specified in the AML/CTF Rules; and

(e) the banking services are not of a kind specified in the AML/
CTF Rules.

For this purpose, **banking service** includes anything that, under the
AML/CTF Rules, is taken to be a banking service for the purposes of
this definition.

Customer/Client

'Customer/Client', in relation to a bank, means a person in whose name
an account is opened or intended to be opened, or for whom the bank
undertakes or intends to undertake any transaction without an account being opened;

Customer Identification Programme

An Anti-Money Laundering provision requiring in part that companies must check their customers against lists of known money
launderers.

Designated Non-Financial Businesses and Professions

'Designated Non-Financial Businesses and Professions' means:

- Casinos (which also includes online casinos);

- Real estate agents;

- Dealers in precious metals;

- Dealers in precious stones.

- Miners and Dealers in Precious Stones and Metals

- Dealers in Luxury Goods such as dealers in jewellry, electronics, and furniture.

- Chartered/Professional Accountants, Audit Firms and Tax Consultants 'mean' those licensed to practice by appropriate licensing authorities.

- Clearing and Settlement Companies.

- Legal Practitioners (sole practitioners, partners and employed professionals within professional firms)

- Trust and company service providers – when they prepare for or carry out transactions for a client concerning the following activities:

  a. acting as a formation agent of legal persons;

  b. acting as (or arranging for another person to act as) a director or secretary of a company, a partner of a partnership, or a similar position in relation to other legal persons;

  c. providing a registered office, business address or accommodation, correspondence or administrative address for a company, a partnership or any other legal person or arrangement;

  d. acting as (or arranging for another person to act as) a trustee of an express trust or performing the equivalent function for another form of legal arrangement;

    e. acting as (or arranging for another person to act as) a nominee shareholder for another person.

- Estate Surveyors and Valuers, means those that provide professional valuation services

- Hospitality industry means hotels and restaurants

- Casino, Pool Betting, and Lottery.

- Supermarkets

Designated Non-Financial Institutions

'Designated Non-Financial Businesses and Professions' also means "Designated Non-Financial Institution

Designated Threshold

Amount of transaction above which might be reported to authorities and be subject to analysis as money-laundering or terrorist finance.

E-currency

'E-currency' means an internet-based, electronic means of exchange that is:

  (a) known as any of the following:

      (i) e-currency;

      (ii) e-money;

(iii) digital currency;

(iv) a name specified in the AML/CTF Rules; and

(b) backed either directly or indirectly by:

(i) precious metal; or

(ii) bullion; or

(iii) a thing of a kind prescribed by the AML/CTF Rules; and

(c) not issued by or under the authority of a government body; and includes anything that, under the regulations, is taken to bee-currency for the purposes of this Act.

Enhanced Due Diligence

'*Enhanced Due Diligence*' refers to additional steps of examination and caution that financial institutions are required to obtain or take to identify their customers and confirm that their activities and funds are legitimate.

Financial Institutions

'*Financial institutions*' means any natural or legal person who conducts as a business one or more of the following activities or operations for or on behalf of a customer:

1. Acceptance of deposits and other repayable funds from the public.

2. Lending.

3. Financial leasing.

4. Money or value transfer services.

5. Issuing and managing means of payment (e.g. credit and debit cards, cheques, traveller's cheques, money orders and bankers' drafts, electronic money).

6. Financial guarantees and commitments.

7. Trading in:

   (a) money market instruments (cheques, bills, certificates of deposit, derivatives etc.);

   (b) foreign exchange;

   (c) exchange, interest rate and index instruments;

   (d) transferable securities;

   (e) commodity futures trading.

8. Participation in securities issues and the provision of financial services

Financial Intelligence Unit

Financial Intelligence Unit (FIU)—A centralized Government agency that collects, records, analyzes, disseminates and sometimes investigates suspicious financial activity and STRs.

Funds Transfers

'Funds Transfers'—The terms funds transfer refers to any transaction carried out on behalf of an originator person (both natural and legal) through a financial institution by electronic means with a view to making an amount of money available to a beneficiary person at another financial institution. The originator and the beneficiary may be the same person.

Know Your Customer

'Know Your Customer (KYC)' is used to describe a set of money laundering control policies and procedures that are employed to determine the true identity of a customer/client and the type of activity that will be 'normal and expected' for the customer, as well as to detect activity that should be considered 'unusual' for the particular customer.

Know Your Customer's Customer

'Know Your Customer's Customer (KYCC)' is a term used to describe a set of money laundering control policies and procedures used to determine the identities of the account holders of a respondent bank in a correspondent banking relationship or of the sub-account holders of a payable-through account.

Know Your Employee

'KYE'—Know your employee means understanding an employee's background, conflicts of interest and their susceptibility to money laundering complicity.

Money

'Money' includes:

(a) physical currency; and

(b) money held in an account, whether denominated in a country's currency or any other currency; and

(c) money held on deposit, whether denominated in a country's currency or any other currency; and

(d) e-currency, however amounts of the e-currency are expressed.

Opening

'Opening' in relation to an account, means creating the account. To avoid doubt, it is immaterial whether:

(a) the account number has been given to the holder of the account; or

(b) the holder of the account, or any other signatory to the account, can conduct a transaction in relation to the account.

Money or Value Transfer Services

'Money or value transfer services (MVTS)' refers to financial services that involve the acceptance of cash, cheques, other monetary instruments or other stores of value and the payment of a corresponding sum in cash or other form to a beneficiary by means of a communication,

message, transfer, or through a clearing network to which the MVTS provider belongs. Transactions performed by such services can involve one or more intermediaries and a final payment to a third party, and may include any new payment methods. Sometimes these services have ties to particular geographic regions and are described using a variety of specific terms, including hawala, hundi, and fei-chen.

Payable through Accounts

'*Payable through accounts*' refers to correspondent accounts that are used directly by third parties to transact business on their own behalf.

Person

'*Person*' means any of the following:

(a) an individual;

(b) a company;

(c) a trust;

(d) a partnership;

(e) a corporation sole;

(f) a body politic.

Physical Currency

'*physical currency*' means the coin and printed money that:

(a) is designated as legal tender; and

(b) circulates as, and is customarily used and accepted as, a medium of exchange in the country of issue.

Politically Exposed Person

'politically exposed person' means an individual:

(1) who holds a prominent public position or function in a government body or an international organisation, including:

    (a) Head of State or head of a country or government; or

    (b) government minister or equivalent senior politician; or

    (c) senior government official; or

    (d) Judge of the High Court of a country, a Federal Court or a Supreme Court of a State or Territory, or a Judge of a court of equivalent seniority in a foreign country or international organisation; or

    (e) Governor of a central bank of a country; or

    (f) senior foreign representative, ambassador, or high commissioner; or

    (g) high-ranking member of the armed forces; or

(h) board chair, chief executive, or chief financial officer of, or any other position that has comparable influence in, any State enterprise or international organisation; and

(2) who is an immediate family member of a person referred to in paragraph (1), including:

(a) a spouse; or

(b) a de facto partner; or

(c) a child and a child's spouse or de facto partner; or

(d) a parent; and

(3) who is a close associate of a person referred to in paragraph (1), which means any individual who is known (having regard to information that is public or readily available) to have:

(a) joint beneficial ownership of a legal entity or legal arrangement with a person referred to in paragraph (1); or

(b) sole beneficial ownership of a legal entity or legal arrangement that is known to exist for the benefit of a person described in paragraph

(4) In these Rules:

(a) *domestic politically exposed person* means a politically exposed person of an Australian government body;

(b) *foreign politically exposed person* means a politically exposed person of a government body of a foreign country;

(c) *international organisation politically exposed person* means a politically exposed person of an international organisation.

(5) In this definition *international organisation* means an organisation:

(a) established by formal political agreement by two or more countries and that agreement has the status of an international treaty; and

(b) recognised in the law of the countries which are members of the organisation.

Note: The term de facto partner is defined in the Acts Interpretation Act 1901and the terms 'foreign country' and 'government body' are defined in the AML/CTF Act.

Red Flag

'*Red Flag*' is an alert that signals possible money-laundering or terrorist financing. Red flags require investigation and possibly filing of STR.

Risk Matrix

'*Risk Matrix*' means a document or chart that allows financial institutions to perform a money laundering risk assessment at the start of a business or customer relationship.

Senior Management

'Senior management' means directors (or board) and senior managers (or equivalent) of a firm who are responsible, either individually or collectively, for management and supervision of the firm's business. This may include a firm's Chief Executive Officer, Managing Director, or other senior operating management personnel (as the case may be).

Shell Banks

'Shell Banks' refers to a bank incorporated in a jurisdiction in which it has no physical presence and which is unaffiliated with a regulated financial group.

Terrorist Financing

'Terrorist financing' is the financing of terrorist acts, and of terrorists and terrorist organisations.

Transaction

'Transaction' means a purchase, sale, loan, pledge, gift, transfer, delivery or the arrangement thereof and includes –

(i)   opening of an account;

(ii) deposits, withdrawal, exchange or transfer of funds in whatever currency, whether in cash or by cheque, payment order or other instruments or by electronic or other non-physical means;

(iii) the use of a safety deposit box or any other form of safe deposit;

(iv) entering into any fiduciary relationship;

(v) any payment made or received in whole or in part of any con-tractual or other legal obligation;

(vi) any payment made in respect of playing games of chance for cash or kind including such activities associated with casino; and

(vii) establishing or creating a legal person or legal arrange-ment.' —

INDEX

Countries identified by credible sources as lacking appropriate AML/CFT laws, 5.2
Countries identified by credible sources as providing funding or support for terrorist activities, 5.3
Countries identified by credible sources as having significant levels of corruption, 5.4

Customer Risk
Enhanced due diligence, 3.2, 4.1.2.2
Simplified due diligence, 3.3
Standard due diligence, 3.1, 4.1.2.1

D

Direct Discrimination
Differential treatment, 9.2.1
No objection and reasonable justification, 9.2.3
No reasonable relationship of proportionality, 9.2.4
Prohibited grounds, 9.2.2

E

Enhanced Due Diligence
Enhanced on-going monitoring, 3.2.2, 4.1.2.2.2
Senior management approval, 3.2.1, 4.1.2.2.1

H

Human Rights
Direct discrimination, 9.2
Right to respect for private and family life, 9.1

R

Record Retention Requirements
Preservation of records, 8.2.1

Right to Respect for Private and Family Life
Family life, 9.1.2
Private life, 9.1.1

Risk-Based Approach
Country or geographic risk, 2.3
Customer risk, 2.1
Product risk, 2.2

Rule-Based Approach
AML/CFT record retention requirements, 8.2
Suspicious transaction reporting, 8.1

S

Standard Due Diligence
Beneficial owners, 3.1.2
Natural persons, 3.1.1

Suspicious Transaction Reporting
Potentially suspicious activity that may indicate money laundering, 8.1.1
Confidentiality of STRs, 8.1.2

T

Terrorism Financing

Detrimental effects of money laundering and terrorist financing, 1.8

Terrorism financing, 1.6

Terrorism financing and money laundering, 1.7

Training and Awareness

Training methods and assessment, 7.1

ABOUT THE AUTHOR

Ehi has so much passion for legal writing, lecturing/teaching and research. Ehi recently published an article on Money Laundering. The Article titled 'A Critical Analysis of the Anti-Money Laundering Measures adopted by BitGold Inc.' has been endorsed by professionals in the Anti-Money Laundering Industry.

Ehi has edited LLM dissertations, PhD theses and professional books on Money Laundering Law.

Ehi received an award from the Top Executives in the Law, Legal & Information Services Industry for his publications in the legal world.

Ehi has been involved in many extra-curricular activities. In December 2012, Ehi worked with Cardiff Digs/Environmental Champions as a Student Volunteer on a variety of projects. The projects focused on waste and recycling, housing and energy efficiency, sustainable travel, fair-trade, environmental tasks including river clean ups, green police and much more. In August 2013, Ehi registered as a Millennium Volunteer (MV) in the Placement Program organised by Cardiff Digs/Environmental Champions and received a 50 hours certificate by the Welsh Government to that effect.

Printed in Great Britain
by Amazon